Bhagavad Gītā

Home Study Course

(Text in Sanskrit with transliteration, word-to-word and verse meaning, along with an elaborate commentary in English based on Śaṅkara-bhāṣyam)

Volume 1

Introduction

Gītā Dhyānam

Context of Gītā

Chapter 1

Swami Dayananda Saraswati
Arsha Vidya

Arsha Vidya
Research and Publication Trust
Chennai

Published by :
Arsha Vidya Research and Publication Trust
4 'Srinidhi' Apts 3rd Floor
Sir Desika Road Mylapore
Chennai 600 004 INDIA
Tel : 044 2499 7023
Telefax : 2499 7131
Email : avrandpt@gmail.com
Website : www.avrpt.com

ISBN : 978-93-80049-30-4
ISBN : 978-93-80049-39-7 (Set of 9 Volumes)

New Edition & Format	: July	2011	Copies : 1200
1st Reprint	: July	2012	Copies : 1000
2nd Reprint	: March	2015	Copies : 1000

Design & Layout :
Graaphic Design

Printed at :
Sudarsan Graphics Pvt. Ltd.,
27, Neelakanta Mehta Street
T. Nagar, Chennai 600 017
Email : info@sudarsan.com

Preface

I am very happy that the 'Bhagavad Gītā Home Study Course' will now be available in nine compact volumes so that one can carry a given volume while travelling. As I said in my foreword for the last edition, I want the readers to be aware that these books do not constitute another set of books on the Bhagavadgītā. They are different in that they are edited transcript-pages of classroom discussions; they are presented to the reader as a program for self-study. If this is borne in mind, while reading, one can enjoy the same attitude of a student in the classroom, making oneself available to the whole process of unfoldment of the content of the words of Bhagavān. The study will then prove to be as rewarding as directly listening to the teacher. This attitude would prove to be *ātma-kṛpā*. Once this *kṛpā* is there, the other two, *śāstra-kṛpā* and *īśvara-kṛpā* would follow.

The enormous job of patient editing of the pages, thousands of them, and presenting them, retaining the original words and content without any compromise, was done by Dr. Martha Doherty. These books have created a number of committed students of the Bhagavadgītā, thanks to Martha's invaluable contribution to the teaching tradition of Vedanta. I also congratulate the staff of our Publication division ably led by Ms. K. Chandra, a dedicated student of Vedanta.

Swami Dayananda Saraswati
Arsha Vidya
June 19 2011

Content of Volumes 1 - 9

Key to Transliteration and Pronunciation of Sanskrit Letters

Sanskrit is a highly phonetic language and hence accuracy in articulation of the letters is important. For those unfamiliar with the *Devanägari* script, the international transliteration is a guide to the proper pronunciation of Sanskrit letters.

अ	*a*	*(but)*	ट	*ṭa*	*(true)**3
आ	*ā*	*(father)*	ठ	*ṭha*	*(anthill)**3
इ	*i*	*(it)*	ड	*ḍa*	*(drum)**3
ई	*ī*	*(beat)*	ढ	*ḍha*	*(godhead)**3
उ	*u*	*(full)*	ण	*ṇa*	*(under)**3
ऊ	*ū*	*(pool)*	त	*ta*	*(path)**4
ऋ	*ṛ*	*(rhythm)*	थ	*tha*	*(thunder)**4
ॠ	*ṝ*	*(marine)*	द	*da*	*(that)**4
लॅ	*ḷ*	*(revelry)*	ध	*dha*	*(breathe)**4
ए	*e*	*(play)*	न	*na*	*(nut)**4
ऐ	*ai*	*(aisle)*	प	*pa*	*(put)* 5
ओ	*o*	*(go)*	फ	*pha*	*(loophole)**5
औ	*au*	*(loud)*	ब	*ba*	*(bin)* 5
क	*ka*	*(seek)* 1	भ	*bha*	*(abhor)**5
ख	*kha*	*(blockhead)**1	म	*ma*	*(much)* 5
ग	*ga*	*(get)* 1	य	*ya*	*(loyal)*
घ	*gha*	*(log hut)**1	र	*ra*	*(red)*
ङ	*ṅa*	*(sing)* 1	ल	*la*	*(luck)*
च	*ca*	*(chunk)* 2	व	*va*	*(vase)*
छ	*cha*	*(catch him)**2	श	*śa*	*(sure)*
ज	*ja*	*(jump)* 2	ष	*ṣa*	*(shun)*
झ	*jha*	*(hedgehog)**2	स	*sa*	*(so)*
ञ	*ña*	*(bunch)* 2	ह	*ha*	*(hum)*

.	*ṁ*	*anusvāra*	(nasalisation of preceding vowel)
:	*ḥ*	*visarga*	(aspiration of preceding vowel)
*			No exact English equivalents for these letters

1.	Guttural	–	Pronounced from throat
2.	Palatal	–	Pronounced from palate
3.	Lingual	–	Pronounced from cerebrum
4.	Dental	–	Pronounced from teeth
5.	Labial	–	Pronounced from lips

The 5th letter of each of the above class – called nasals – are also pronounced nasally.

Contents

Gītā Dhyānam

Verse 1

Verse 2

Verse 3

Verse 4

Verse 5

Introduction

It is said that a human birth is not easy to achieve. If we look at it from an evolutionary standpoint, there are millions of years between the ape and the human being. In other words, the monkey did not become a person overnight. Even from the standpoint of reincarnation, where human birth is said to be a result of one's own past actions, *karma*, it is not easy. And once we have this human body, whether it be due to *karma* or to the natural selection inherent in evolution, we are no longer in the hands of nature. We have the free will, a rare capacity, to initiate a further process of evolution. The whole process, then, is in our own hands.

An animal, on the other hand, is fulfilled once it survives a few years and produces an offspring. The cow, for example, need not do anything more than reach physical maturity in order to be an adult. It need not do anything to be evolved emotionally. There is no such thing as an emotionally mature cow. The only goal of a cow's life is to survive to adulthood and, as an adult, to survive as long as it can. Once it has become an adult, the cow is mature in every way.

A human being also has to become an adult physically. Otherwise, one's life is unfulfilled. To become an adult physically, all you need is to survive by appeasing your hunger and thirst, and avoiding fatal accidents and diseases. You need not do anything special. The process is a very natural one, made possible by the survival instinct common to all living beings. After a few years, you find that you have become an adult.

Until you are a physical adult, you are in the hands of nature, which takes care of your physical growth until you can no longer say, 'I am a child.' Emotional maturity, however, does not happen in the same way. Unlike physical maturity, emotional growth is purely in your own hands. Unlike a cow you need not be mature just because you happen to have an adult physical body. Inner maturity is a process that you have to initiate because you are a human being enjoying a faculty of choice.

The four human pursuits

What is fundamentally sought after by every human being is called *puruṣārtha* in Sanskrit. Although each individual seeks something peculiar, there are four ends that everyone seeks, whether he or she is an Eskimo in Alaska or someone living in a remote village in India. These four ends are *artha, kāma, dharma* and *mokṣa*.

Artha and kāma

The two universal ends most commonly sought after are security, *artha* and *kāma*, pleasure. That which gives you any kind of security, emotional, economical or social, is called *artha* in Sanskrit. *Artha* may be in the form of cash or liquid assets, stocks, real estate, relationships, home, good name, title, recognition, influence, or power of any kind. Such accomplishments boost one's ego and, therefore, also provide some security for the ego. Although each person seeks various forms of security at a given time, that he or she is seeking security is common to all.

Seeking pleasure is another *puruṣārtha* called *kāma* in Sanskrit. It also takes many forms. For instance, sensory pleasures may be anything from seafood or icecream onwards. Examples of intellectual pleasures are those derived from playing games, solving puzzles or riddles, and studying certain bodies of knowledge. Thus, we have varieties of pleasures.

Anything that satisfies your senses, that pleases your mind, touches your heart and evokes in you some appreciation, is *kāma*. For instance, any form of pleasure you derive from your home or from a relationship is *kāma*. Music and travel are also *kāma*, not *artha*, because by pursuing them, you are seeking pleasure and not security. You do not go to Hawaii or Bahamas to seek security. In fact, you lose some security, in the form of money, when you go to these places. Because you happen to have some money, you travel for pleasure, not for security.

You also derive pleasure from seeing the stars on a beautiful night, enjoying the sunrise, a flower, a playing child, or a beautiful painting. Because this pleasure is neither sensory nor intellectual, we call it aesthetic pleasure. Even though such pleasures go beyond one's senses and intellect, they are still *kāma*.

Dharma

Dharma, the third *puruṣārtha*, is neither *artha* nor *kāma*. *Dharma* is a word with many meanings, as we shall see. Here, it refers to the pleasure born of harmony, the pleasure derived from friendship, sharing, helping another person and so on.

For instance, when you are able to relieve someone's suffering, you experience a joy that is not *kāma*. This form of pleasure is different from both *artha* and *kāma* in that you do not seek out a person in pain in order to derive some pleasure. It is not the same as going to Hawaii or to a concert. When you happen to come across someone in pain, you are able to alleviate the person's discomfort, and you feel happy.

A doctor who does not work purely for financial gain, enjoys this kind of pleasure. Charity also works in the same way. Those who are able to discover joy in such work, I would say, have an inner growth, understanding and sensitivity on their part. This sensitivity is also required to understand love, for to love another person totally is to understand the other person, for which one should be educated, cultured. If a person has not learned through experiences, and is not cultured, what kind of joy can he or she get out of life? For such people, there can be only sensory pleasures like eating, for example. But many simple joys are lacking in their lives. Thus, the gain in one's life commensurates with what one knows.

A professor of medicine, in his introductory class, said, 'What your mind does not know, your eyes do not see.' What he meant was, without medical knowledge the cause for a disease would continue to elude a person, even though the symptoms are everywhere. The eyes may see the symptoms, but the mind does not know. In life too, the more you know, the brighter life is, because you cannot see more than what you know. It does not imply that you should necessarily get more out of life. Only that your life is to be lived properly, fully, which implies a lot of understanding.

Living does not simply mean dragging yourself around from day-to-day, from bed to work, back home and to bed again. The whole process repeats itself until the weekend comes. Then you drag yourself to some recreation in the hope of forgetting yourself, which is why recreation becomes so important. In fact, your whole life can be a recreation. Someone once asked a Swami, 'Swamiji, do you not take any holidays? You seem to be working everyday.' In fact, the Swami's life is one long holiday.

If you enjoy what you do, life is very simple. If you do not enjoy what you do, then you have to do something in order to enjoy, which can be very costly. On the other hand, any pleasure that comes out of your maturing process is a different type of joy. Not hurting someone or doing the right thing at the right time, for instance, gives you joy, if not immediately, later. Suppose, you have postponed doing something like the laundry, vacuuming or letter writing, the day you decide to do it, and do it, you find that there is a joy in finally having done it, a joy that is neither pleasure nor security. It is just doing what is to be done; it is *dharma*, a very big topic that we will discuss later. For now, it is enough to know that as you grow in your understanding, your *dharma* also grows.

So, *artha*, *kāma* and *dharma* are three of the four *puruṣārtha*s. Because of the importance we place on *dharma*, the order can now be reversed as *dharma*, *artha* and *kāma*. *Dharma* accounts for your maturity. The more mature you are, the more *dhārmika* you become. In order to be mature, an understanding of *dharma* and conformity to it becomes of prime importance in your life. Thus, *dharma* occupies the first place among these three human ends. Without violating *dharma*, doing what is to be done, you pursue *artha* and *kāma*, security and pleasure. This is how these three universal human pursuits are to be understood.

Mokṣa

Even though *mokṣa* comes last, it is a very important *puruṣārtha*, as we shall see. *Mokṣa* is recognised as a pursuit only by few people in any given generation. Some appreciation, maturity or insight about life and its struggles is required to understand *mokṣa*. People do not discerningly pursue it, although everyone is, in fact, always seeking freedom in one form or other.

Though you think of freedom in a very positive way, the word *mokṣa* is actually defined in a negative sense. There is something binding you, from which you want to become free and that freedom is *mokṣa*. For instance, a man who is not in jail has freedom, whereas if he is in jail, he does not. Because he cannot choose to come out, he has lost his freedom of mobility and wants to gain it. He wants freedom from the shackles of jail.

If you are using crutches because of a leg fracture, you want freedom from the crutches. Similarly, an infant requiring the help of the wall or mother's hand in order to stand, wants to be free of the wall or the hand and, therefore, strives to stand on his or her own. So, freedom is always freedom from something.

Mokṣa means freedom from something I do not want. And because *mokṣa* is a *puruṣārtha*, a human end common to all, wanting to be free is not peculiar to me alone. Everyone wants to be free from things that are common to all. That I am attached to particular forms of security, *artha*, reveals a fact about myself, that I am insecure. That I also seek pleasure, *kāma*, reveals I am restless and I am not satisfied with myself. I have to do something in order to please myself, which means that I am displeased with myself. If I am always seeking security and pleasure, when will I make my life? When will I really be able to say, 'I have made it !' I can say that only when I see myself as secure and I am pleased with myself. Then I am free; I have *mokṣa*.

Mokṣa does not mean salvation. In fact, there is no word in Sanskrit for salvation, which is just as well, since salvation implies some condemnation of myself. It implies that someone has to salvage me, save me, which is not what is meant by *mokṣa* at all. The word *mokṣa* refers only to the freeing of myself from certain fetters. The basic ones are the notions that 'I am insecure,' and 'I am displeased with myself.'

I must see myself as secure and be pleased with myself as I am. Only then do I have *mokṣa*. If I am secure and pleased with myself, what situation is going to change that? I require no security or a situational change whatsoever to be secure and at peace.

This should be understood well. I spend my entire life manipulating the world to please myself. In the process, I find that two hands and legs, five senses and a mind are not enough to contend with all the factors involved. There are just too many events and situations as well as natural forces, over which I seem to have no control.

Mokṣa is freedom from seeking

With my limited powers and limited knowledge, I find that I can never measure up to the demands of gaining the securities and pleasures that I seek, which is why life seems to be a problem. Only when I reach thirty-nine or forty, when I undergo what is sometimes referred to as the 'midlife crisis,' do I begin to understand this. Even though I may think my marriage or my job is my crisis, actually I am the crisis. My crisis has nothing to do with marriage or any other situations in my life. The tendency, however, is to find a scapegoat for every problem I have, and the immediate scapegoat available is often my partner in life.

When you look into your various pursuits – *artha, kāma* and *dharma* – you find that, what you really seek is none of these. You seek only freedom from being a seeker. Everyone is a seeker pursuing *artha* and *kāma* mainly and, to some extent, *dharma*. But, ultimately everyone is seeking only *mokṣa*. Therefore, *mokṣa* alone is the real end. In other words, freedom from being insecure is what you seek when you seek security. When you seek securities, you are not really seeking securities themselves. You are seeking freedom from being insecure. This distinction should be clearly understood.

The shift in emphasis that this distinction represents is what we call learning. Seeking security is very natural. For an uninformed person who does not think about or understand his or her own ideas and urges, security is a particular thing and is always taken to be outside of oneself. That 'I am insecure' is a totally accepted conclusion for such a person, a conclusion that is never doubted or questioned.

Various philosophies have arisen from this insecurity. For instance, one person says, 'Money will not give you security,' while another person says, 'It will, but only here on earth, not later.' Later security, we are told, can only be gained by doing certain prescribed acts. Thus, we have varieties of religions and philosophies, all of which have been born out of accepting, 'I am insecure,' and security is something that is outside of oneself.

Even as a child, one's security depends on the constant availability of protection, love and care of one's parents. On the other hand, once the child has grown up, the situation is reversed. Now the parents' security depends on the attention of the child. Parents often feel neglected by their grown up children who are now occupied with their own lives. Once a child has grown up, security is no more in the parents; it lies elsewhere.

As a child I was insecure and now also I am insecure. There is a constant shift in what I take to be securities, which is considered to be a normal life for everyone. No one, however, deserves to have this problem. Security is not the problem. That I lack something is not the problem. The problem is 'I' lack. This difference must be seen clearly.

What I lack is always variable – I lack iced tea, I lack children, I lack a house. What I lack is always peculiar to me at a given time and place in my life. It differs from individual to individual, from culture to culture. However, the 'I lack' is common to all and is entirely different from what I lack. I may lack a healthy body, a taller body, a thinner body, a turned-up nose, longer eyelashes or a different skin colour. And this may only be the beginning of an endless list! But the fact that I conclude 'I lack' is universal.

For instance, what can you do if your height is less than you would like it to be? The most you can do is to wear high-heeled shoes, which does not really make you any taller. In fact, in the eyes of others you may be shorter. It is only when you are being recruited for a basketball team that anyone else thinks about your height. Height is your complex. I do not think about your height until you get into high-heeled shoes and try to walk. Only then do I see your height because you have drawn my attention to it, and I immediately cut it down by a few inches. I may actually reduce it more than the actual height of your heels. You not only fall short of my expectation, but you also become shorter than what you really are!

So, if you have a complex with reference to your height, you are stuck. If you were a wire or something stretchable, your height could be increased, but no such stretching is possible. Similarly, there are lot of things that you are stuck with because the things you are not, known and unknown, are countless. And what you lack you can never totally fulfil. The more you go after what you lack, the more you breed what you lack because what you lack has a knack of multiplying itself. It is like going to the supermarket to pick up few things you lack and coming home with a few more desires to be fulfilled when you get your pay cheque the following week. This is why we say desire is like fire that leaves a black trail after it. No matter how much you feed it, fire never says, 'Enough!' Similarly, human beings can never say 'enough' to securities and pleasures.

A discriminative analysis of dharma, artha and kāma leads to mokṣa

So, when are you going to completely fulfil your *artha*s and *kāma*s? I am not saying you should not seek out security; that is not the emphasis here. We are only trying to understand the very pursuit itself. Money definitely has its value. But, if you think that there is security in money or in anything else, the process of seeking becomes endless. The insecure you, the one who wants to be secure, does not really become secure by the addition of what you consider to be securities. No one can say, 'I am secure,' even with all possible securities.

As long as you require crutches, the sense of insecurity centred on you will remain with you. Feeling secure because you have crutches does not mean you are secure. You feel secure only because of the crutches, whereas the sense of insecurity centred on you remains.

Suppose, you are insecure, and what you think as secure is also as insecure as you are. For instance, if one insecure person marries another insecure person in order to be secure, the result is not security. All that results is a marriage between two insecure people. Can there be a greater hell anywhere? When two such people come together, it is a problem because insecurity plus insecurity do not make security; there is only double insecurity.

There is a story about a man who, as he was bathing by the side of a river, slipped and was swept away by the current. Because he could not swim, he prayed, 'Oh! Lord, please help me!' Just then a log came along and, catching hold of it, the man said, 'My God! God is great!' Then he realised that the log had fur on it, and hands too. He had thought he was holding on to a log, but now he realised that the 'log' was holding on to him. Yet, he thought that the Lord was saving him. He found, however, that the Lord was a grizzly bear that had fallen from a tree, was also swept up by the current. Once he realised he was holding on to a bear, he wanted to escape, but the bear already had too tight a hold on him.

Similarly, you do not know which holds what or who holds whom. You may have thought you were holding on to something, only to find that you cannot give it up, which means it is holding you. It is a problem. Any habit is the same. An alcoholic was once a free person. When he or she took the first drink, the person poured the alcohol into the glass and, holding on to the glass, drank from it; no problem. However, after some time the person finds that he or she does not drink at all. As soon as 'Happy Hour'[1] arrives, the bottle tells the person, 'Come here,' and he or she goes like a zombie. Then the bottle says, 'Come on, pick me up!' And the person picks it up. It says, 'Come on, pour me into the glass. Drink!' And the person drinks. Then it

---

[1] The time in a bar when drinks are served at reduced prices

says, 'One more, one more.' The person takes more and more alcohol without his volitional control. Who is this person? Is he or she the one who was previously free? Does the person take to the drink or does the drink take to the person?

In so many situations, no one knows who holds on to what. I see no difference between the grabber and the grabbed, the holder and the held. Even inert things like drinks, cards or dice have the capacity to grab me; what to say of relationships, since people are equally insecure. Therefore, an insecure me plus anything in this world that happens to be within the framework of time is not going to make me secure. I need to understand this well. We are not trying to develop a particular attitude here, just a simple appreciation of facts.

That I am insecure is a fact and that I seek securities is also a fact. What I consider secure is not secure because it is also finite. This too is a fact.

I may think, by giving away whatever securities I have, I will become secure. One man did this. He gave away his house, his business, his bank balance and went to a Swami. But the Swami was insecure and wanted to have a following of disciples. Previously, the man was on a husband-trip, father-trip, a business-money trip, and now he is on another trip, a *svāmi-ātmā* trip, minus a house, wife, children, money and so on. To think that subtraction is going to help, when addition does not, is nothing but a lack of understanding. If this is *artha*, then *kāma* is also the same.

No pleasure is going to be lasting. For instance, if you take music, you buy a recording of a hit song. Why is this song a hit? Because, like a hit man, it knocks off all the other songs out of the running. Last month's hit song has been hit and is no longer a hit song. It only gathers dust on your tape deck. You do not bother about it any more.

Similarly, your attitude is always changing. What made you happy before no longer provides the same joy. You get tired of everything. Even if God were around you all the time, you would eventually want some privacy. This constant changing is natural because you are basically displeased with yourself. Therefore, you are pleased only now and then. The only silver lining in life is your hope. It is all that keeps you going. Perhaps hope is nature's way of enabling you to survive that you can discover nature herself.

Suppose, these moments of pleasure, which are so few and far between, are denied to a given person, and they are not there at all, do you think a self-conscious human being, the displeased human being, would want to live? He or she would surely commit suicide. In spite of these moments of pleasure, if a person thinks there is no possibility of being happy, either because of a loss of some kind or an apprehension of some great calamity, the person would choose not to live. This is the thinking behind all suicides.

So, moments of pleasure are worthwhile because they keep you going. The hope is you will discover that you do not need a mother-in-law to be displeased; you need only yourself. If you close the doors, put aside the world and sit in an easy chair and try to be with yourself, you will then understand whether[2] you are pleased with yourself. You will find that you do not require a world of perception, a world of books or any thing to be displeased. All that you require is yourself. After just a few minutes of sitting with yourself, you want to get up and go out or take a shower; anything other than sitting with yourself.

To be displeased, then, requires nothing but yourself. It is not the world that displeases you; you are displeased with yourself. Whatever pleases you is going to be time-bound, all of which we will see as we study the eighteen chapters of the Bhagavadgītā.

Any *kāma*, pleasure, you pick up is limited by nature, in terms of time, content and degree. But, the one who is displeased remains so in spite of occasional moments of pleasure. Therefore, you have now discerned the problem to be the conclusion about yourself that, 'I am displeased.' It is a fact that is not going to be altered just because you pick up moments of pleasure. That you are insecure does not change merely because you acquire or give up securities. The only solution is to see yourself as secure and pleased. But how is it possible to do this?

If, with all these securities and pleasures, you are displeased with yourself, how are you going to see yourself pleased without them? Here, the teaching called Vedanta comes in and

---

[2] Whether or not is a common expression but the correct usage is only 'whether' without being followed by 'or not'. Whether one likes this, grammatically this is right. (Swamiji)

tells you that your problem is not one of lacking something, but of not knowing that you do not lack anything. It converts all your pursuits into a pursuit of knowledge.

In the vision of Vedanta, there is no reason for you to be displeased with yourself because you are totally acceptable to yourself, not in terms of attitude, but in reality. It is not a belief. It is a fact, and a discoverable fact. What can be discovered is a fact, and the discoverable fact here is that you lack nothing. You are totally free. This is the vision of the self and the heart of Vedanta, the heart of this teaching. The problem 'I lack' is thereby converted into ignorance, the cause of which you do not know for the time being. Until you come to know, the vision assumes the status of a promise.

Vedanta defines the problem as not what you lack, but that you lack. It says that you are the solution because you are the problem.

There are two types of problems. One has its solution outside the problem and the other has its solution within the very problem itself. For instance, the solution to the problem of feeling cold is outside the problem. You have to cover yourself, go to the fireside, or go out into the sun. You may even decide to go to the Bahamas. When the solution to a problem is outside, it means you need to do something to solve the problem. If hunger is your problem, you have to feed the hunger by eating food, which is also outside. The solution to a jigsaw puzzle, however, is within the problem, within the puzzle itself as the solution is within the problem. In fact, there is no problem. When you do not understand something, it is a problem for you, whereas when you do understand there is no problem; understanding is the solution. In the vision of Vedanta you have no problem.

You may then ask, 'How can I recognise that I do not have a problem?' It seems to be one more problem, adding to the ones I already have. But is it? The problem of self-non-acceptance is not there because in the vision of Vedanta, the self is acceptable. What else do you want really? The only problem a human being has is self-non-acceptance. Therefore, you are the problem and you are the solution. Now your pursuit becomes one of knowing yourself and it can be a game, fun all the way. This is teaching.

A discriminative analysis of *dharma*, *artha* and *kāma* leads you to the fundamental human problem. Once this human problem has been discerned, you will take special steps to resolve it, even though you may continue to pursue *artha*, *kāma* and *dharma*. The solution to this fundamental problem is called *mokṣa*.

Mokṣa is not an equivalent to salvation, as is commonly thought. Nor is it some kind of accomplishment other than yourself. As freedom from something, however, *mokṣa*, could be considered a negative accomplishment of sorts. Nevertheless, there is nothing more positive than *mokṣa*.

Once we say 'freedom,' the question is, 'Freedom from what?' The answer is simply, 'freedom from something I do not want.' No one wants freedom from what he or she wants. Therefore, no one wants freedom from *artha*, securities, and *kāma*, pleasures. One wants *artha*, *kāma* and a little bit of *dharma* plus *mokṣa*.

Mokṣa is not freedom from *artha* or *kāma*. What *artha* provides, *mokṣa* cannot provide. But what *mokṣa* provides cannot be provided by *artha, kāma* and *dharma* combined. A person who has *mokṣa* also has the freedom to pursue the other three human ends, namely *artha, kāma* and *dharma*, if he or she chooses so. This is real freedom and not freedom from these pursuits.

Artha and kāma are for one's own sake

Who undertakes these pursuits? The person called *puruṣa* in Sanskrit, meaning any person young or old, man or woman, Indian or American. This *puruṣa*, the person, is the one who is after *artha* and *kāma*.

A human being never undertakes a deliberate activity without having a purpose. Even involuntary actions have a purpose. Here, we are talking only about those actions that are voluntary. Voluntary, deliberate actions always presuppose a desirer, whose desire is never for the action as such, but for the result, the object of desire. There is always some end in view.

An object that you have cannot become an object of desire, if you know you have it. However, you may have something and not recognise that you have it. Therefore, it may become an object of your desire. So, the clause, 'If you know you have it' is important here. For instance, you cannot desire a head over your shoulders, since you already have one. Even if you desire so, no one can fulfil it, not even the Lord. In spite of all your devotion and prayers, if you were to ask the Lord why he has not fulfilled your desire, he could only say, 'I cannot give you what you already have in spite of my knowledge, power, or resources. The incapacity to give you a head over shoulders is because you are asking for something you already have.'

How can even God give you one? If you want one more head, being God, he can give you a second head, although I do not know how a second head is going to help you, if the one you already have has not helped you! But he can give it to you. You will have to tell him, of course, where would you like to have it. However, do not ask him to give you a head over your shoulders. What you have, he cannot give you.

Although you cannot desire an object that you know you have, you can always desire an object that you do not have. There are many things that you do not have such as green card, new house, another job, promotion, wife, husband, child, a trip to a particular place; anything you do not have, you can desire. Thus, what you do not have can become an object of your desire.

Without a purpose, there is no effort, no deliberate activity. Therefore, the *puruṣa*, the person, undertakes activities for accomplishing different ends, mainly *artha* and *kāma* but also *dharma*. If this is so, there is a very important question to be asked, 'Do I want *artha* and *kāma* for the sake of *artha* and *kāma* themselves?' The answer to this question is what distinguishes the entire Vedic vision of a human life from one's usual way of looking at it.

Is *kāma* for its own sake? Is it for the sake of pleasure? Is it just for fun? If so, then with or without it, you are the same.

You go for it just because you go for it. In other words, it is nothing more than a fancy. But is this really the case? Are *artha* and *kāma*, which you seek in life, for their own sake or are they for your sake? The Veda says, '*ātmanastu kāmāya sarvaṁ priyaṁ bhavati*, every object of my desire is for my sake alone.'[3]

You only desire what you know. You do not desire an object that is unknown to you. For instance, you do not desire for '*gagabugain*.' An unknown *gagabugain* cannot be an object of desire. In fact, there is no such thing as *gagabugain*. No amount of coaxing will cause you to get into your car and go to buy *gagabugain*. But you always have a reason for getting into your car. Some desire is always being fulfilled. Thus, an unknown object does not become an object of desire.

Only known objects become objects of desires. There are of course, some known objects for which you do not have a desire – scorpions, disease like cancer and so on. In fact, the more you know of such objects, the more you want to get rid of them. Also, an object that has been known and loved by you need not always be desirable to you. You may have no desire for it whatsoever a few years down the road. No one undertakes a course of action without an end in view. Whether the end is right, can only be discovered later. You may change your view or give it up altogether, for a variety of reasons. We have all done this. But what is desirable now, you will definitely seek out. Therefore, one who desires a particular end, any *artha* or *kāma*, does so for his or her own sake.

---

[3] *Bṛhadāraṇyakopaniṣad* 2.4.5

Suppose you say, 'No, Swamiji, it is not for my sake; it is for the sake of my son.' It only means that your 'me' has become a little extended, but it always reduces to 'me.' Your 'me' can extend to the community in which you live, to your religion, and to your nation also. It is your ego, an extended ego, and more the extensions, healthier the ego. Yet, the end is always for your sake alone.

Even if you offer a prayer, for whose sake is the prayer? For God's sake? Is God in such difficulty that you have to pray for him also? If God requires your prayer in order to survive, then to whom should you pray? If you are praying to God for God's sake, then for God's sake, please give it up! When you say, 'For God's sake,' it is only an expression. You do not do anything for God's sake.

It is also often said that you should 'Serve God.' Is it that, God has too much work to do and therefore needs your help? Of course not. Your service and your prayer is for your sake alone. There is nothing wrong with that. If you pray for your mother, father, children, humanity and all living beings, you do so because you can be happy only if others are happy. How can you be happy if everyone else is unhappy?

You see this in games, for instance. In tennis, you always start with love, like marriage, and then fight to the bitter end. One person wins and the other loses. The one who wins, throws his or her racket into the air and says, 'Wonderful! I won!' But the one who loses never throws his or her racket into the air, although it may be thrown to the ground in a gesture of defeat. And when the winner approaches the net, still ecstatic and gasping for breath, to shake hands with the loser, the elation subsides a little, because every human heart knows what it is to be on the other side. Thus, when others are unhappy, you cannot be happy.

Desiring *artha* and *kāma*, you then make certain efforts. If these efforts do not seem to be enough, you make another effort called prayer. Prayer is neither *artha* nor *kāma*; it is *dharma*. Through prayer, you want to gain some invisible result that will give you *artha* and *kāma*. Although spiritual seekers do not pray for *artha* and *kāma*, they do pray for knowledge and maturity, which again is for one's own sake alone. This aspect of the human personality is very important and is basic to the vision of Vedanta.

When you know whatever you do is for your own sake, everything becomes meaningful. You find that what you do has its place and everything falls into place. Nothing is more efficacious than anything else, for no one action is more important than another. Each action becomes important in its own sphere and is meant for producing its own result. Can you say that the ears are better than the eyes or that the eyes are better than the ears? No, you require both. If I see you shouting at me but cannot hear what you are shouting, I cannot respond to you properly. Eyes have their own sphere, as do the ears. Similarly, each organ – the kidney, liver, heart, lung and so on – has its own sphere, each one as important as any of the others.

However, in order for everything to fall into its place, the starting point must be proper. Here, the proper starting point is knowing that any action you perform is always for a given end and that end is for your sake alone. Vedanta takes this statement one step further to cover important relationships. A wife is dear to her husband not for her sake, but for his sake. Similarly, the husband becomes dear to his wife for her sake, not for his sake. If you understand that everything you do is for your sake alone, then even your relationships would be very objective. You will not go about saying, 'I did so much for you,' the starting point for all kinds of trouble.

Discerning mokṣa as the end in life

That I want *artha* and *kāma* reveals I am an insecure and unhappy person from two different standpoints. What do I really want? Do I want the actual *artha* and *kāma*, the objects themselves, or do I want security and happiness? Because I want security and happiness, all *artha*s and *kāma*s are reduced to security and happiness alone.

If I am insecure, I naturally seek security, and if I am unhappy, I seek happiness. However, it is not the security itself that I want. What I really want is freedom from insecurity. In terms of security, I am wanting. In terms of fullness and happiness also, I am wanting. Therefore, I want freedom from being a wanting person. In order to be free from being a wanting person, I have to see myself as secure. I have to see myself as one who does not lack anything. I can see myself in this way when I have no sense of lack.

If I am insecure and unhappy, and see myself as secure and happy because of some kind of self-hypnotism, for instance, then I am under yet another delusion. It is better to be insecure than to be deluded into thinking that I am secure. If I know I am insecure, then at least I can be objective and thereby understand my problems.

So, one has to be secure in order to see oneself as secure. To be able to say, 'I am happy,' one has to be happy to understand the happiness I talk about. One can, therefore, see oneself as secure and happy either by becoming so or by already being so. I am using two different words here, 'becoming' and 'being' for a reason. One generally sees oneself as insecure and unhappy and then tries to become secure and happy. The whole process of living, the struggles in one's life, are but a process of becoming. Being insecure one seeks to become secure.

In the final analysis, people are after the same thing. I may seek various ends, but over the shoulders of these seemingly different ends, I see two common ends – being secure and being happy. My hope is that one day I will become secure and happy. Therefore, even when I am seeking *artha* and *kāma*, I am seeking freedom from being insecure and unhappy. This must be clearly understood.

Given that everyone wants freedom from being a wanting person, everyone wants *mokṣa*. When you put it this way, it looks as though *mokṣa* is just another end. In fact, it is not another end. It is **the end**, the end behind all ends. You refer to *mokṣa* as another end, another *puruṣārtha*, only because you do not recognise it as the only end, even though you seek freedom from insecurity. Recognising this end is the culmination of your life, the end of *saṁsāra*, your insecurity and unhappiness.

The culmination of your life is not ageing. It is the ability to discern yourself as one who is secure and happy. Discerning is part of growing up. Once you have discerned the fact of your being secure and happy, even though you may continue your *artha* and *kāma* pursuits, you have taken the necessary step for *mokṣa*. However small the step, the step has been made. Having 'stepped into' this teaching, the necessary step has been taken.

You should not be alarmed by the word *mokṣa*. You need not worry about what will happen to your family if you study and become enlightened. Believe me, your family will be happy because they will no longer have to deal with your insecurities and unhappiness. Also, by trying to gain enlightenment, the pressure you were feeling will definitely be less because you now have something better to accomplish in life. Otherwise, life is a problem.

Marriage, for example, cannot be an end itself. If it is, there will be problems, and the marriage will end. Marriage is a means, not an end, whereby both the husband and wife seek freedom from insecurity. Freedom from insecurity is their common end and they help each other. Together as companions, they make the journey. This most significant aspect of marriage is acknowledged in seven steps of a Hindu marriage ceremony. Only when these seven steps have been taken, has the marriage taken place. Each of the seven steps represents one aspect of the couple's journey, for which there is a destination, *mokṣa*.

Discerning *mokṣa* as the end in life and seeking it makes your life meaningful. It does not prevent you from seeking *artha* and *kāma*. In fact, without that life is just a rat race. You should always remember that the truth of rat race is, even after a race, the winning rat continues to be a rat. The vision is now clear. Freedom is seeing yourself as a secure and happy person, free from being insecure and unhappy.

The whole struggle in life stems only from insecurity and unhappiness. You think that by adding some security, you will become secure. In this way, life is one of becoming. In the process, you become hurt, aged, and have all kinds of things happen to you. If the fundamental problem is not discerned, your life is wasted. All that is achieved is that one human life has been spent. The good thing is, the Veda says, you always have another chance, and another, and another! While this may provide some satisfaction, it is not a solution to the fundamental problem.

Now, if there is no 'becoming free,' and you have to be free, then you must already be free. If you are already free and you seek freedom, then you are seeking something that you already are. You know that you want freedom, but you do not know that you are free. Therefore, not knowing 'I am already free' is the problem.

There is a means of knowledge for knowing the self

If there is ignorance of yourself, then in order to know, there should be a means of knowledge. It is a fact that what can be known by one means of knowledge cannot be known by another means of knowledge. For example, what can be known by the eyes, in terms of colour and form, cannot be known by the ears, in terms of sound. Similarly, what can be inferred, can only be inferred at a given time and place.

The basic means of knowledge available to you for knowing things other than yourself is perception. But the self cannot be an object of perception like *śabda*, sound; *sparśa*, touch; *rūpa*, form or colour; *rasa*, taste; and *gandha*, smell. Only those objects which have the attributes of sound, form, colour, smell, taste and touch can be known as objects of your senses; whereas the self is the one who uses this means of knowledge, perception. So, you cannot employ perception as a means of knowledge to know yourself.

Your perception can be enhanced by microscope, telescope and various other instruments, thereby gathering better data and increasing your capacity to make more accurate inferences based on perception. They definitely question your previous understanding. For instance, because you see the sun rising in the eastern sky and setting in the west, you conclude from your perceptual data that the sun rises and sets, and the earth is stationary. However seeing the sun move, does not mean that it moves. The sun can appear to be moving, but if you go to the North pole, you will see that the sun does not move from east to west. You now have better data because of which you revise your earlier conclusion. This new conclusion then becomes the basis for additional data and inferences.

Similarly, if you put a stick in a glass of water, the stick looks bent. You may think that the water has the capacity to bend the stick, but when you pull it out, you see it is not bent. Your conclusion or knowledge now is that it does not bend, that it only appears to be bent while in the glass of water. Perception is negated by conclusive knowledge. That the stick appears to be bent when it is not, is now understood as an optical illusion. Conclusions based on better data are valid and arrived at through a means of knowledge, *pramāṇa*, inference in this case.

The question now is, can the self, who uses inference and perception, become an object for either of these means of knowledge? It cannot. Yet, at the same time, I must know myself.

I do know that I exist. To know this, I do not require a means of knowledge. All I need to know is what I am. Am I as I conclude? Am I insecure? What are the reasons for concluding that I am insecure? More of this will be seen in detail, later. For now, it is enough to know that ignorance is the main reason that I see myself as insecure. Ignorance is the main reason for any error. But here, the error is typical. Wherever an error is typical, there are other incidental reasons that make it so. Suppose, you mistake a rope for some other object, what kind of a mistake do you make? You do not take the rope to be an elephant. Such a mistake is not possible. But you could take the rope to be a snake or any number of other similar looking objects. You cannot, however, mistake it for something totally dissimilar.

Similarly, there is self-ignorance leading to typical conclusions on the part of every being, that I am insecure, unhappy and so on. There are incidental causes for such conclusions as well as the prime cause, ignorance, which we are dealing with here. Knowledge alone can dispel ignorance. It cannot take place without a means of knowledge, even knowledge that is picked up accidentally, like the knowledge of Penicillin, for example. Knowledge picked up accidentally does not preclude a means of knowledge. In fact, there was a great deal of knowledge leading to the accidental discovery of Penicillin, the greatest discovery of the century, I would say, since it has revolutionised the quality of human life. Infections that were once fatal succumb to this wonder drug. Innovative surgeries such as heart transplants can now be performed, thanks to Alexander Fleming who stumbled upon this particular knowledge.

'Stumbling upon,' serendipity, is also a means of knowledge. If the scientist who discovered Penicillin had not been qualified, he would not have had the knowledge to question why the strain of bacterium, he was culturing, had been destroyed by a particular fungus. When he found the bacteria dead, he would have just said, 'They died. Better luck next time.' Instead he had the capacity to look into the whole situation. Using the proper means of knowledge, experiments and so on, he concluded that this particular fungus destroys bacteria.

Knowledge itself is never stumbled upon. All that is stumbled upon is a particular situation leading to knowledge. For knowledge to take place, you have to recognise the situation and this recognition is what is meant by knowledge. But, the self can never be stumbled upon, even if you remove all your thoughts, as some people maintain. Which self will you stumble upon? Who is it that is stumbling and what is it that is being stumbled upon? If you are ignorant of yourself and remove all the thoughts you previously had, what will you be? You will still be ignorant, without thoughts. Then, if you conclude that you are enlightened because you have removed all thoughts, the conclusion will be a thoughtless conclusion.

You need to know this. The enlightened mind is not brought about by the elimination of thoughts. Knowledge always comes because of an appropriate means of knowledge. There is no way of altering knowledge and there is no replacement for a means of knowledge. Therefore, what can be known by a given means of knowledge can be known only by that means of knowledge. There is no accommodation here. If you have to see a colour, what accommodation can there be? Only the eyes will see colour; your nose certainly will not. There is no other means for knowing colour except the eyes.

You may ask, 'Because I cannot stumble upon myself, will I not remain ignorant in spite of anything I do? And if so, is it not enough just to be a devotee? Why should I study all these books? Why should I have this knowledge? As a devotee, will I not gain *mokṣa* when I die?'

You may think, because of your devotion you will go to heaven and sit with God. However, you will still be ignorant. In addition, how long will it be before you become bored there and want to come back? On the other hand, the reward for all your prayers, offered either in this life or in previous lives, is stumbling upon the means of knowledge for knowing the *ātmā* or even understanding what a means of knowledge is. It is all stated in the Vedas.

Veda as a means of knowledge

What is the means of knowledge to know the self then? We have seen that it has to be other than perception and inference. So it can only be an external means – words. For facts that we cannot know by perception and inference, words, *śabda*, can be a means of knowledge. And those words are called Veda. They are with us, meaning, they are with humanity. We refer to them as 'revealed' and look upon them as a means of knowledge for truths that can be neither inferred nor perceived.[4] The acceptance of Veda as a *pramāṇa* is what is meant by *śraddhā*.

Suppose, I were to say, 'The Veda says that there is such a thing as heaven,' can you prove it? Can you disprove it? If it can be proven, it is not knowledge exclusive to the Veda. Since you cannot prove or disprove it, the Veda is the *pramāṇa* for knowing about heaven. Anything that cannot be proved or disproved is the sphere of the Veda and is its definition as well. That there is a heaven, that there is an afterlife, that there is not an end of everything and everyone, cannot be proved. Nor can you prove

---

[4] प्रत्यक्षेणानुमित्या वा यस्तूपायो न बुध्यते एतं विदन्ति वेदेन तस्माद् वेदस्य वेदता (ऋग्वेद भाष्या)
pratyakṣeṇānumityā vā yastūpāyo na budhyate etaṁ vidanti vedena tasmād vedasya vedatā (*Ṛgveda-bhāṣya*)

People know through the Vedas what cannot be known through perception or inference. Therefore the Vedas are a means of knowledge.

that there are invisible results called *puṇya* and *pāpa* accrued to your account for all your actions, right and wrong.

The Veda says that *puṇya* is the result of good action and *pāpa* is the result of wrong action. The Veda also says, along with some supporting logic, that *pāpa* accrued to your account has to be paid for with pain. It is called the law of *karma*. Can you disprove such statements? Can you prove them? You can neither prove nor disprove them.

There are a number of other things mentioned in the Veda. For instance, you are told that by performing a specific ritual, you will receive a specific result, either immediately or later. Suppose, you perform a ritual called *putrakāmeṣti* for the sake of having a child. You have made every effort possible and the best medical advice available has assured you that there is no reason for you not to have a child. But something is denying you this particular gift. Since you are dealing with an unknown factor, and you want a specific result, you perform a specific prayer, not a broad-spectrum prayer. This specific prayer takes care of the unknown factor that is denying you the gift of the child, and a child comes to you. All of this is stated in the Veda. Because this ritual and its results is given by the Veda, you accept it along with all other statements made therein. The spheres covered in the Veda are only those that are not available for perception and inference.

The first portion of the Veda deals with various rituals, prayers, *karma*, *puṇya*, *pāpa* and so on, and is called the *pūrvabhāga* or the *karma-kāṇḍa*. The end portion of the Veda deals with facts about the nature of the self that cannot be stumbled upon by any other means of knowledge at our disposal. It is called the *jñāna-kāṇḍa* or Vedanta or the *uttarabhāga*.

When something is beyond our inference or perception, we do not mean it is beyond the mind. We mean it is not available for our inference or perception. Yet, it has to be known and any knowledge takes place only in the mind. Therefore, where does self-knowledge take place? Only in the mind, *manasā eva anudraṣṭavyam*. Since any knowledge has to take place in the mind, we cannot go 'beyond the mind' to gain self-knowledge.

Self-knowledge is peculiar in that, it is not knowledge of an object. It is knowledge of oneself for which the means of knowledge is the last portion of the Veda, in the *Upaniṣad*s, collectively called Vedanta. Any statement that reveals the truth of oneself, the nature of oneself, with all fallacies removed, is Vedanta, whether it is in Sanskrit, some tribal dialect or any other language. Although the literal meaning of Vedanta is 'the end of the Veda,' the word 'Veda' itself means a 'body of knowledge.' This body of knowledge is available for the humanity. All that one has to do is make use of it.

How has this knowledge come about? We can say, it has come about by revelation. But to do so, we require some understanding of the word 'revelation.' Anyone can say, 'I had a revelation yesterday.' God seems to come in dreams and tell people all sorts of things. I can also say I had a dream in which God came; but, in my dream, God said, 'I never come in dreams!'

The statement, 'The entire Veda and hence Vedanta is a revealed knowledge,' is not an immature statement, as we will come to understand. The entire Veda is a body of knowledge that was not authored by any person. It was revealed to the *ṛṣi*s directly, which is why the *ṛṣi*s are not the authors of the Veda. They are the seers of the *mantra*s – *mantra-draṣṭāraḥ* and not *mantra-kartāraḥ*. Hence the Vedas are considered to be *apauruṣeya*, not born of human intellect. They are considered to be a *pramāṇa* because they reveal something that is not available to us through perception or inference, be it the knowledge of various means and ends in the *karma-kāṇḍa*, or the knowledge of the self in the end portion of the Vedas. So, my definition of Vedanta is that, it is a means of knowledge, a *pramāṇa* in the form of words. The sphere of this means of knowledge is 'you.' It talks about 'you.'

You now have a means of knowledge that you did not have before. You only have perception and inference, which you cannot press into service to know yourself. Naturally, you then look for an appropriate means of knowledge and find that there is none available to you other than the one that is outside of you.

An appropriate means of knowledge must tell you something valid about yourself. In other words, it cannot be fallacious. When something is said about you, it can either be true or untrue, something that is subject to personal validation. The word 'revelation' here is to be understood in terms of an appropriate means of knowledge. The first step towards self-knowledge, then, is accepting Vedanta as a revealed means of knowledge.

How do we know that Vedanta is a means of knowledge? What is the proof? Is there a proof for a means of knowledge? If Vedanta is a means of knowledge for the self, it requires neither inferential nor perceptual proof. All that is required is, it should not contradict what you know perceptually or inferentially .

Vedanta cannot be disproved as a means of knowledge and it requires no proof other than self-validation. Let us suppose that a man, aged thirty-five, who was born blind, undergoes a new surgical procedure that will enable him to see. The surgery is considered to be a success. There are no complications and the doctors are convinced that the man will see. After removing the bandages the doctor says, 'Please open your eyes.' But keeping his eyes closed tightly, the man says, 'Doctor, I will open my eyes only when you prove that I can see.' What can the doctor do now? He is being asked to prove that the man's eyes are a means of knowledge, that they are capable of sight. But how can he do that? He can only say, 'I think you will be able to see. The surgery went very well and there is no reason why your eyes should not see.' Even if the doctor forces the man's eyes open, the only proof that he will be able to see is the sight registered by the eyes themselves.

Vedanta says that you are the solution to your problem and that there is no other solution. You have already tried to resolve the problem in a number of different ways. Vedanta does not promise anything. It does not say you will become the solution; it says you are the solution. To become the solution implies some commitment and investment. You may find it or you may not, since every 'becoming' is fraught with uncertainty.

In the vedic vision of the reality, everything that is known and unknown is Brahman, and that Brahman you are, *tat tvam asi*. Gaining this vision, you find yourself free from all the limitations imposed upon you due to ignorance and error.

Two committed lifestyles

To gain this vision, the Veda prescribes two committed lifestyles. One is a life of activity, *pravṛtti-mārga*, and the other a life of renunciation of activity, *nivṛtti-mārga*. Śaṅkara introduces his *bhāṣya* to the Bhagavadgītā with the exposition of this two-fold *dharma* as it is revealed by the Veda. Here, *dharma* can be understood as a religious or as a spiritual pursuit.

The Veda talks about action or activity, *karma*, meaning not only religious activities, but also those that we consider as secular. All activities, whether religious or secular, are considered to be *dharma*, and thereby become duties. This is what is meant by the lifestyle of *pravṛtti*, whereas the lifestyle of *nivṛtti* is called renunciation, *sannyāsa*.

The lifestyle of *pravṛtti* is two-fold, *pravṛtti* for achieving security and pleasures, here and in the hereafter, and a *pravṛtti* for the purpose of one's own maturity, for the purification of oneself, *antaḥ-karaṇa-śuddhi*. The same acts of prayers and other religious activities are done for both purposes.

So there are two types of people who follow the *pravṛtti-mārga*. Both follow the Veda, but one group does so for the purpose of gaining immediate pleasures and securities. This group also follows the Veda for unseen results of good deeds to be converted into better forms of security or pleasure later, either here or in the hereafter. The second group of people follow the Veda and engage in various actions for the sake of *antaḥ-karaṇa-śuddhi* with *mokṣa* as their end in view. People belonging to both these groups accept the Veda as a means of knowledge, *pramāṇa*, and are called *vaidika*s. And because they are *vaidika*s, they are referred to as believers, *āstika*s.

In English, we use the words 'atheist' and 'theist' purely with reference to whether a person believes in God. It is not so in *vaidika-dharma*. Here, one may believe in the Veda and not believe in a personal God at all. Such a person interprets the Veda in a manner that there is no such Īśvara, no creator at all. So, there can be a *vaidika* who accepts the Veda as a *pramāṇa*. Such a person is an *āstika*, a believer, who believes in the Veda but does not believe in God as a person.

For us, *āstika* means someone who believes in the Veda as a *pramāṇa* and *nāstika* is one who does not. Given this definition, there are many *nāstika*s, people who do not accept the Veda as a *pramāṇa* and who are religious. For instance, a follower of Buddha, although a *nāstika*, should not be dismissed as irreligious. Such people are religious in their own way. However in our view, a Buddhist is a *nāstika*, based on our definition of *āstika* and *nāstika*. Similarly, a person who follows Mahavira, a Jain, is also a *nāstika*. The *sāṅkhya* philosopher, Kapila, and his followers, on the other hand, are *āstika*s, *vaidika*s. They accept the Veda as a *pramāṇa* but they do not accept Īśvara. The one who follows the Vedic rituals, but does not accept Īśvara, is also an *āstika*.

Although Buddhists and Jains are *nāstikas*, they both believe in *karma*. They believe there is an afterlife and that there is such a thing as *nirvāṇa*, liberation, which is gained after a number of births. It is their belief and they have their own arguments to support it.

When *mokṣa* is the end in view, the two committed lifestyles, *pravṛtti-mārga* and *nivṛtti-mārga*, must be properly understood. They are stated very clearly in the Vedas and are again presented in the *Gītā* as well as by Śaṅkara in his opening commentary.

Allowing the means of knowledge to work

If I am the solution, I have no reason either to deny what Vedanta says or to prove that it is correct. Just as, in our earlier example, the man had to open his eyes to prove that he could see, so too, the only proof that Vedanta is a means of knowledge is in allowing it to work. I should let the words do their magic on me. 'Words' refer to certain knowledge born of the words. Words are not just words. They can reveal and thereby remove your ignorance.

Words need not always give rise to indirect knowledge; they can also give direct knowledge. When the Veda talks about heaven, the knowledge is definitely indirect. In fact, it is a belief. There is a description giving you some indirect knowledge about heaven, if indeed there is one. Every tradition has its own description of heaven and you understand it from that description.

The Veda reveals the self by saying that it is beyond words and, at the same time, uses words to make you see the truth of yourself. Therefore, the self is not 'beyond words' in the usual sense of the term. It is something entirely different, highly technical, as we will see; it may take some time to understand.

When words are about an object away from yourself, the knowledge is indirect and when they are about an object around yourself, the knowledge is direct. For instance, I hold up an orange. You know it is a fruit but you do not know what kind of fruit it is. When I tell you it is an orange, you come to know that it is an orange. Now you want to know how it tastes and I tell you how it tastes. It is not enough. You have to taste it actually. You also have to taste some other oranges as well. Only then you come to know more or less, all about an orange. When you smell an orange, peel it and eat it, not knowing that it is an orange, and I say, 'This is an orange,' the knowledge is direct knowledge, immediate knowledge.

I now ask, 'Do you exist or not? 'I exist. I am,' you say. Then I ask, 'Who are you?' There are many answers to this question, all of which reveal, 'I am insecure.' However, I say, 'You are secure.' This is not just a statement. I have a whole methodology of teaching. I take you through all the steps logically and then I say, 'Therefore, you are secure.' Is this knowledge immediate, direct, or mediate, indirect? It is immediate, direct knowledge. Vedanta is, therefore, a *pramāṇa*, a means of knowledge, and you have no other way to proceed except to expose yourself to it, taking it as a means of knowledge. You need to understand exactly what Vedanta is saying. If you do not understand, if you have questions, then you should make an effort to understand.

If what Vedanta says is untenable, you should see how untenable it is and examine the untenability. Perhaps it is your understanding that is untenable and what is said is tenable. If it is the case, then, you need to correct your understanding and keep correcting it, thereby seeing what Vedanta has to say.

Gītā as a means of knowledge

The *Gītā*, of course, is not as voluminous as the Vedas, which contain all the *Upaniṣads*. The *Upaniṣads* are the original source book which are understood with the help of books like the *Gītā* that presents the same material very cogently in an easily understood form. This is why the *Gītā* is referred to as the *gītā-śāstra*.

The *Gītā* contains seven hundred verses in eighteen chapters, the first chapter and the initial few verses of second chapter providing the context. We then have the entire *gītā-śāstra* in seventeen chapters wherein the two-fold *dharma* of a committed lifestyle for *mokṣa* is unfolded. Because the *Gītā* is a book, *grantha*, that unfolds this *dharma*, it is looked upon as a *pramāṇa-grantha* even though the *Upaniṣads* are the *pramāṇa*, not being born of a given intellect. The *Upaniṣads*, meaning the Vedas, form the means of knowledge. But the *Gītā* is also looked upon as a *pramāṇa* because it upholds and unfolds what the Veda, the *śruti*, says. If the *Gītā* said anything that is not in keeping with the *śruti*, then it would definitely not be considered a *pramāṇa-grantha*. The *Gītā* would not be studied, nor would Śaṅkara have written a commentary on it.

The *Gītā* is accepted as a *pramāṇa-grantha* because of its affinity and fidelity to the Veda. Lord Kṛṣṇa himself confirms in the *Gītā* that, what he is saying has already been said in the Veda. Further more, the *Gītā* is presented by Vyāsa who is considered to be the editor of the Vedas.

The four Vedas, collectively referred to as the Veda, existed even before Vyāsa. He was the one who grouped them properly so that a designated person in a given family could study one particular Veda and then hand it over to each succeeding generation. Because Vyāsa knew the Vedas so well, he was considered to be all-knowing, *sarvajña*. In the middle of the vast, beautiful word tapestry of his epic Mahābhārata, Vyāsa presented the wisdom of the Vedas in the form of the *Gītā*. It shines in the midst of the much larger work like a pendant jewel. These eighteen chapters are, therefore, considered to be an authentic *pramāṇa*.

The first argument for the *Gītā* being a *pramāṇa* is that it does not contradict what the Veda says. It expounds and illustrates what the source book says. The second argument is that it is presented by Vyāsa. Thirdly, Vyāsa presents Kṛṣṇa as an *avatāra* of the Lord. Therefore, Kṛṣṇa is looked upon as an *avatāra*, a particular form that the Lord assumed for achieving certain limited ends.

If the concept of *avatāra* is accepted, then Kṛṣṇa as an *avatāra* is Lord Nārāyaṇa, Īśvara himself. So when Kṛṣṇa talks in the *Gītā*, Īśvara, the Lord, is talking. What is said is the word of Bhagavān, *bhagavad-vacana*, and Bhagavān is telling us what the Veda says. This again makes the *Gītā*, a *pramāṇa-grantha* for the believers. When Bhagavān himself is talking about what is said in the Vedas, what else do we want? Because the *Gītā* is *bhagavad-vacana*, the word of Bhagavān, it is a *pramāṇa*.

Meaning of Bhagavān

Bhagavān[5] is the one who has *bhaga*, the six-fold virtues in absolute measure. These are – all-knowledge, *jñāna*; total dispassion, *vairāgya;* the capacity to create, sustain and resolve, *vīrya;* absolute fame, *yaśas;* all wealth, *śrī*; and overlordship, *aiśvarya*.

To have all-knowledge, *jñāna*, is to be free from all ignorance. The one who has all-knowledge does not require a mind, perception or other means of knowledge with which to know. If we require a mind to know, there is always ignorance. Whoever is endowed with a mind in order to know cannot be Bhagavān. We will see later how it is possible to be one with Bhagavān. *Bhaga*, therefore, is *jñāna*, all-knowledge.

Total dispassion is also called *bhaga*. The one who has total, absolute dispassion, *vairāgya*, has no longing, no insecurity. He or she is full. *Vīrya* is absolute power, *śakti*, meaning the capacity to create, to sustain, and to resolve. The one who has this absolute power is called the Almighty.

Absolute fame, *yaśas*, means all fame, including your own or anyone else's. It is also *bhaga*. For example, the one who is

---

[5] भगः अस्य अस्ति इति भगवान्

bhagaḥ asya asti iti bhagavān – the one who has *bhaga* is called Bhagavān. It is said in the *Viṣṇu-purāṇa:*

ऐश्वर्यस्य समग्रस्य वीर्यस्य यशसः श्रियः । ज्ञानवैराग्ययोश्चैव षण्णां भग इतीरणा ॥

aiśvaryasya samagrasya vīryasya yaśasaḥ śriyaḥ jñānavairāgyayoścaiva ṣaṇṇāṁ bhaga itīraṇā (*Viṣṇu-purāṇa*: 6.5.74)

Total and absolute overlordship, power, wealth, dispassion, fame and knowledge are known as *bhaga*.

endowed with the ability to sing, may gain some fame, a ray of glory, but that fame belongs to the Lord, the one who has all-fame. The Lord also has all-wealth, all-resources, *śrī*. Any wealth you may have really belongs to Bhagavān. You are only the trustee of whatever resources you happen to have.

Finally, the one who is not caused, who is not ruled by anyone, who is not subject to the laws of someone else, has the *bhaga* called *aiśvarya*, overlordship. We, as individuals, have to go by the laws of nature; we cannot go against them. Even an engineer who is responsible for planning, commissioning, and running a thermal plant cannot touch a live wire without facing the consequences. In other words, the engineer cannot behave as he or she likes merely because he or she caused the electricity to be generated. It was because of the laws alone that the engineer was able to generate electricity in the first place.

The one who does not subject himself to the law or laws of another is the Lord. If the Lord is ruled by someone else, then that someone else becomes the Lord; and it is this Lord that we are talking about. These six absolute virtues, then, constitute *bhaga* and the one who has this six-fold *bhaga* is Bhagavān.

Bhagavadgītā – the Lord's song

There are varieties of *Gītā* – the *Anugītā, Uttaragītā, Kāmagītā, Pāṇḍavagītā, Haṁsagītā, Siddhagītā, Rāmagītā, Uddhavagītā, Gaṇeśagītā* and so on, but the most popular one is the Bhagavadgītā.

The title 'Bhagavadgītā' means the song, *Gītā*, of the Lord, Bhagavān. It is considered a song because it is in the form of verse and therefore pleasing. It has only two meters, *anuṣṭubh* and *triṣṭubh*, making the *Gītā* easy to recite and remember. The *Gītā* is also pleasing because it has a subject matter that is highly desirable to all.

The word, 'Bhagavadgītā' is feminine in gender because the Veda, that is *śruti*, is feminine; what is said in the *śruti* is said in the *Gītā*, further revealing it. And who is Bhagavān here? Kṛṣṇa is Bhagavān. Kṛṣṇa is the one who has proved that he has the six-fold *bhaga*s and is, therefore, looked upon as Bhagavān. Once you understand the meaning of Bhagavān as the one who has *bhaga*, Kṛṣṇa being Bhagavān presents no problem at all.

Subject matter of the Gītā

We can look at the title Bhagavadgītā in another way – as a song that has Bhagavān as its subject matter. It is similar to saying 'Electronic knowledge,' knowledge whose subject matter is electronics. So, we can take the title Bhagavadgītā to mean either Bhagavān's *Gītā* or a *Gītā*, song, that has Bhagavān as its subject matter.

The Bhagavadgītā, with Bhagavān as its subject matter, actually has two aspects, because both a life of activity and a life of renunciation are presented. One is *yoga-śāstra* in that it talks about *karma-yoga* and the other is *brahma-vidyā*, knowledge of Brahman. Its subject matter, therefore, implies both activity and the renunciation of activity.

Since both the lifestyles are meant for *brahma-vidyā*, *brahma-vidyā* is its real subject matter. It is this *brahma-vidyā* that is pursued by a *sannyāsī* to the exclusion of all else – a *sannyāsī* being the one who has given up all *karmas*.

While a *sannyāsī* pursues only *brahma-vidyā*, a *karma-yogī* pursues *brahma-vidyā* plus *karma*. How does a *karma-yogī* pursue *karma*? With an attitude whereby the *karma* that is done becomes *yoga* for him or her. Because both *brahma-vidyā* and *karma-yoga* are found in the *Gītā*, its subject matter is two-fold, *brahma-vidyā* and *yoga-śāstra*.

Brahma-vidyā means the knowledge of 'what is.' What is Brahman? What is Īśvara, the Lord? What is the reality of the world, *jagat*? What is the nature of the individual, *jīva*? What is the truth of oneself, *ātmā*? What is the relationship between the *jīva*, the *jagat* and Īśvara? What is the reality of each of them? Is there anything common among them? Are they all one or are they separate entities? *Brahma-vidyā*, knowledge of Brahman, reveals all of this.

To gain this *brahma-vidyā*, there are certain qualifications mentioned, which *karma-yoga* alone can provide. To help one gain these qualifications, *karma-yoga* is discussed in detail in the *Gītā*. Because both *karma-yoga* and *brahma-vidyā* are dealt with, the *Gītā* is considered complete and referred to as *gītā-śāstra*.

There is one particular verse praising the *Gītā* –'*Gītā sugītā kartavyā kim anyaiḥ śāstra-vistaraiḥ*, the *Gītā* has to be studied well; what is the use of studying other elaborate works?' The completeness of the subject matter unfolded by the *Gītā* is highlighted here.

People always say that whenever they are in trouble, they go to the *Gītā* and their problem is solved. Maybe they do find answers in the *Gītā* because they can read into it whatever they want. Be that as it may, the *Gītā* has something of its own to give. Do you want what it has to give? That is the question.

To know what the *Gītā* says requires enquiry, *vicāra*. In the introduction to his commentary on the *Gītā*, Śaṅkara says:

तदिदं गीताशास्त्रं समस्त-वेदार्थ-सार-सङ्ग्रहभूतं दुर्विज्ञेयार्थम् ।

tadidaṁ gītāśāstraṁ samasta-vedārtha-sāra-saṅgrahabhūtaṁ durvijñeyārtham.

The sense of the *gītā-śastra*, which is in the form of the essence of the meanings of all the words of Vedas, is difficult to grasp.

तदर्थ-आविष्करणाय अनेकैः विवृत-पद-पदार्थ-वाक्यार्थ-न्यायम् अपि अत्यन्त-विरुद्ध-अनेकार्थत्वेन लौकिकैः गृह्यमाणम् उपलभ्य अहं विवेकतः अर्थनिर्धारणार्थं संक्षेपतः विवरणं करिष्यामि ।

tadartha-āviṣkaraṇāya anekaiḥ vivṛta-pada-padārtha-vākyārtha-nyāyam api atyanta-viruddha-anekārthatvena laukikaiḥ gṛhyamāṇam upalabhya ahaṁ vivekataḥ arthanirdhāraṇārthaṁ saṅkṣepataḥ vivaraṇaṁ kariṣyāmi.

By many commentators, in an effort to clearly expound its meaning, this has been expounded in the form of treatises that deal with the words of this text, the meanings of the words, the meanings of sentences, the logic involved, and so on. Seeing that they are fraught with vagueness and contradictions, in order to ascertain the correct meaning with due discrimination, I am writing this brief commentary.

Need for a Guru

The essence of any knowledge is sometimes expressed too cryptically to be understood. Because the *Gītā* is the essence, one naturally has to know the entire *śāstra* to fully appreciate what the *Gītā* is saying. Even though Arjuna had certain background, it was not easy for him to understand. He had to ask questions. If it was not easy for Arjuna, it is definitely not going to be easy for someone in our own time who does not have the same background, being far removed from both Arjuna and the Vedas. For such a person, the *Gītā* will be as difficult to understand as any other text of Vedanta. The knowledge of oneself is in the form of words. But since the subject matter is something very unique, the knowledge is not easily accessible through words. At the same time, words are employed to reveal the self immediately. Therefore, one requires not only the teaching, Vedanta as *pramāṇa*, but also a teacher, a *guru*.

There are two letters in the word, *guru*, '*gu*' meaning darkness or ignorance, and '*ru*' meaning the one who removes it. Thus, a *guru* is one who removes darkness of ignorance by teaching the *śāstra*. The teaching is the *śāstra* and the teacher is also the *śāstra*. As a teacher, then, I do not use the *śāstra*; rather, what I teach is *śāstra*.

What does this mean? The teaching itself comes to life when it is handled in a certain way. Otherwise, all you have are so many dead words. Even though the teaching is a *pramāṇa*, there is a methodology employed for unfolding the words. A teacher, a *guru*, is one who is able to unfold the meaning of these words. The words are already there and their meanings are already there. They need only to be unfolded for your comprehension, just as an artist unfolds his vision on the canvas.

The problem then is, who is the first *guru*? I answer that question by asking, 'Who is the first father?' When you tell me who the first father is, I will tell you who the first *guru* is. Either way, it is the same. If you say that the Lord, the creator, is the father, then he also must have a father, which means that he cannot be the creator. Therefore, there is no father for the one whom you call the Lord.

Someone claimed that the first father was a monkey, which is an inferential conclusion. You will find, however, that this monkey also had a father, who had a father, who had a father, until finally you give up. Because you are into infinite regression, you had better give up! Or, you may decide that the first father was one who was not a son. He was only a father whom we call the Lord.

If we assume that the father is the Lord, then, the first *guru* is not going to be different from that Lord. And, from the Lord downward, there is a teacher-student lineage, *guru-śiṣya paramparā*. The entire *paramparā* is praised in the following verse:

सदाशिवसमारम्भां शङ्कराचार्यमध्यमाम् ।
अस्मदाचार्यपर्यन्तां वन्दे गुरुपरम्पराम् ॥

sadāśivasamārambhāṁ śaṅkarācāryamadhyamām
asmadācāryaparyantāṁ vande guruparamparām

I salute the lineage of teachers, beginning with Śiva, the Lord, (linked by) Śaṅkarācārya in the middle, and extending down to my own teacher.

When you salute the teacher, your salutation goes to the Lord in whom the lineage has its beginning. To point out one of the links, Śaṅkarācārya is mentioned as being in the middle, meaning somewhere in the flow between the Lord and one's present teacher. The word 'middle' having been used, there must also be an end. If the begining is Lord Śiva meaning the Lord, one who is all fullness, all-knowledge, and the middle is Śaṅkarācārya, then who is the end? My teacher, *asmadācārya*.

Because I am here today, I know there has been no break in the flow between the first father and myself. Similarly, since this knowledge is coming to me right now, I know it has been kept alive by one teacher giving it to another and, thus, there has been no break between my teacher and the Lord. I salute this *guru-paramparā*.

To choose a *guru* can also be a problem. Do you find the teacher with the longest or the whitest beard? So much is said by so many, everyone claiming to know the truth. Given all this confusion, first and foremost, I would say that the best teacher is one who looks at the whole human problem as an error.

If someone says you have a problem, then that person is going to manipulate you. If, however, the person says that the problem that you seem to have is an error, then he or she is objective. And, if the problem is real, no one will be able to resolve it.

If the situation is factually real, how can it be changed? If I am really an inadequate and limited person, then there is no way of my solving the problem of inadequacy with or without help. The limited is always limited. But here, there is no need to say, 'If I am a fraction of the whole, I will always be a fraction of the whole.' If I am the whole, the conclusion that I am a fraction is an error and the way out is to see myself in the proper light. Thus, the one who says the problem is an error and that it is a universal error, not your own personal error, may be a *guru*.

In order to know that I am the whole and, therefore, acceptable to myself, it is said, 'May one go to a teacher, *gurum abhigacchet*.' What kind of a teacher? The Veda itself says that, the teacher should be one who is well informed in this teaching and who is well rooted in this knowledge – one who is a *śrotriya* and a *brahma-niṣṭha*.[6] But how do I know whether someone is well informed or not? If I want to study higher mathematics and do research in topology, I need only find someone who

---

[6] तद्विज्ञानार्थं स गुरुमेवाभिगच्छेत् समित्पाणिः श्रोत्रियं ब्रह्मनिष्ठम् (मुण्डकोपनिषद् १.२.१२)

tadvijñānārthaṁ sa gurumevābhigacchet samitpāṇiḥ śrotriyaṁ brahmaniṣṭham. (*Muṇḍakopaniṣad* 1.2.12) For gaining that knowledge, may one properly approach a teacher who is a *śrotriya* and a *brahma-niṣṭha*.

has studied higher mathematics and specialised in topology. If I find a person who has published numerous credible papers on topology, I can assume that he or she knows the subject matter. I can then decide to study with this person until he or she proves otherwise.

In *guru*-seeking, however, there is a problem because this knowledge, being spritual knowledge, is different. How do you know the person has this knowledge and has undergone the discipline of learning unless you already know something of it yourself?

The society should be informed enough for one to be able to find out whether a person knows or only pretends to know. The person could also be deluded, not pretending to know, but thinking he or she knows. Such people do not know what they do not know.

Previously, in Indian society, this was not a problem because everyone is supposed to become a *sannyāsī* eventually. One did not start another life after retirement. But nowadays, people plan their retirements early. Still, the best retirement plan to be ever conceived is *sannyāsa*, which was meant to be the last stage of one's life. Having been married and so on, the time comes when one just walks out, not because of a quarrel or because one wants to marry another person. Walking out is considered a part of married life and is appreciated by both the husband and wife as its ultimate aim. At this stage, they have matured and are independent enough for a life of *sannyāsa*.

This kind of retirement plan requires no social security, only the maturity to walk out as a renunciate. Since the Indian society respects the *sannyāsa* stage of life and the Veda enjoins it, naturally the basic needs of a *sannyāsī* are taken care of by the society. Although some people postpone this stage of life, everyone is expected to become a *sannyāsī* in the end.

To be a *sannyāsī* means you already have the knowledge or you are seeking it. Even as a householder, you are supposed to study in order to gain self-knowledge. Once a person becomes a *sannyāsī*, he or she has no daily duties, except studying and teaching. In every village, you will find a few *sannyāsī*s permanently staying there, or who keep coming and going, so that the society knows who they are; just as you know who is a professor of mathematics and who is not. To do research in mathematics or electronics, you have no doubt with regard to the person to whom you should go to, and which institution you should attend. So, there is no problem in choosing a teacher for this knowledge in society.

If you know exactly what you are seeking, to that extent you can know whether the person who is recognised as having the knowledge, knows or not. However, if people do not know these things, then they are totally gullible, in spite of their expertise in other fields. For such people, anyone can pass as a *guru*.

A person who has undergone this discipline of knowledge is a scholarly person, *śrotriya*. A *guru* is a scholar, whereas a scholar need not be a *guru*. To be a *guru*, a committed pursuit is also necessary. One who is committed to this knowledge is called a *brahma-niṣṭha*. This is an important point to understand.

If the knowledge is used to gain security, the person is insecure. Moreover, because the knowledge is 'I am secure,' the person does not really know anything about it and is, therefore, not qualified to teach it. Such a person is self-seeking and has no knowledge to give you. All that he or she can give is a collection of words, for which you do not require a teacher. You need only a book and a dictionary!

The teacher you require is one who employs these words and makes them meaningful. To do this, a teacher must necessarily be free from being insecure so that he or she is not seeking recognition or security. The proof of a teacher's knowledge is in the teaching methodology, in the person's communicative ability and the content of what he or she communicates. Thus, you go to a teacher who is well informed and committed to this teaching and who has no other pursuit.

How should you go to a teacher? With an attitude that indicates you are ready to serve the teacher, meaning, you are ready to do what is to be done in order to gain this knowledge because of your love for it. Nothing is too much and no distance is too far. This attitude is not damaging to you because you have chosen the right teacher. Hence, there is no question of the person exploiting you if he or she is a *guru* – true to the definition of the word *guru*. A *guru* exploits no one. Thus, you will do whatever you can do. It is your attitude. Only then can the teaching begin.

Gītā as a dialogue

The entire *Gītā* is a dialogue. In fact, all the teaching is in the form of a dialogue, although the methodology of the teaching does not necessitate the presentation of characters and the dialogues between them. After all, we are not interested in knowing the names of the teacher or the taught. We are only interested in the teaching itself. However, the characters involved in the dialogue are presented in the form of a story, an *ākhyāyikā,* in order to tell us something about ourselves.

We find the same approach in the *Upaniṣad*s where many names of people are cited. If *'tat tvam asi*–that thou art,' is the message, why not just talk about that message? Why are all these stories brought in? Only to reveal the method of teaching, the *sampradāya*, how we have to learn, and what type of knowledge it is.

Four types of dialogue

There are different types of dialogues. One is a discussion involving two or more people who are interested in finding out the facts about a subject matter; they are exploring. In this type of discussion, there is no teacher-student relationship. Each person is equally placed, even though one person may know a little more than the others about the subject matter. They are interested in understanding. This kind of discussion among equals or any collective study among students is called *vāda*. It is naturally healthy and is traditionally an important component of study. It is said that a student gains a quarter of his knowledge by such discussion.[7]

There are two types of unhealthy dialogue that we should be aware of. One is the dialogue that takes place between two people who are already committed to different beliefs. Such a discussion, called *jalpa,* is governed purely by each person's wit. Any discussion between two fanatics falls into this category. Each of them is convinced that the other person is totally wrong and tries to win over the other to his or her particular belief, although there is no basis for the discussion.

Suppose, you have a belief and I have another belief. Your belief may be right and mine may be wrong. On the other hand, my belief may be right and yours may be wrong. Or both of us may be wrong. Both of us may be right also. How, then, can either of us insist that 'I alone am right?' The difference between a believer and a fanatic becomes obvious here.

The difference between a scientist and a believer is also worthy of notice. One may adhere to a belief, but everyone must neccesarily have a mind that is open to explore and know. That open, enquiring mind, the mind of a scientist, is an entirely different mind from that of a believer.

---

[7] With reference to gaining any empirical discipline of knowledge, there is a verse that says:

आचार्यात् पादमादत्ते पादं शिष्य स्वमेधया । पादं सब्रह्मचारिभ्यः पादं कालक्रमेण च ॥

ācāryāt pādamādatte pādaṁ śiṣyaḥ svamedhayā
pādaṁ sabrahmacāribhyaḥ pādaṁ kālakrameṇa ca

A student obtains one quarter from the teacher, one quarter by one's own intelligence, one quarter from the fellow students, and one quarter in time. The third quarter refers to *vāda*.

We can and must respect the beliefs of others, but we cannot have a discussion based on such beliefs. Both of us may be wrong. A discussion between two people, both of whom are committed to certain beliefs, is purely a dialogue between two missionaries. It is better to respect the other person's belief and have a simple human relationship. Discussions are useless. All you can do is ask, 'What is your belief?' Some people are curious. If you are curious you can ask, but I myself would not ask because the other person is acceptable to me along with his or her beliefs. I need not know what they are. This is a healthy attitude to have towards a person. But any discussion, *jalpa*, based on beliefs, is useless. No one wins and no one loses. Each person always comes back with better arguments. Therefore, *jalpa*, discussions, are useless; they have no value.

There is another type of discussion called *vitaṇḍā*, wherein one person makes a statement with which the other person always disagrees. Why? Merely because the other person said it. Due to jealousy or some other reason, one person always tries to prove the other wrong. Such a discussion is also useless.

Dialogue between teacher and student

A fourth type of discussion, one that concerns us here, is called *saṁvāda*, a discussion between a teacher and a student, *guru-śiṣya-saṁvāda*. In the teacher-student relationship, the student has already accepted the other person as a teacher and, therefore, looks up to him or her. Although there is a dialogue between them, the attitude is entirely different, the discussion being based on the student's acceptance that, 'I am a student and this person is my teacher.' This attitude prevails until or unless the person, thought to be a teacher, proves to be otherwise.

The moment you discover the person has nothing to teach, you can become friends. However, when you have to learn from someone, you look up to that person. If you do not understand what the teacher is saying, you give the benefit of doubt to the teacher, even though he or she may sometimes appear to be contradictory, seeming to have said something previously that is not in harmony with what is being said now, as we will see in the *Gītā*.

In a *guru-śiṣya-saṁvāda*, the subject matter can be anything. Here, in the *Gītā*, the subject matter is *brahma-vidyā* and *yoga śāstra*; in one word, Vedanta. The *guru* is Bhagavān Kṛṣṇa, referred to as Vasudeva's son, and the student is Arjuna, called Pārtha here because he is Pṛthā's son. He is also called Kaunteya, the son of Kuntī. Arjuna has a number of other names such as Dhanañjaya, Savyasācī, Guḍākeśa and so on, but Arjuna is his popular name.

Between Arjuna, the student, and Lord Kṛṣṇa, the teacher, there is a discussion and the *Gītā* is the body of knowledge being taught. Therefore, the *Gītā* is called a *saṁvāda*.

Giving the benefit of doubt to the teacher

If it looks as though the teacher is being contradictory, then the student gives the benefit of doubt to the teacher. It is what is expected of a student. As a student, one need not take the blame upon oneself.

The teacher can be asked a question, 'Previously such and such was said and now this is being said, why is this difference? You said Brahman is without qualities, *nirguṇa* and now you say it is with qualities, *saguṇa*. How can Brahman be *saguṇa?* You say it is beyond the mind, and that it is not available as an object for the mind. At the same time, you say, one sees oneself, the *ātmā* with the mind, *manasā paśyati*. How can one see the *ātmā* with the mind? And how is one going to know that one is seeing the *ātmā?*' It looks as though the *śruti* herself is contradictory. To say that Brahman cannot be objectified by the mind but has to be recognised by the mind seems to be a contradiction. But it is not a contradiction; it is perfect. If it looks like a contradiction to the student, then he or she can ask a *praśna*, question, and when the student waits for the right time to ask a question, it is called *paripraśna*, based on his or her faith, *śraddhā*, in the teacher.

As a teacher, one cannot contradict oneself. A teacher who contradicts himself or herself does not know the subject matter. Nor can a teacher simply learn along with a student and teach, since it creates situations wherein both the teacher and the student may suddenly discover a new fact never known to either of them before, a fact that contradicts everything they have known thus far. This is not why one goes to a teacher. Teaching is not meant to be exploratory. Therefore, the teacher should know exactly what he or she is talking about and not be contradictory.

The attitude implied by the term *guru-śiṣya-saṁvāda* is especially relevant here. Since the entire teaching is itself a means of knowledge, it is not a philosophical speculation.

Moreover you are not attracted to this kind of learning out of a simple academic interest. The teaching has a value and the value is yourself alone. The teaching is about you. You have a value for freedom and this value makes you want to know. As a person, you want to be free and you want to learn for no other purpose than to be free. Since there is a value, and the teaching itself is a means of knowledge, there must necessarily be certain attitude on your part towards this teaching and the teacher.

That the teaching has to come from a teacher in the form of a dialogue is because it is something to be understood, something to be followed and not swallowed. In a belief, there is nothing to follow, only something to swallow, something to accept totally, without question. Any questioning that may take place is meant only to establish what the belief is, which is not really questioning at all. This is why there are so many attempts to establish historical proofs that a certain person existed. Whether someone existed is not the issue. The teaching is the issue.

If you look into the teaching and you are interested in what is being taught, your whole attitude and approach will be different. Here, a dialogue implies a teaching that is received from a teacher, meaning that the knowledge has to be received from a teacher and the subject matter has to be understood.

Two types of subject matter

There are two types of subject matter – *sādhya-viṣaya* and *siddha-viṣaya*. *Sādhya* is that which is yet to be accomplished and is accomplished by doing something, by an action. For instance, if you want to know how to go to heaven, first you have to know what heaven is and then you have to decide to buy a ticket. You are told that *puṇya*, the ticket for heaven, can be gained by doing good deeds. You must also hold on to the *puṇya* you have earned, which means that you must not do any improper actions, *pāpa*, while you are earning your ticket to heaven. Only then will you go to heaven after death. All this is very straightforward for a person who has *śraddhā* in the Veda being a *pramāṇa* and is not something that can be logically arrived at.

Any question related to *sādhya* is only to understand how to do something, like cooking for example. An Indian woman who wants to know how to make pizza will ask a few questions. The situation is very simple. You just tell her how to do it a few times until she knows how, and the topic is over. It is just a matter of whether she has understood what you have said. There is an order governing how everything is to be done. Certain elements are involved and, therefore, must be understood. What has to be done is also to be understood; and that is the end of it. One may do it or not do it. By practice, one eventually acquires the knack of it. If a person keeps on making pizza, hopefully with some sympathetic people around, he or she will certainly master the art of pizza making.

This is *sādhya*, then. There is no questioning here. When the subject matter is something you have to accomplish later, when it is dealing with means and ends, *sādhana* and *sādhya*, questioning is not part of the whole approach. It is true even if the subject matter is a Vedic ritual.

Again, when it comes to actions there are many choices available. You can do it this way or that way; you need not do it at all; or you can entirely do something else and achieve the same result.[8]

There is more than one way to go to heaven. There are hundred different ways, of which one can choose any. Why anyone would want to go is another matter. Thus, when a *sādhya-viṣaya* is involved, there can be choice. But this is not so with a *siddha-viṣaya*.

There is no choice in knowledge

There is no choice involved, however, when what is to be accomplished is already accomplished, *siddha*, but not understood. Unlike action, knowledge is not open to choice; it is always true to its object. For example, knowledge of an apple is always true to the object, apple, even if you will it to be otherwise. Nor do you have a choice in knowledge, once the means of knowledge and the object of knowledge are aligned. If your eyes are open, and if they are not defective, and if the mind is not elsewhere, you will necessarily see what is in front of you. What choice do you have?

To know an already accomplished fact requires proper questioning in order to remove whatever that may be blocking the knowledge from taking place. Why should you be denied

---

[8] कर्म – कर्तुं शक्यम् अकर्तुं शक्यम् अन्यथा वा कर्तुं शक्यम् ।

karma – kartuṁ śakyam akartuṁ śakyam anyathā vā kartuṁ śakyam

Action– may be done, may not be done or may be done differently.

the knowledge of yourself once it is unfolded? What exactly is the obstruction? Is it that you do not follow what is being said? Once the obstructions have been identified, they have to be removed one by one, because you are Brahman. The whole pursuit, then, is one of removing all doubts.

Since it is the knowledge of an already accomplished fact, the knowledge has to be immediate. It cannot be indirect. If it does not happen in spite of the teaching, then there is some obstruction, which is in the form of error, vagueness or doubt. The obstructions are removed in the dialogue between the teacher and the student.

Significance of questioning

Where there is understanding involved, questioning is imperative. It does not mean that you should question all the time. What is meant is that a questioning mind is necessary because without questioning you can never gain clarity. Therefore, the teaching itself consists of a number of questions. As teachers, we ourselves raise questions and keep answering them. If the student still has questions, he or she should ask those questions in order to know, since we are not dealing with a simple belief here. And if we find that something is a belief, we can say, 'This is a belief,' thereby ending the matter.

We do not try to establish a belief, beyond establishing that it is a belief. For example, the statement, 'This is my mother,' is a belief because there is no way of proving it. How do you know two babies were not switched? There may be a lot of corroborative evidence, but still it is a belief. It is not direct perception. There are many beliefs and there is nothing wrong with beliefs, as long as we understand them as beliefs. However, there are also many things we have to know, and where we have to know, questions are very important and are allowed. The *Gītā* is presented as a dialogue between a teacher and a student to emphasise that the subject matter is one for understanding, not for believing.

Commentaries on the Gītā

Śaṅkara says that he is writing this commentary on the *Gītā* so that people can analyse and understand what the true meaning of the *gītā-śāstra* is, although it had already been elaborately commented upon by others. The earlier commentaries, no matter how definitive they were, sometimes differed from one another; and in some cases, they were even opposed to each other. Since these various works were confusing to those who did not have a clear understanding of the *śāstra*, Śaṅkara decided to undertake this work in order to clarify what the *Gītā* is actually saying.

Since Śaṅkara's time, there have been numerous commentaries and translations in various languages with varying degrees of clarity. None has matched Śaṅkara's analysis of the *Gītā*. His commentary is extremely cogent and consistent from the begining to the end. For instance, whenever the topic of *bhakti* comes up, he discusses it in its proper context. Wherever Īśvara is mentioned, even though Lord Kṛṣṇa uses the first person singular, Śaṅkara makes it very clear that, what was meant was the Lord, Īśvara, Paramātmā.

When the *Gītā* is analysed properly, the analysis must be rational. It should not go against reason. A commentary on the *Gītā* should be in keeping with the words that are there. It should honour all the rules of grammar and syntax. What was said before and what is said later should also be taken into account.

Since the *Gītā* is a book that contains only what is said in the *Upaniṣads*, there is all the more reason for any commentary on it. Nothing should contradict the source book. Our understanding of the *Gītā* should definitely be in keeping with all these various factors. Only then can there be real understanding. Whether the *Gītā* says this or that is something that must be understood. We are not trying to make the *Gītā* say what we want to say. We are trying to understand what it says, and for this we need to enquire and be objective. This is why before approaching the *Gītā*, a few verses called the *Gītā-dhyānam* are sung in praise of it, whereby we invoke Mother *Gītā* to reveal the truth contained in the *gītā-śāstra*. These verses are a prayer to the *Gītā* herself, to the *Gītā* as the mother *śruti* and to the *Gītā* as Bhagavān, the Lord. It is only after we have invoked the *Gītā* in this way, do we try to extract the exact meaning of what the *Gītā* has to say.

The *Gītā* is like a mirror, just as the *Upaniṣads* are a mirror of words wherein we can see ourselves very clearly. If the world is not separate from me and if Īśvara also is not separate from me, then I should be able to see this truth in the words of the *Gītā*. The prayer is for the sake of understanding the *Gītā* properly, which is understanding myself.

In the brief discussion of the *Gītā-dhyāna* verses that follow, you will come across sentences requiring further elucidation and more clarity in order for you to enjoy their meaning completely. This clarity will come as the *Gītā* is unfolded.

Gītā Dhyānam

In praise of Gītā

Verse 1

ॐ पार्थाय प्रतिबोधितां भगवता नारायणेन स्वयं
व्यासेन ग्रथितां पुराणमुनिना मध्येमहाभारतम् ।
अद्वैतामृतवर्षिणीं भगवतीमष्टादशाध्यायिनीम्
अम्ब त्वाम् अनुसन्दधामि भगवद्गीते भवद्वेषिणीम् ॥ १ ॥

om pārthāya pratibodhitāṁ bhagavatā nārāyaṇena svayaṁ
vyāsena grathitāṁ purāṇamuninā madhyemahābhāratam
advaitāmṛtavarṣiṇīṁ bhagavatīmaṣṭādaśādhyāyinīm
amba tvām anusandadhāmi bhagavadgīte bhavadveṣiṇīm (1)

Om – name of the Lord; *amba bhagavadgīte* – O Mother Bhagavadgītā!; *bhagavatā nārāyaṇena* – by Bhagavān Nārāyaṇa; *svayam* – himself; *pārthāya* – to the son of Pṛthā; *pratibodhitām* – (you who were) taught; *purāṇa muninā vyāsena grathitām* – (you who were) faithfully collected and reported by the ancient sage Vyāsa; *madhye-mahābhāratam* – in the middle of the Mahābhārata; *advaita-amṛta varṣiṇīm* – (you who have) the nature of showering the nectar of non-duality; *aṣṭādaśa-adhyāyinīm* – (you who are) in the form of eighteen chapters; *bhavadveṣiṇīm* – (you who are) the destroyer of the life of becoming, *saṁsāra*; *bhagavatīm* – (you who are) the Goddess; *tvām anusandadhāmi* – I repeatedly invoke

Om. Goddess Mother Bhagavadgītā! I repeatedly invoke you who were taught by Bhagavān Nārāyaṇa himself for the sake of Arjuna, the son of Pṛthā (Kuntī), (you who were) faithfully collected and reported by the ancient sage, Vyāsa, (and placed) in the middle of the Mahābhārata, (you who are) in eighteen chapters, you who have the nature of showering the nectar of non-duality, and who is the destroyer of the life of becoming (*saṁsāra*).

Gītā invoked as mother

Any beginning is considered to be auspicious. Since the word 'Om' is the name of Bhagavān, the Lord, it is an auspicious way to begin these verses in which we invoke the Lord's help as we begin our study of the *Gītā*.

A mother is a symbol of love, affection and spontaneous care, is someone who always prays for your welfare, who never lets you down when you are in trouble. It is also true of the Vedas because, with great compassion, the Veda takes into account the need for the human being to achieve various things in life and talks about the various means and ends for you to achieve them. Finally through self-knowledge in the *Upaniṣad*s, the person gets out of the pursuit of means and ends. Therefore, the Veda or the *śruti* is given the status of a mother. And because the *Gītā* says exactly what the Vedas say, it is also looked upon as a mother.

In this opening verse, the *Gītā* is invoked in this way: O Mother! I invoke you. I meditate upon you again and again as a mother of blessing.

The *Gītā* was taught to Arjuna. He is called Pārtha in this verse because he is the son of Pṛthā, another name for his mother Kuntī. Because the *Gītā* was taught for Arjuna's sake, Arjuna is said to be its cause, *nimitta*.

Kṛṣṇa as teacher of Gītā

Bhagavān Nārāyaṇa, the Lord, taught the knowledge contained in the *Gītā*. It was not taught by any other *guru*, but directly by Nārāyaṇa. Even though every *guru* is considered to be Nārāyaṇa, this verse makes it clear that all-knowledge Lord himself, as Kṛṣṇa, was the teacher of the *Gītā*.

There are many ways of looking at the meaning of the word Nārāyaṇa, one of which is particularly relevant here. The word *nara* is used to refer to a human being. It also means indestructible, that which always remains, not destroyed, *na rīyate iti naraḥ*. Nara, therefore, can only refer to that which pervades everything and is timeless, *ātmā* in Sanskrit. *Ātmā* here refers to 'I' the essence of the subject who performs various actions and enjoys various forms of experiences. It is an entirely different meaning from what we commonly understand by the word 'I.' Therefore, the real meaning of the word *nara*, human being, is to be understood from the *śāstra*, to be the all-pervasive and timeless *ātmā*, *paramātmā*.

Narasya idaṁ nāram, that which belongs to the *nara* is *nāra* or *jagat*, the world. The world is born out of the all-pervasive, timeless *paramātmā*, is sustained by *paramātmā* and goes back to *paramātmā*. *Nāra*, then, is the entire world. And, *nāram eti iti* Nārāyaṇa, the one who knows the *nāra*, the world is Nārāyaṇa, the omniscient Lord, Parameśvara. Therefore, the same *ātmā*, the *nara-ātmā*, the human being, is the omniscient *paramātmā*, Parameśvara, the Lord. Because this omniscient Nārāyaṇa is the one who is teaching Arjuna here, everything that is taught in the *Gītā* is considered valid. Nārāyaṇa is the one who knows everything and is also the one to be known through Vedanta.

Vyāsa as a reporter

How would we know about the Lord's teaching to Arjuna without Vyāsa? Any gospel is the report of a disciple and, therefore, its accuracy depends on the disciple. If the disciple is adept, he or she will report properly. If the disciple has limitations, then there will be problems with the report.

In the *Gītā*, the reporter is very important. Nārāyaṇa taught and Arjuna heard; but it was Vyāsa who reported it all. The reporter here is not an ordinary person, as we shall see in a later verse. Vyāsa is the one who is capable of elaborating a brief statement into one thousand verses, complete with intricate details and cogent arguments.

Vyāsa is described here as a *purāṇa-muni*, an ancient sage. A *muni*, a *manana-śīla*, is a person who is capable of bestowing careful thought over a particular subject matter. The word *purāṇa* can also mean the ancient legends based on the teaching found in the Vedas. Vyāsa gathered these legends together and, remaining faithful to the Vedic vision, put them into writing called *purāṇa*s. Therefore, he is referred to as *purāṇa-muni*.

Since the subject being taught in the *Gītā* was so well-known to him, Vyāsa had no problem with reporting it properly. Where did Vyāsa report what was taught by the Lord to Arjuna? He presented it in the middle of the epic Mahābhārata, in the *Gītā,* in eighteen chapters.

Gītā – the nectar of non-dulaity

What is the subject matter of the *Gītā*? What did Lord Nārāyaṇa teach Arjuna? What was taught is described as a shower of *amṛta,* nectar. Nectar generally comes only in drops, but in the *Gītā,* nectar is showered upon us. What kind of nectar is it? All nectars are sweet to taste but do not last forever. The nectar that is showered by the *Gītā* is different. Not only does it provide happiness here, but also showers us with the *amṛta* of *advaita,* non-duality. Here, the word *amṛta* is used in the sense of that which gives you immortality. The knowledge here frees you from mortality in the form of life and death.

In non-duality there is no second thing. Therefore with this knowledge, any fear is eliminated. Only in duality can there be fear. Fear cannot exist in non-duality because there is no second thing to fear.

That you are everything, that there is nothing other than you, is not an ordinary subject matter. This is what is meant by non-duality. Non-duality means that you are the whole. That which gives you this vision is the nectar of non-duality. Nectar is used here because, just as nectar is something to be tasted, to be experienced, non-duality is something to be understood to be yourself.

The Goddess *Gītā* showers the nectar of non-duality upon you. This shower of nectar is the vision of non-duality. It is the message of the Lord. The *Gītā* is Bhagavatī, the Goddess, and is not separate from Bhagavān's vision. She knows that Kṛṣṇa is Īśvara, the Lord, and along with him she blesses you because she gives you this knowledge. In this verse the *Gītā* is addressed as the one who has eighteen chapters. It is said, 'O *Gītā*! the one with eighteen chapters, I salute you.'

The nectar of non-duality destroys the *bhava*, the *saṁsāra*, completely. *Bhava* means a life of becoming with all of its problems and fears, a life of sorrow, bondage, birth and death. This teaching is, therefore, the medicine for *saṁsāra*, that by which the whole *saṁsāra* is destroyed. The destroyer of *saṁsāra* and the nectar of non-duality go together and refer to the *Gītā* as the mother who destroys the *saṁsāra* by showering the nectar of non-duality.

In the first verse we salute the mother *Gītā* by meditating upon her, by invoking her, before we start our study. Also, we cannot think about the *Gītā* without thinking about Vyāsa, Kṛṣṇa and Arjuna, called Pārtha in this verse. The second verse, therefore, is addressed to Vyāsa.

Verse 2

Vastness of Vyāsa's intellect

नमोऽस्तु ते व्यास विशालबुद्धे फुल्लारविन्दायतपत्रनेत्र ।
येन त्वया भारततैलपूर्णः प्रज्वालितो ज्ञानमयः प्रदीपः ॥ २ ॥

namo'stu te vyāsa viśālabuddhe
phullāravindāyatapatranetra
yena tvayā bhāratatailapūrṇaḥ prajvālito
jñānamayaḥ pradīpaḥ (2)

viśāla-buddhe – one who has a vast mind; *phulla-aravinda-āyata-patra-netra* – one whose eyes are beautiful like the soft petals of a lotus; *vyāsa* – O Vyāsa!; *yena tvayā* – by you; *bhārata-taila-pūrṇaḥ* – filled with the oil of Mahābhārata; *jñānamayaḥ* – in the form of knowledge; *pradīpaḥ* – the lamp; *prajvālitaḥ* – was well lighted; *te* – to you; *namaḥ astu* – let (my) salutation be

> Bhagavān Vyāsa! Salutation be unto you, the one who has a vast mind, whose eyes are beautiful like the soft petals of a lotus, by whom (you) was lighted the lamp of knowledge, filled with the oil of Mahābhārata.

Shakespeare's intellect has been described as the 'Platform of the world,' upon which its drama unfolds. He was able to write excellent characterisations for the stages of the world. Similarly, in this verse, Vyāsa is described as one whose intellect, knowledge is vast. He wrote thousands of verses; they simply flowed out of him.

There is a story told that when Vyāsa was planning to write the Mahābhārata, he wanted to dictate the epic to a stenographer. Because there was no shorthand at that time, stenographers had to write very quickly in longhand. But no human being could take dictation from Vyāsa because his mind was so quick and clear. He just reeled out the verses and no one could hope to keep up with him. So he asked Lord Gaṇeśa to be his stenographer.

Gaṇeśa agreed on the condition that Vyāsa would not stop dictating once he began. Vyāsa agreed and he also had a condition that Gaṇeśa should understand everything he said, in every sense. Agreeing to this condition, Gaṇeśa pulled out one of his tusks, sharpened it, and with it wrote down Vyāsa's Mahābhārata on palm leaves. That is why Lord Gaṇeśa is portrayed as having only one tusk.

In the Mahābhārata you will find, for the most part, simple, descriptive verses. Once in a while there will be a verse which is profound, a purple verse with different meanings. Vyāsa did this so that he could have a breather. Because Gaṇeśa understood so easily what was being written, Vyāsa had to compose a difficult verse whenever he wanted a break. If we count these verses, we can find out how many times he stopped. By the time Gaṇeśa figured out the meaning, Vyāsa had his time and was ready to begin again. This is Vyāsa.

Vyāsa had big beautiful eyes. They are described in this verse as being like a fully blossomed lotus, eyes that were clear and pleasing. Vyāsa is also compared here to a lamp that sheds light, the light of knowledge. This lamp is very well lit. He is, therefore, the one who lights the lamp of knowledge for us.

The lamp that was lit by Vyāsa is filled with the oil of the Mahābhārata. This epic is considered to be the fifth Veda because it is true to the knowledge found in the Vedas. It seems to have been written for the sole purpose of lighting up this knowledge.

When a small object is presented against a much larger background, its beauty is often more evident. The Mahābhārata is like a canvas from whose vast background the Vedic knowledge emerges. Knowledge is the lamp and the epic is its fuel. The fuel is for the lamp; the lamp is not for the fuel.

This verse is paying tribute to Vyāsa, who lit up the wisdom of the Vedas with the oil of the Mahābhārata. So, unto you, Vyāsa, who lit the lamp of knowledge with this epic fuel, my salutation.

Verse 3

प्रपन्नपारिजाताय तोत्रवेत्रैकपाणये ।
ज्ञानमुद्राय कृष्णाय गीतामृतदुहे नमः ॥ ३ ॥

prapannapārijātāya totravetraikapāṇaye
jñānamudrāya kṛṣṇāya gītāmṛtaduhe namaḥ (3)

prapanna-pārijātāya – unto the one who is the wish-fulfilling tree for those who surrender to him; *totravetra-eka-pāṇaye* – unto the one who holds a whip in one hand; *jñāna-mudrāya* – unto the one who has the symbol of knowledge in the other; *gītā-amṛta-duhe* – unto the one who milks the nectar that is the *Gītā*; *kṛṣṇāya* – unto Lord Kṛṣṇa; *namaḥ* – my salutation

My salutation to Lord Kṛṣṇa, who is a wish-fulfilling tree for those who surrender to him, who holds a whip in one hand and has the symbol of knowledge in the other, (and) who milks the nectar that is the *Gītā*.

Kṛṣṇa – the wish-fulfilling tree

In this verse, Lord Kṛṣṇa is likened to a wish-fulfilling tree said to be found in heaven. Whatever you wish for, while sitting under this tree, appears immediately in front of you. Kṛṣṇa is this wish-fulfilling tree for those who have surrendered unto him. To them he is the giver of everything.

Kṛṣṇa's control

In one hand, Kṛṣṇa is holding the whip with which he drives the horses. His other hand assumes the gesture symbolising knowledge. It means that Kṛṣṇa does not give up the job of a charioteer when Arjuna wants to be taught. Right in the middle of the battlefield, when Arjuna wants to know, Kṛṣṇa assumes the role of a teacher.

Knowing very well that Arjuna would fight, Kṛṣṇa did not drop the whip. Arjuna dropped his bow and arrows, but Kṛṣṇa kept the whip in his hand. He loosened the reins for the interim period, but everything was under control. Unto the one who thus holds the symbol of knowledge, I offer my salutation.

Symbol of knowledge

We offer our salutations, not to the symbol of knowledge, but to the one who has this knowledge of non-duality, which cannot be negated. The symbol of knowledge, *jñānamudrā*, is formed by joining the three fingers and separating them from the index finger. The index finger then joins with the thumb to form a circle.

The index finger, also called the accusing finger, stands for the self and usually joins the other three, representing the body, mind and senses. By separating them out, we see that the body, mind and senses are all *anātmā*, 'not I'. One generally thinks that these are *ātmā*, but they are not. They are all *anātmā* and are, therefore, to be understood as such. Whatever is not *anātmā* is the self and is revealed by the teaching as identical with the limitless Brahman, represented by the thumb.

Without the thumb, the fingers cannot grasp anything. It is important that the thumb be away from the fingers in order to do so. Similarly, the limitless Brahman is away from, unattached to, the body, mind, and senses. At the same time, without the limitless Brahman, the body, mind, and senses have no being, much less any function.

Previously, we thought of ourselves as limited. When we have the knowledge of non-duality, symbolically shown as a cricle created by the index finger and the thumb, the sense of limitation is gone. Just as a circle has no begininning and no end, we know ourselves to be limitless.

Kṛṣṇa – the giver of nectar that is Gītā

The *Gītā* is likened to milk and Kṛṣṇa is the one who provides the milk. From where does the milk come? From the *śruti*. Therefore, all the Vedas, the *Upaniṣads*, are likened to a cow, its milk being the *Gītā*. Unto Kṛṣṇa the one who gives out the nectar that is the *Gītā*, my salutation.

Verse 4

सर्वोपनिषदो गावो दोग्धा गोपालनन्दनः ।
पार्थो वत्सः सुधीर्भोक्ता दुग्धं गीतामृतं महत् ॥ ४ ॥

sarvopaniṣado gāvo dogdhā gopālanandanaḥ
pārtho vatsaḥ sudhīrbhoktā dugdhaṁ gītāmṛtaṁ mahat (4)

sarva-upaniṣadaḥ – all the *Upaniṣads*; *gāvaḥ* – cows; *gopāla-nandanaḥ* – joy of cowherds; *dogdhā* – one who milks; *pārthaḥ* – Arjuna; *vatsaḥ* – calf; *sudhīḥ* – one whose mind is clear; *bhoktā* – the partaker (of the milk); *mahat gīta-amṛtam* – invaluable, timeless *Gītā*; *dugdham* – milk

The *Upaniṣad*s are the cows; the one who milks is Kṛṣṇa, the joy of cowherds; the calf is Arjuna; the partaker (of the milk) is the one whose mind is clear; and the invaluable, timeless *Gītā* is the milk.

The first two verses praised the *Gītā* and Vyāsa. Because the *Gītā* was taught to Arjuna by Lord Kṛṣṇa, he is praised in the third verse as the teacher of *Gītā*, as *gītācārya*. In the fourth verse, the nature of the *Gītā* and the Lord are both mentioned. This is the subject matter of the *Gītā* and it is being praised here.

Upaniṣads as a cow and Gītā as its milk

All of the *Upaniṣad*s are taken into account in the *Gītā*. To present the *Gītā* as the essence of the *Upaniṣads*, a popular imagery is used in this verse. Here, the cow, a symbol of wealth and sanctity, is presented to represent all of the *Upaniṣad*s.

Together, they form the body of the cow. If the *Upaniṣad*s are the cow, then its milk is the *Gītā*.

Kṛṣṇa as gopāla-nandana, the joy of cowherds

Who is the milkman? Nowadays, milking is done by machines, but previously it was not easy to coax milk from a cow. The cow has its own moods and will not yield for just anyone. In this verse, Kṛṣṇa is acknowledged as the best milkman. Born into the family of a milkman, in a cowherd community, Kṛṣṇa did not need to be taught how to milk a cow. Even from cows with empty udders, Kṛṣṇa was able to get milk. Just as he could get milk from a cow, Kṛṣṇa was able to milk the *Upaniṣad*s. He knows exactly what the subject matter is. In fact, he is the subject matter. Since he knows the subject matter so well, he is the best one to milk the *Upaniṣad*s.

Milk is the essence of the cow in that many things a cow eats are all converted into milk. In the same manner, the *Upaniṣad*s talk about a variety of topics, but it is converted into the milk of *vedānta-śāstra* or *brahma-vidyā* and *yoga-śāstra*. These are the two most important topics in all of the *Upaniṣad*s. They form the milk and there can be no better milkman than Kṛṣṇa.

Lord Kṛṣṇa is referred to here as *gopāla-nandana*, the joy of cowherds. The word '*go*' in Sanskrit, not only means cow; it also means 'words' and 'earth.' The one who gives meaning to all of these words is Lord Kṛṣṇa and the one who nourishes and sustains the earth with life is also Lord Kṛṣṇa. In this verse, he is also referred to as the milkman who is the joy of all cowherds because he is the nourisher and protector of cows.

Arjuna, the cause of the Gītā

A cow produces milk for the sake of its calf. Here also, there must be a calf to generate the milk that is the *Gītā*. Arjuna, Pārtha, is the *vatsa*, the calf, because he is instrumental in drawing the *Gītā* out from Kṛṣṇa. Just as the cow's milk is born for the sake of the calf, the *Gītā* was born for the sake of Arjuna.

Since the calf cannot take all of the milk produced by the cow, there is extra milk for the people. In the same way, Arjuna acquired the milk of the *Gītā* and others are also the partakers of it.

The timelessness of the subject matter

Unlike the milk from the cow, the milk of the *Gītā* is endless. The enjoyer of this milk is the one whose mind is clear and who has discrimination. The person who is capable of enquiry, *sudhī*, is the partaker of this milk.

The *Gītā* is likened to milk because it is nourishing to all. Milk is a complete food, a universal food. The message of the *Gītā* is also universal. It is applicable to everyone at any time or place because it deals with facts that do not change with time or place.

That which does not change is the very subject matter of the *Gītā* and is, therefore, described here as *amṛta*. There are many meanings for the word *amṛta*, but the one that is most relevant here is 'that which is not subject to death.'

Whatever is not bound by time, does not undergo any change, that which immortalises you, nourishes you, makes you happy, is considered to be *amṛta*. Anyone can take it; it is applicable to all. This timeless, nectarine *Gītā* is described here as something that becomes more available the more it is given. The milk of the *Gītā* is knowledge. The more knowledge you give, the more you have because, as you keep giving, the knowledge becomes clearer for you.

Verse 5

वसुदेवसुतं देवं कंसचाणूरमर्दनम् ।
देवकीपरमानन्दं कृष्णं वन्दे जगद्गुरुम् ॥ ५ ॥

vasudevasutaṁ devaṁ kaṁsacāṇūramardanam
devakīparamānandaṁ kṛṣṇaṁ vande jagadgurum (5)

vasudeva-sutam – the son of Vasudeva; *kaṁsa-cāṇūra-mardanam* – the destroyer of Kaṁsa and Cāṇūra (demonic kings); *devakī-parama-ānandam* – the greatest joy of Devakī (Kṛṣṇa's mother); *jagad-gurum* – the teacher of the world; *devaṁ kṛṣṇam* – Lord Kṛṣṇa; *vande* – I salute

I salute Kṛṣṇa, the Lord, the world-teacher, the son of Vasudeva, the destroyer of Kaṁsa and Cāṇūra, and the greatest joy of Devakī.

Kṛṣṇa as a teacher of the world

In the fifth verse, Kṛṣṇa is presented as the teacher of the world, *jagad-guru*. A teacher can only be a teacher of the world if he or she has universal message. Also, one can teach only those people who want the subject matter he or she is teaching. For instance, only those who are interested in calculus will go to a teacher of calculus. A universal message is relevant to everyone, everywhere, even though not everyone will be interested in it.

Here, the message of the *Gītā* can be given to anyone because it is relevant to everyone. Kṛṣṇa is not considered to be a teacher merely because he is accepted as such, but because he has a message acceptable to all. This we must know. It is a message that is extremely valuable to everyone. Without it, one's life is a search that never comes to an end. The message which Kṛṣṇa gives in the *Gītā*, is what makes him a *jagad-guru*.

Kṛṣṇa for the purpose of meditation

As a teacher of the world, Kṛṣṇa is looked upon as a person with qualities or attributes, only for the purpose of meditation. When what is being discussed is free from all attributes, it is a matter for knowledge; it is something to be understood. But when a particular form with a set of attributes is being talked about, such as Kṛṣṇa as a person, it is purely for the purpose of meditation.

In this verse, some historical facts are given about Kṛṣṇa to create a figure for meditation. He is described as the son of Vasudeva, *vasudeva-suta*. At the same time, he is the Lord, *deva*, father of all, including Vasudeva. Obviously, he is not an ordinary son. If he were, we would not meditate upon him.

Kṛṣṇa as the destroyer of evil

Kṛṣṇa is also referred to here as the destroyer of evil. We should know that there is no evil beyond our own minds and that there is no such thing as an evil mind. There is only wrong thinking that needs to be corrected. Kṛṣṇa, as the Lord, is the chastiser of wrongdoers. By giving them what they deserve, he removes this evil of incorrect thinking.

Kṛṣṇa as the source of happiness

Kṛṣṇa is the greatest joy of his mother, Devakī. He is the most attractive, the one who is the source of all happiness. Anything that attracts, *karṣati* is Kṛṣṇa; anything that attracts is happiness. What pleases you attracts you because it makes you happy, which is why the source of happiness is the focus of complete attraction. O Kṛṣṇa! teacher of the world, whose message is universal, I salute you.

Verse 6

भीष्मद्रोणतटा जयद्रथजला गान्धारनीलोत्पला
शल्यग्राहवती कृपेण वहनी कर्णेन वेलाकुला ।
अश्वत्थामविकर्णघोरमकरा दुर्योधनावर्त्तिनी
सोत्तीर्णा खलु पाण्डवै रणनदी कैवर्तकः केशवः ॥ ६ ॥

bhīṣmadroṇataṭā jayadrathajalā gāndhāranīlotpalā
śalyagrāhavatī kṛpeṇa vahanī karṇena velākulā
aśvatthāmavikarṇaghoramakarā duryodhanāvarttinī
sottīrṇā khalu pāṇḍavai raṇanadī kaivartakaḥ
keśavaḥ (6)

bhīṣma-droṇa-taṭā – with Bhīṣma and Droṇa as its banks; *jayadratha-jalā* – with Jayadratha as its water; *gāndhāra-nīlotpalā* – with Gāndhāra (Śakuni, the prince of Gāndhāra) as the blue lily; *śalya-grāhavatī* – with Śalya as the shark; *kṛpeṇa vahanī* – with Kṛpa as the force of the water; *karṇena velākulā* – with Karṇa as its breakers; *aśvatthāma-vikarṇa-ghora-makarā* – with Aśvatthāma and Vikarṇa as its killer whales; *duryodhana-avarttinī* – (and) Duryodhana as its whirlpools; *sā raṇa-nadī* – that river of battle; *pāṇḍavaiḥ* – by the Pāṇḍavas; *khalu* – indeed; *uttīrṇā* – was crossed over; *kaivartakaḥ* – the boatman (being); *keśavaḥ* – Lord Kṛṣṇa

> With Bhīṣma and Droṇa as its banks, Jayadratha, as its water, Gāndhāra (Śakuni) as the blue lily,[9] Śalya as the shark, Kṛpa as the force of the water, Karṇa as its breakers, Aśvatthāmā and Vikarṇa as its killer whales, and Duryodhana as its whirlpools, the river of battle was indeed crossed by the Pāṇḍavas, because the boatman was Kṛṣṇa.

Pāṇḍavas

The Pāṇḍavas, Pāṇḍu's sons, were five in number. The oldest son was Yudhiṣṭhira, also called Dharmaputra. The second son was Bhīma. Arjuna, who appears in the *Gītā*, was the third son. The fourth and fifth were Nakula and Sahadeva.

---

[9] The blue lily is deceptive. It looks like a lotus but it is not one.

The river of battle

It is said that the Pāṇḍavas crossed the river of battle, *raṇanadī*, which is described poetically in this verse. Every river must have two banks within which the water flows. Without the banks there would be no river at all. Bhīṣma and Droṇa are the two banks of this river of battle.

Bhīṣma, Arjuna's grandfather, was the eldest in the family and a man of great vows. He was considered to be invincible even though he was an old man. Bhīṣma was such a great warrior that he never lost a battle; only trickery could destroy him. Droṇa was the greatest archer, the *guru* who taught archery to Arjuna and his brothers, as well as his cousins.

Both Bhīṣma and Droṇa were in Duryodhana's ranks against the Pāṇḍavas. Duryodhana took care of them during the thirteen years that the Pāṇḍavas were in exile. He pampered them so much that they felt obliged to him. And he made sure they felt obliged. Bhīṣma and Droṇa were his strength and, because of them, he thought he could win the war.

He had one more important ally in Karṇa. Therefore, these three people were the indirect causes of this war. Without them, Duryodhana would definitely not have embarked upon it.

In a river, there are always whirlpools. In this verse, Duryodhana is likened to a whirlpool because anyone who went near him got sucked in. Once caught in a whirlpool, it is very difficult to get out. Bhīṣma, Droṇa, Kṛpa, his uncle, all of them got sucked in. Even though they were very kind to the Pāṇḍavas, Duryodhana was able to drag them into his grip because he was such a scheming person.

Although Bhīṣma and Droṇa were the banks of this river of battle, the river would have been empty if Jayadratha and his huge army had not been there. Jayadratha provided the manpower and was, therefore, the water.

There are areas in the river where the water collects and remains. This is where the blue lilies grow, making the river not only beautiful but difficult to move through because of their entangling stalks. The prince of *Gāndhāra*, Śakuni is referred to here as the blue lily.

The river being described was one that had sharks in it. Śalya is likened to a shark and is called the great grabber. He was Karṇa's charioteer and was considered the greatest driver. A charioteer is very important in a battle. He must not only have great expertise in driving, but he must also encourage the warrior, whose chariot he is driving. But during the battle with the Pāṇḍavas, Śalya discouraged Karṇa as much as he could because of the promise he had made earlier to the Pāṇḍavas.

The current in this river was very fast. Its speed was provided by Kṛpa. Because of Karṇa, it was full of breakers. Aśvatthāmā, the son of Droṇa, was a great archer and also a killer. Vikarṇa was one of the hundred sons of Dhṛtarāṣṭra. These two, Aśvatthāmā and Vikarṇa, were the yougest and are described as killer whales.

Crossing the river of battle

To cross such a terrible river is not easy. It is only possible by boat. Swimming across is impossible because of all the whales, whirlpools and breakers. Even a boat may not make it.

However, there is a way. If Kṛṣṇa is our boatman, we can cross this river of *saṁsāra*. We too face the various problems mentioned here; we have whirlpool of problems, breaker like problems, whale of problems, credit card problems and so on. If Lord Kṛṣṇa is the boatman, we will definitely make it.

Verse 7

पाराशर्यवचःसरोजममलं गीतार्थगन्धोत्कटं
नानाख्यानककेसरं हरिकथासम्बोधनाबोधितम् ।
लोके सज्जनषट्पदैरहरहः पेपीयमानं मुदा
भूयाद्भारतपङ्कजं कलिमलप्रध्वंसि नः श्रेयसे ॥ ७ ॥

pārāśaryavacaḥsarojamamalaṁ gītārthagandhotkaṭaṁ
nānākhyānakakesaraṁ harikathāsambodhanābodhitam
loke sajjanaṣaṭpadairaharahaḥ pepīyamānaṁ mudā
bhūyādbhāratapaṅkajaṁ kalimalapradhvaṁsi naḥ śreyase (7)

pārāśarya-vacaḥ sarojam – the lotus born of the water of the words of Parāśara's son, (Vyāsa); *gītā-artha-gandha-utkaṭam* – having the meaning of the *Gītā* as its sweet fragrance; *nānā-ākhyānaka-kesaram* – with its many stories as stamens; *hari-*

kathā-sambodhana-ābodhitam – fully blossomed with the revealing stories of the Lord Hari; *loke* - in the world; *sajjana-ṣaṭpadaiḥ* – by the honey-bees who are right thinking people; *aharahaḥ* – day after day; *mudā* – happily; *pepīyamānam* – being relished; *kali-mala-pradhvaṁsi* – the destroyer of the blemishes of *kali-yuga*; *amalam* – spotless; *bhārata-paṅkajam* – the lotus of Mahābhārata; *naḥ śreyase* – for our good; *bhūyāt* – may it be

> May the spotless lotus, Mahābhārata – born of the water of the words of Vyāsa, the son of Parāśara, having the meaning of the *Gītā* as its sweet fragrance, with its many stories as stamens, blossoming with the revealing stories of the Lord Hari, relished happily day after day by the honey bees who are the right thinking people of the world, and which destroys the blemishes of *kali-yuga* (may this lotus of Mahābhārata) – be for our good.

In praise of Mahābhārata

This is a verse in praise of the Mahābhārata itself. It says, 'Let it be for the good of all people. Let this beautiful lotus epic be for *mokṣa*, liberation, the most desired end.' It destroys all of the problems of *kali-yuga*. *Kali* is that which is selfish. Any evil is called *kali*. *Kali-yuga* is a *yuga*, a time period, when people become easily caught up in their own likes and dislikes, *rāgās* and *dveṣa*s.

The Mahābhārata has a number of guidelines for people to follow. It talks about ethics – personal, social and political values, and even logistics through interpretative illustrations.

What kind of a lotus is the Mahābhārata? Just like any other lotus, it is born of water. It comes from the water of words. This water of words springs forth from Vyāsa, the son of Parāśara. Also, this word lotus is as clean as the lotus in the pond. It has the strong, sweet fragrance of the meaning of the *Gītā*.

A meaning is something silent; it is something that you understand. You can repeat a word because it is a sound, but its meaning is always silent. You can see a flower, but the smell cannot be seen anywhere. You can only sense it. Similarly, the meaning of the *Gītā* makes the whole Mahābhārata waft with fragrance. This epic is the lotus that exudes the fragrance of the meaning of the *Gītā*.

There are many small stories within stories. These stories are like the rows of stamens of the lotus. The stamens of the saffron flower are the most fragrant, while the stamens of the lotus are known for their beauty. If the *Gītā* is the fragrance of the Mahābhārata, then the stories are the stamens which impart beauty to it.

Because of Kṛṣṇa's presence in the Mahābhārata, it is the Lord's story. Without it, the Mahābhārata would be a lotus that had not yet bloomed. The opening of a bud generally requires the sun; here the Lord's story is the Sun. It opens up the Mahābhārata with devotion. It provides the light necessary for this opening.

The *Gītā* is being enjoyed happily. People are drinking deeply from it, taking more and more, day after day. Who are these people? They are likened to an insect with six legs, the honey bee, for instance. Human beings have five sense organs plus a thinking intellect. Some extra intellect is necessary to extract the nectar from the epic flower that is the *Gītā*. The people who enjoy the *Gītā* are, therefore, thinking people, those who use their intellects.

Let this *Gītā*, which is the destroyer of all problems in *kali-yuga*, of the problems caused by likes and dislikes, be for the good of all people.

The next verse is in praise of the Lord, which says, 'I salute the Lord who is all *ānanda*, joy, fullness, whose form and expression are *ānanda*, and who is Lord Kṛṣṇa.'

Verse 8

मूकं करोति वाचालं पङ्गुं लङ्घयते गिरिम् ।
यत्कृपा तमहं वन्दे परमानन्दमाधवम् ॥ ८ ॥

mūkaṁ karoti vācālaṁ paṅguṁ laṅghayate girim
yatkṛpā tamahaṁ vande paramānandamādhavam (8)

yat-kṛpā – whose grace; *mūkam* – the mute; *vācālam* – eloquent; *karoti* – makes; *paṅgum* – one who is lame; *girim* – mountain; *laṅghayate* – causes to scale; *tam* – him; *paramānanda-mādhavam* – Kṛṣṇa, the Lord of Lakṣmī (wealth) whose nature is fullness; *ahaṁ vande* – I salute

I salute Kṛṣṇa, the Lord of Lakṣmī (wealth), whose nature is fullness, whose grace makes the mute eloquent and the lame scale the mountaintops.

Mādhava is another name for Lord Kṛṣṇa, one who has all the resources and wealth with him, who is Bhagavān, the Lord. I salute Bhagavān who is Mādhava, whose expression and essential nature is fullness, *ānanda*.

Lord's grace and the result of prayer

This verse adds something more – grace, *kṛpā*. Grace is something that is earned. It is not something that the Lord randomly distributes day by day. If he did, he would be partial, which is not the case. Grace is a graceful expression for *karma-phala*. *Karma* is what you do and *phala* is the result of what you do.

Prayer is also a *karma*, an action. Because it is an action, it necessarily produces a result. The result is two-fold, seen, *dṛṣṭa-phala* and unseen, *adṛṣṭa-phala*.

One example of a seen result is the psychological benefit of prayer. The very fact that you are able to pray is itself a benefit. Also as a result of prayer, there can be a psychological benefit of having someone upon whom you can rely. Any individual has limitations, whereas the one you pray to is looked upon by you as limitless. Even without understanding, the Lord is looked upon as someone who is omniscient.

No one undersands totally what it means to be omniscient, to be all-knowledge. To understand all-knowledge one must be all-knowledge. However, our knowledge is limited. From this limited knowledge we can always know a little more, but that also will be limited. What we can very easily understand is limitation in knowledge. So, we are able to appreciate that an omniscient person is free from limitation with respect to knowledge. This is known as appreciation of omniscience.

Who is the omniscient person? Is he or she another kind of person or one of us? So, there is a great deal of knowledge to be known in order to appreciate Īśvara, the Lord. We invoke this Īśvara in the form of prayer.

Prayer is a *karma* and it produces an immediate result, a visible result. That you are able to invoke the Lord is the result. You have someone to rely on, someone who is all-power, almighty, all-knowledge, unlike anyone else. From this, you gain certain strength, knowing that you can draw on this power to the extent that your capacity to draw allows. It is like having a huge reservoir of water. You need not bring all the water at once; it does not matter that your receptacle is small. Just knowing that there is so much water in the reservoir gives you so much strength.

Thus, the immediate benefit you experience, because you are able to pray, is that there is someone for you who is all-knowledge, upon whom you can draw whenever and as much as you want. This is *dṛṣṭa-phala,* the seen result. You experience it even as you pray. There is also an *adṛṣṭa-phala,* the unseen result of prayer. It is what we call grace, which accounts for benefits that we cannot attribute to a particular day's prayer.

Invisible result of prayer

Grace is earned in the same way that you earn anything else. Since you are not able to relate to an unexpected result to a given course of action on your part, in the immediate past, we are constrained to call this result, grace. Grace is able to convert a mute into the eloquent and enables a lame person to climb a mountain.

Kālidāsa, the celebrated poet, was considered to be a mute, but because of grace, he began pouring out verses. Similarly, Vālmīki became a great poet because of grace. In day-to-day life, we often hear various stories of the disappearance of incurable diseases. Cancer suddenly vanishes and no one knows how. We call it grace because the causes are not known. You can call such happenings as grace, accident or chance. However, a perceptive person, with maturity and understanding of Īśvara, appreciates these unseen results as grace.

In a prayer, what you really release is an invisible force causing *adṛṣṭa-phala,* the unseen result. The very system, the laws, that produce results which are not visible to us are reorganised by prayer. Certain elements are introduced through prayer into this invisible system, causing it to reorganise itself. However, we do not know how it will be reorganised which is why the results are said to be caused by grace.

Grace, therefore, is something that we receive purely as a result of our own *karma,* actions, done either in our immediate past or in the remote past. Because of this result, grace, certain situations happen in our favour. What is generally taken to be impossible is made possible by grace. In fact, the whole life is like that; the impossible is made possible.

In this verse, I salute Bhagavān, by whose grace the mute becomes eloquent, the lame scales mountaintops and by whose grace the impossible is made possible.

The final verse of *Gītā-dhyānam* describes the various beings who praise this all-knowledge Lord.

Verse 9

यं ब्रह्मा वरुणेन्द्ररुद्रमरुतः स्तुन्वन्ति दिव्यैः स्तवैः
वेदैः साङ्गपदक्रमोपनिषदैर्गायन्ति यं सामगाः ।
ध्यानावस्थिततद्गतेन मनसा पश्यन्ति यं योगिनो
यस्यान्तं न विदुः सुरासुरगणा देवाय तस्मै नमः ॥ ९ ॥

yaṁ brahmā varuṇendrarudramarutaḥ stunvanti divyaiḥ stavaiḥ
vedaiḥ sāṅgapadakramopaniṣadairgāyanti yaṁ sāmagāḥ
dhyānāvasthitatadgatena manasā paśyanti yaṁ yogino
yasyāntaṁ na viduḥ surāsuragaṇā devāya tasmai namaḥ (9)

Brahmā – Brahmāji; *varuṇa-indra-rudra-marutaḥ* – Varuṇa, Indra, Rudra, and Marut *devatās*; *divyaiḥ stavaiḥ* – with divine hymns; *yam* - whom; *stunvanti* – praise; *sāmagāḥ* – the singers of the *Sāmaveda*; *vedaiḥ* – with the Vedas; *sāṅga-pada-krama-upaniṣadaiḥ* – with the full complement of the limbs (of singing) in the order of *pada*, *krama* and the *Upaniṣads*; *gāyanti* – sing in praise; *yam* – (of) whom; *yoginaḥ* – contemplative people; *dhyāna-avasthita-tad-gatena-manasā* – with a mind resolved in him in a state of meditation; *yam* – whom; *paśyanti* – see clearly; *sura-asura-gaṇāḥ* – the celestials as well as demons; *yasya antam* – whose nature; *na viduḥ* – do not know; *tasmai devāya* – unto him, the Lord; *namaḥ* – my salutation

> My salutation to the Lord whom Brahmā, Varuṇa, Indra, Rudra and the Marut *devatā*s praise with divine hymns, the one whom the singers of the *Sāmaveda* praise by singing with the full complement of the limbs (of singing) in the order of *pada*, *krama* and the *Upaniṣad*s, the one whom contemplative people see with minds resolved in him in a state of meditation and whose nature the celestials and demons do not know.

The word *deva* has different meanings. The root meaning is that which is effulgent. *Deva* can refer to any God, a celestial, or even a sense organ. The Lord is also called *deva*, meaning the one who is all-knowledge. Unto this Lord, my salutation.

Praise by exalted beings

Who is this Lord? He is the one about whom all the Gods, from Brahmāji downward, sing hymns of praise. In addition to Brahmāji, the verse specifically mentions the *deva*s – Varuṇa, Indra, Rudra, and the Marut *devatā*s. Even though these *deva*s are exalted beings, they are still *jīva*s, individuals, occupying special positions. Their songs in praise of Īśvara are found in the Vedas.

Praise by scholars

Those who are able to sing the *Sāmaveda* also praise the Lord. To sing the Vedas, one must have the knowledge to do so.

Six other disciplines of knowledge are required, called the *ṣaḍaṅgas*, the six limbs. They are – phonetics, *śikṣā*; grammar, *vyākaraṇa*; rituals, *kalpa*; etymology, *nirukta*; prosody, *chandas* and astronomy with astrology, *jyotiṣa*. The reciters of *Sāmaveda* with the full knowledge of these six limbs, sing in praise of the Lord, the hymns of *Sāmaveda* in the form of *pada* and *krama* along with the *Upaniṣad*s which reveal the truth of the Lord.

Praise by contemplative people

There are contemplative people who meditate upon the truth of Īśvara, whom they see very clearly. How do they see? With their minds. What kind of mind? A mind that is in a state of contemplation, a mind that is absorbed, tranquil and subtle. These people contemplate, again and again with minds that are awake to the true nature of the Lord, which they have come to appreciate through listening to and analysing Īśvara, the teaching.

Praise by others

There are people who praise the Lord as one with form and attributes. The whole creation with all of its glories is nothing but the Lord's form. There are others, *yogīs*, who see the Lord as formless, whose nature is not known by either Gods or demons. Even though these Gods are exalted beings, they do not necessarily know that they are limitless. Being a God or a celestial does not mean that the person is enlightened. Self-knowledge is not something that comes with an exalted position. They must have a means of knowledge, a *pramāṇa*, to know this truth about themselves.

Thus, salutations are offered to the Lord, who is praised by the Gods and demons alike – the demons also praise the Lord to gain various powers by his grace – and by the singers of the *Sāmaveda*, whom the contemplative people realise in their meditation and whose glories even Gods and demons know not.

So, these nine verses praise the *Gītā* in general. First, the Mahābhārata, in which the *Gītā* is placed, is praised. Then Lord Kṛṣṇa is praised as a boatman because of whose tact and grace the Pāṇḍavas were able to cross the great river of battle with all its hurdles.

The *Gītā* herself is also praised and Vedavyāsa, the chronicler of the Mahābhārata, is praised because of whose grace we now have the *Gītā*. Arjuna is recognised in these verses as being its *nimitta*, cause. Without him, there would be no *Gītā*. Because Arjuna asked for it, we have the Lord's Song, the Bhagavadgītā.

Life as we know it, that is *saṁsāra*, is considered to be a river of battle, *raṇanadī*, in which people drown. The verses do not tell us how this river can be crossed. Nor do they mention Kṛṣṇa's grace. We simply need to understand that the boatman is Kṛṣṇa, the Lord. Kṛṣṇa is the one whose grace enables us to cross.

Having invoked the Lord's help by this prayer to the *Gītā*, we can now commence our study. Before we begin the first chapter, we will see briefly the context, in which the *Gītā* is set, and its purpose.

Context of the Gītā

A large-scale battle between two factions of the royal clan of the Kurus, in the days of Kṛṣṇa, provided the context for the Bhagavadgītā. The people belonging to this Kuru clan were called Kauravas. The battle was waged between one hundred sons of Dhṛtarāṣṭra, collectively referred to as Dhārtarāṣṭras, and the five sons of Pāṇḍu called Pāṇḍavas. The entire Mahābhārata, in which the *Gītā* is placed, is a piece of literature, drama. Thus, the author, Vyāsa had the freedom to use his imagination creatively. He did this by weaving the whole tapestry of this huge epic around a few historical events and characters.

Kauravas

When Dhṛtarāṣṭra and Pāṇḍu, the sons of Vicitravīrya came of age, Bhīṣma had to install one of them as the king to rule the Kauravas. Although Dhṛtarāṣṭra was older than Pāṇḍu, he was not eligible to rule because he was blind. According to the *dharma-śāstra*, which states exactly who can and cannot rule, ruling a kingdom being a very responsible and difficult job, a king should have all his faculties intact. Pāṇḍu, therefore became a ruler. Pāṇḍu was a great man and he ruled well. He respected his older brother, Dhṛtarāṣṭra, and gave him the full status of a king, even though he could not actually rule. Pāṇḍu went on a *digvijaya* – going in all the directions and conquering the rulers of various kingdoms and bringing them under one's subjugation – and brought in wealth and prosperity to the kingdom. He also extended the frontiers of his kingdom.

Once Pāṇḍu decided to go to the forest along with his wives Kuntī and Mādrī and a huge retinue, to hunt and enjoy the life of living in the forest. There, he came across a pair of deer which were sporting together. Without thinking, he shot arrows at them and mortally wounded them. At that instant the pair of deer took on their original forms of a *ṛṣi* and his wife. They had assumed the form of deer and were cavorting freely. Then the *ṛṣi*, by the name Kindama, cursed Pāṇḍu, that, if ever he would unite with his wife, he would die instantaneously and hence would never be able to beget children. After this Pāṇḍu renounced his kingdom and took to an ascetic way of life in the forest along with his wives. He observed many kinds of austerities and his wives Kuntī and Mādrī also practised the austerities along with him. Thus, all three of them lived a life befitting the *vānaprasthāśrama*.

The fact that he could not beget any children was a source of great sorrow to Pāṇḍu. His wife Kuntī had been given a *mantra* as a boon by the sage Durvāsa once, when she had served him very well. This *mantra* had the power to bring any God to her and bless her with a son. Therefore, at Pāṇḍu's behest, she gave birth to three sons, Dharmaputra, Bhīma and Arjuna, using the *mantra*. She also helped Mādrī to beget the twins, Nakula and Sahadeva, using the *mantra*. Later, being unable to resist the temptation when Pāṇḍu tried to approach Mādrī, the *ṛṣi*'s curse took effect and he died. Because she had been instrumental in causing Pāṇḍu to die, Mādrī put an end to her life by committing *satī* after entrusting her two sons to the care of Kuntī. After this the *ṛṣis* in the forest brought Kuntī, and the five sons of Pāṇḍu, to Hastināpura and entrusted them to the care of the elders of the Kuru clan. The entire Kuru clan accepted the five brothers as the rightful heirs of Pāṇḍu. Bhīṣma entrusted Droṇācārya with the task of education and training in archery and warfare of all the princes – the hundred sons of Dhṛtarāṣṭra and the five sons of Pāṇḍu. After their education was completed, they all demonstrated their skills in public during their graduation ceremony. Then by the unanimous decision of all the elders, Dharmaputra, the oldest of the Pāṇḍavas, was installed as the crown prince and was entrusted with the responsiblity of ruling the kingdom.

Dharmaputra, also known by the name Yudhiṣṭhira, was committed to a life of *dharma*, to what was right, even at the cost of his own welfare. Because Dharmaputra was born by the grace of Lord Yama, he was also called Dharmarājā. The second son was Bhīma, a man of valour and strength. He was born by the grace of Lord Vāyu. He also had a great heart and was committed to *dharma*.

Then there was Arjuna, the most versatile of them all. Not only a master archer, Arjuna had a thorough grasp of logistics. He knew all about warfare, how to organise an army, how to advance, how to fight. There is a *śāstra* for all of this, explaining the various ways to arrange an army into appropriate formations, *vyūha*s, so that when the front lines are gone, there are other lines to back them up. All of this requires a lot of study and understanding. Besides being an expert in warfare, Arjuna was very adept in performing fine arts.

He was a great dancer, musician, and a man of great name and fame, committed to *dharma*.

Nakula, a younger brother to these three, was also an archer. Sahadeva, the youngest, was considered to be a wise man, a *jñānī*, and a great astrologer. Nakula and Sahadeva were twins born to Mādrī by the grace of the twin Gods, Aśvini-kumāras, the celestial physicians. When it became obvious that war with Duryodhana was inevitable, Dharmaputra asked Sahadeva when the Pāṇḍavas should begin the war against their cousin, Duryodhana, so as to win. Sahadeva gave his brother a certain time. Duryodhana, having the same respect for Sahadeva and his integrity, also asked for an appropriate time to begin the war against the Pāṇḍavas. Sahadeva naturally gave Duryodhana a time meant to make the war go in his favour. This one episode alone, in the Mahābhārata, presents Sahadeva as an extraordinary person with all the additional qualifications of a prince, such as skill in archery and warfare. However, thanks to Lord Kṛṣṇa's grace, Duryodhana could not start the war on time.

Together, Dharmaputra and his four younger brothers, committed to the law of *dharma*, ruled the kingdom very well and all the citizens were very happy. One and all showered praise and accolades on the Pāṇḍavas. This marked the beginning of all the problems because the sons of Dhṛtarāṣṭra, especially Duryodhana, were very jealous of them and did not accept the Pāṇḍavas as rulers. They did whatever they could to see that the Pāṇḍavas were always in trouble even though, as princes, the Dhārtarāṣṭras (sons of Dhṛtarāṣṭra) were treated very well by the ruling Pāṇḍavas.

Duryodhana's jealousy

The Pāṇḍavas grew up in the same palace with their cousins, the hundred sons of Dhṛtarāṣṭra. Even as children, Duryodhana and his brothers were jealous of the Pāṇḍavas and would gang up and try to destroy them. Therefore, the Pāṇḍavas always grew up in the midst of great jealousy and constant fighting. They tried to understand that their cousins were jealous and accommodated them as best they could.

Now that the people were happy that Dharmaputra was their crown prince, Duryodhana's jealousy knew no bounds. From the time Dharmaputra became the crown prince, Duryodhana began scheming for the throne. He plotted with his uncle Śakuni,[10] Karṇa,[11] and his brothers to kill the Pāṇḍavas. With the silent approval of Dhṛtarāṣṭra, Duryodhana plotted to kill the Pāṇḍavas at Vāraṇāvata. Dhṛtarāṣṭra sent them to Vāraṇāvata under the pretext of asking them to preside over an *utsava*. Duryodhana had already built a palace made

---

[10] Śakuni was the brother of Gāndhārī, Duryodhana's mother. He was the vile schemer who advised Duryodhana in his actions against Pāṇḍavas.

[11] Karṇa was actually the son of Kuntī, born to her by the grace of Lord Sun, when she had experimented with the *mantra* given by sage Durvāsa to her when she was a young unmarried girl. When the child was born, being afraid of the society, she placed the child in a basket and floated it away in the river Gaṅgā. This child was found and raised by a charioteer as his son. Karṇa was very valorous and grew up into a fine archer. He came to the graduation ceremony of the Kuru princes to prove himself and gain some acceptance. He challenged Arjuna. But he was not allowed to participate on the grounds that he was not a *kṣatriya*. When he thus stood humiliated, Duryodhana came to his rescue and crowned him as the King of Aṅgadeśa. Since then he became the most devoted friend of Duryodhana.

of inflammatory substances for their stay and had sent one of his agents with the instruction that at an opportune moment he should set fire to the palace so that it would look like an accident. This would lead to the end of the Pāṇḍavas.

But Vidura[12] who already knew about this plot warned them and made secret arrangements for their escape. Everybody assumed that the Pāṇḍavas had perished in the fire. Except Vidura no one knew of their escape. The Pāṇḍavas lived incognito for sometime and went to the *svayaṁvara* of Draupadī, who was the daughter of the King of Pāñcāla. Arjuna won the test and all five of them married Draupadī and came back to Hastināpura.

This time the elders of the Kuru family decided to put an end to the conflict by dividing the kingdom into two halves, one each for the Dhārtarāṣṭras and the Pāṇḍavas. The most undeveloped and unproductive part of the country called Khāṇḍavaprastha was given to Pāṇḍavas as their share. Hastināpura itself with the developed productive lands around it went to the Dhārtarāṣṭras. But they accepted the deal and went to Khāṇḍavaprastha. With the help of Lord Kṛṣṇa, Lord Indra and the divine architects, the Pāṇḍavas made the land fertile and built a very beautiful capital for themselves. It was called Indraprastha. Yudhiṣṭhira sent his brothers in all directions for *digvijaya* and they in turn brought in wealth and made their country prosperous and powerful.

---

[12] Vidura was another brother of Pāṇḍu and Dhṛtarāṣṭra. He was born to a servant maid and was not entitled to rule the kingdom. He was a minister to the king and was a great soul. He was *dharma* incarnate. Many a time he tried to give good advice to Dhṛtarāṣṭra.

Dharmaputra was asked by Vyāsa to perform a great *yajña* called *rājasūya*, in which money and food were to be distributed. In that *yajña*, Duryodhana was in charge of distributing the money. He was known to be generous and if it was someone else's money, he gave even more. Everyone participated in the *yajña* in some way or other and this was Duryodhana's contribution to it.

After the *yajña*, people began praising Dharmaputra and his brothers. This made Duryodhana even more jealous. He could not bear to see the prosperity of the Pāṇḍavas. He wanted Indraprastha for himself. But he knew he could not win in a war with the Pāṇḍavas. Śakuni advised him to invite Dharmaputra for a game of dice and said that he would play on behalf of Duryodhana and win for him Indraprastha and all that the Pāṇḍavas owned. With his father's consent, Duryodhana invited Dharmaputra for a game of dice. Śakuni's plan worked; Dharmaputra lost everything.

Game of dice – Dharmaputra's weakness

Dharmaputra accepted the invitation for a game of dice because it was considered to be a *kṣatriya-dharma* not to refuse an invitation to a game of dice. Apart from that, he had a liking to it. It was his weakness. But he had not bargained for playing against Śakuni who was an expert in the game. Dharmaputra was no match for Śakuni even in a fair game. But Śakuni had no intentions of playing fair. Not knowing that Śakuni had loaded the dice, Dharmaputra thought that with every subsequent throw he would recover what he had lost.

Instead, being goaded by Śakuni to stake more and more, he lost the crown, the kingdom, his brothers, himself and everything– even his wife, Draupadī, who was also considered to be part of his wealth. Śakuni baited Dharmaputra to stake Draupadī in an attempt to regain all that he had lost. A gambler's thinking being what it is, Dharmaputra thought that this at last would work and, in that stake, he lost her too.

All the stories in the Mahābhārata point out either certain human virtues or weaknesses. This story reveals that playing the game of dice is a weakness and that a gambler gambles everything. There is a value here and the value is to be understood. Dharmaputra's weakness was gambling and he paid dearly for it!

The story then continues to tell how Draupadī was drawn into the court where she was insulted and attacked by Duryodhana's brother, Duśśāsana. While she was being disrobed, Kṛṣṇa helped her by continuing to lengthen her sari until her attacker finally became exhausted by his efforts. Although she had sympathetic support, no one else was able to help her because of *dharma*. Dharmaputra had staked his wife and lost her to another. Whatever he did with her or allowed to be done to her was his right. Because of their commitment to *dharma,* the furious Pāṇḍavas had to remain helpless witnesses, controlling themselves from doing anything to stop Duśśāsana's malicious act. Kṛṣṇa's grace was Draupadī's only support which saved her from further humiliation.

Pāṇḍavas' exile

The Pāṇḍavas felt humiliated. The other four brothers were bound by love and honour to Dharmaputra. That prevented them from killing Duryodhana and others then and there. So, they stood there with suppressed anger and frustration and Draupadī appealed to the elders in the assembly for justice. Many signs of ill omens appeared at that time. Then Bhīma declared that he would kill Duryodhana and Duśśāsana in war later. Arjuna declared that he would kill Karṇa. Sahadeva vowed to kill Śakuni. Nakula in turn vowed to kill Śakuni's son. These declarations were terrible and frightening.

Dhṛtarāṣṭra lost his nerve and promised Draupadī he would offer everything back to the Pāṇḍavas; they should forgive and forget and go back to Indraprastha. Then, Bhīṣma, Droṇa and other respected elders too told Duryodhana that what had happened was wrong and that Dharmaputra should continue to rule the kingdom. But Duryodhana would not budge an inch. Then everyone agreed to play one more game with the condition that if the Pāṇḍavas won they would get their kingdom back. If they lost, they would go to the forest for twelve years, during which time Duryodhana would rule the kingdom. After their return, however, the kingdom was to be given back to the Pāṇḍavas.

Duryodhana agreed to this condition with one amendment, that is, for one additional year, the Pāṇḍavas should live somewhere incognito without being recognised by anyone. If any one of them was discovered, they would all have to serve another period of twelve years in the forest, plus one more year living incognito, *ajñātavāsa*. In this way, Duryodhana was certain that he could send the Pāṇḍavas back into exile for thirteen more years because he had so many spies moving about the kingdom. At least one of the Pāṇḍavas would surely be recognised, he thought.

Thus, the Pāṇḍavas lived for twelve years in the forest and one more year incognito in the kingdom of Virāṭa. Each of them got employed in the King's palace – Dharmaputra as a companion to the king, Bhīma as a special cook, Arjuna as the teacher of dance and music to the women. Arjuna had been cursed by the celestial damsel Urvaśī that he should lose his masculinity. Lord Indra had modified that curse to take effect for a period of one year whenever he chose. Thus, Arjuna opted for it to take effect for this period of *ajñātavāsa*. He taught music and dance to the royal ladies of the King of Virāṭa. In this way, the Pāṇḍavas lived out the remaining year unrecognised by anyone.

Duryodhana had suspected their presence in Virāṭa and he engineered a border skirmish in order to bring them out into the open. Arjuna did come out, along with the Prince of Virāṭa. But the one year period had just expired. Bhīṣma was the one who told Duryodhana that according to the lunar calendar, the period was indeed over. However, all that came out of Duryodhana's scheme was that Arjuna gave Duryodhana, his people, Karṇa and others a good scare. It was a great day for Arjuna, one he had been long awaiting.

Pāṇḍavas' return

The Pāṇḍavas came back to claim the kingdom but Duryodhana refused to return it to them. No amount of pleading could convince him to alter his stand. Bhīṣma, along with other highly respected people, advised Duryodhana to return the kingdom; but he refused.

Duryodhana had enjoyed absolute power for thirteen years. Power corrupts, and absolute power corrupts absolutely. Duryodhana was now so corrupt that he would not give the Pāṇḍavas even so much as a square inch of the kingdom. The Pāṇḍavas for their part were willing to accept anything because they wanted to avoid war; therefore they turned to Kṛṣṇa for help. Bhīma, inspite of his vow to avenge Draupadī by destroying his cousins, pleaded with Kṛṣṇa to somehow avoid the war. They all told Kṛṣṇa, "It will be the end of the entire family. We do not want this. We are ready to take anything, but let *dharma* prevail. Otherwise, it is *adharma*, it is not proper. We are supposed to protect *dharma*. Now we have to fight and we do not want to fight. Please make it possible for us to avoid the war."

But even Kṛṣṇa's eloquence, pleading power, and negotiating acumen were of no avail. Duryodhana was too hard a nut to crack. His attitude towards his cousins was based on the fact that they were princes, members of the ruling class. They had valour and were well-armed with weapons. 'Let them fight,' he said, 'and take the kingdom as they should. I am not going to give it back to them. I have declared war. If they want the kingdom, they should meet me in the battlefield in Kurukṣetra and take it back. Otherwise, let them go back to the forest. I will not disturb them there.'

In his role as the mediator, Kṛṣṇa then asked Duryodhana for some kind of compromise. He said, 'Give them one state with five districts. Give them a district with five counties. Give them a county with five villages. Give them a village with five houses. Give them a house with five rooms.' Duryodhana refused to give even one needle-point of land to the Pāṇḍavas.

The issue, therefore, was no longer the kingdom, but a matter of *dharma*, a question of right and wrong. The Pāṇḍavas were the lawful rulers, even though Duryodhana ruled the kingdom de facto. The Pāṇḍavas were the rightful rulers, rulers in exile, and Duryodhana was a usurper who continued to occupy the throne. To allow a usurper to rule the kingdom is to allow injustice, *adharma*, to go unchecked. If the king himself is following *adharma*, what will happen to the kingdom?

Just as a fence, put around a growing crop to keep out stray animals, should not creep into the field and destroy the crop, so too, a ruler should not destroy *dharma*. Rulers, Kings, are all fence-like protectors. If they begin to follow *adharma*, the kingdom will not be fit to live in.

There is a daily prayer that says, *nyāyyena mārgeṇa mahīm mahīśāḥ paripālayantām* – let all the rulers of the world rule their kingdoms following the path of justice. It is said because the word, 'ruler' implies justice. It may be your own son or a cousin by marriage who has done wrong. Nevertheless, the person must be given the punishment that the crime deserves.

It is the duty of a ruler. The Pāṇḍavas were supposed to protect *dharma*, law and order, and Duryodhana had gone against it in every way. *Dharma* and justice had to be reinstated.

Therefore, the Pāṇḍavas could not avoid this war, even though they had explored all possible avenues for avoiding the war. Because Duryodhana would not return the kingdom, Lord Kṛṣṇa had no option but to hand over the challenging gloves to Dharmaputra, saying, 'I am sorry. I could not get even a square inch of land from Duryodhana. I tried everything. The situation is impossible. Here are the gloves. You have to fight. There is no other way.'

War is declared

It was with great reluctance that Dharmaputra accepted the need to fight. In the meantime, both parties had begun gathering whatever support they could. Since Duryodhana was the ruler, he was able to sway people to his side by bribing those who were willing to compromise. Such people are prepared to ignore what is right and wrong when it suits their purpose. Thus, using his money, power, land and position, Duryodhana gathered a large number of people, kingdoms, armies and supplies – everything required to wage a war.

The neighbouring kingdoms felt that if they did not give Duryodhana their support, they would have to face the consequences. Duryodhana was the emperor, whereas they were lesser kings and chieftains. Because they could also have elected to join the Pāṇḍavas, Duryodhana sent his brothers and special messengers to elicit their support. They agreed to join his ranks primarily out of fear. Therefore, the number of people who refused to give him their support, because they lived according to *dharma*, was very few.

There are always a few people in any society who live their lives according to *dharma*. We read in a Tamil verse that it is because of such people that the rains come, the winds blow, and the flowing water still finds its own level, meaning that there is some order in the society. Here too, there were a few people who were not threatened by Duryodhana, still less tempted by his offers because of their commitment to *dharma*. Unbribable and virtuous as they were, these people cast their lot with the Pāṇḍavas.

Dharma of war

War was declared openly. No stealth was involved because, in those days, even war was controlled by *dharma*. There was no such thing as a pre-emptive strike, where, while one side was preparing for war, the other side went in and took them by surprise. Nor could a man without a weapon be struck. If he was in a chariot, the other person also had to be in a chariot before any fighting could occur.

So, there were certain rules that had to be followed and that is how the battle between the Pāṇḍavas and Duryodhana was fought. A time was declared and the fighting did not begin until then. The place was also arranged – Kurukṣetra, located just above Delhi.

As the *Gītā* opens, the forces of Duryodhana and those of Dharmaputra had assembled. Duryodhana's commander-in-chief was the invincible Bhīṣma, the grand old man of the Kuru family. Even though Bhīṣma was a man of *dharma*, he felt obliged to be on Duryodhana's side because he had promised his father that he would always stand by the one who ruled Hastināpura. And at the time of war, rightfully or not, Duryodhana was the current ruler and hence Bhīṣma was obliged to fight on his side.

Although Droṇa had taught archery to both the Dhārtarāṣṭras and the Pāṇḍavas, his heart was with the Pāṇḍavas. But, Duryodhana had made him feel so obliged that Droṇa agreed to join his ranks. Also, Droṇa was extremely fond of his son, Aśvatthāmā; in fact, one could say Aśvatthāmā was his weakness. And Aśvatthāmā was Duryodhana's friend. It was another reason for Droṇa to stay on with Duryodhana. Kṛpācārya was also obliged to stay with Duryodhana. Karṇa, of course, was Duryodhana's friend and very loyal to him. Because of his exceptional expertise in archery, Karṇa was Duryodhana's answer to Arjuna. He had been recognised as a great archer, early on, and Duryodhana had deliberately cultivated him and had given him a small kingdom. This gesture was enough to commit Karṇa to Duryodhana forever.

So, everyone who was in some way obliged to Duryodhana had come to the battlefield to fight for his cause. They were all very well equipped with weaponry, skills, and a thorough knowledge of warfare. Just as armies now have tanks, there were chariots, cavalries, regiments with camels as the mount, regiments with elephants as the mount and infantries. With all this support, Duryodhana was ready.

The Pāṇḍavas were also ready and the war was about to begin. All eyes were upon Arjuna because he was the one everyone wanted to see in action. Even the Gods wanted to see him and the balconies were full! To add to the colour, Kṛṣṇa was sitting right in front of Arjuna as his charioteer. Kṛṣṇa was the added attraction. Arjuna was already the apple of everyone's eye. But to add to that Kṛṣṇa was also there. Therefore, all eyes were upon Arjuna whose chariot was driven by none other than Kṛṣṇa, the Lord himself.

An account to settle

So this was the situation as the *Gītā* was about to begin. Arjuna had a long account to settle with his cousins. From childhood onwards, there were so many occasions when he would have got even with Duryodhana, but his mother would not allow it, nor would his elder brother. The incident involving Draupadī was the final insult. He, therefore, wanted to teach all the Dhārtarāṣṭras a lesson.

All the weapons he had been stockpiling for this day were going to have a chance to express themselves. These were not simple arrows. They were a different type of weaponry; they were all missiles. One came emitting fire, like a napalm bomb. Another one had the ability to neutralise it by dousing it with water. With such missiles, what a fight it would be! Elaborate descriptions of these weapons and missiles are found in the pages of the Mahābhārata.

Arjuna's magnificent weapons had been stockpiled in anticipation of an appropriate occasion in which they could be used. The war of *dharma*, which was about to begin, was just such an occasion. More often than not, war is due to *adharma* on both sides; here, *adharma* was on one side only.

When a warrior fights for *dharma*, all his weapons and skills become useful. They come alive and are not wasted. The warrior will not think he spent his life simply gathering weaponry that was never used. A warrior who does not have an opportunity to fight, having spent fifty or sixty years stockpiling weapons, may develop arthritis and wish he had studied geology instead! He will regret what he has done because he has no proof of his valour. Therefore, for a *kṣatriya* like Arjuna, it was a great day to prove himself. He was a prince who had been nursing a lot of hurts and injustices. For him, the D-Day had come. Having waited so long for this day. Arjuna was naturally one flame of fury.

He ordered Kṛṣṇa to position his chariot in such a way that he could see all those with whom he would be fighting. Arjuna could not have fought with ordinary soldiers. He had to determine which chieftains he must tackle, which ones were his equals. As a good driver, Kṛṣṇa replied, 'Yes, Sir,' and placed the chariot where Arjuna could see all sides.

Arjuna's grief

When Arjuna looked around him, he collapsed, not out of fear but in appreciation of the following fact that the people he was going to destroy were the people whose life and company he would prefer to have. He thought, 'In their absence, my life will be empty. How can I destroy my own family, my own kith and kin? These are the very people who are standing in front of me. How can I destroy all of these people?'

Most of the people Arjuna saw were citizens of this great kingdom. They had all been conscripted by Duryodhana, given a crash training course, and then brought to the battlefield. It was all visible because of their dress. They did not know how to button the shirts of their uniforms properly and their walk was clumsy because of the heavy, unfamiliar military boots. They were obviously new recruits who had come to be fodder for Arjuna's arrows.

Not only were there so many citizens in the opposite camp, but on his own side, too, there were a lot of innocent people. Arjuna then understood that no one was going to be victorious in this war. Because Arjuna and his brothers were committed to the moral order, *dharma*, they did what was to be done and avoided what was not to be done. A word once spoken was fulfilled and their actions were always beyond question. Their life, therefore, was lived according to this *dharma*, whereas, in the case of Duryodhana and his brothers, with the exception of Vikarṇa, it was quite the opposite. They followed a life which was questionable, *adhārmika*. So the fight now was between *dharma* and *adharma*.

This battle is also sometimes interpreted as representing a conflict within the physical body, the body having been brought into being by certain type of *dharma* – good actions. In this interpretation, the body is called *dharma-kṣetra, kṣetra* meaning 'place.'

Knowledge of right and wrong is universal

If the physical body is considered a *dharma-kṣetra*, then Kurukṣetra is your own mind in which there are conflicts between *dharma* and *adharma* – what is to be done and what is not to be done, what is proper and what is not proper. These things you already know, of course, because you have certain innate sense about them. No one can plead ignorance of what is right and wrong. This knowledge is universal.

What do we mean by universal knowledge? All monkeys, for example, born to live on treetops, need to know something about the law of gravity – and they do. If you were to observe the mother monkey, you would see that she has no concern about whether there is a baby holding on to her as she jumps from tree to tree. The baby monkey, however, holds on to its mother's bosom for its dear life. It is definitely afraid of falling, whereas the mother is not. She just keeps leaping from one branch to another, while her baby holds on tight. Suppose, the baby monkey had to undergo some education to know that there is a law of gravity operating, that it must hold on tightly in order not to fall and that if it did fall, it would be injured or it would die. If all of these things had to be taught to monkeys, many of them would die for want of education and the species itself would sooner or later become extinct.

Fortunately, every baby monkey, without being educated, seems to know what is to be done and what is not to be done. Without going to Harvard or Cornell, without joining the Moral Majority, it knows very well that, 'I will fall if I let go of my mother.' 'I will fall' is one piece of truth and, 'if I fall, I may hurt myself,' is the second piece of truth the monkey seems to know. The third piece of truth is, 'To fall and get hurt or be killed is not good for me or for my species.'

Instinctively, then, the monkey knows all this. Since monkeys are made to live on treetops, the minimum knowledge every monkey must have in order to survive is to know, 'I will fall; objects come down; I will be the victim if I do not hold on to the other branch when I leap.' This knowledge must be given to monkeys along with the creation. Only then is there any hope of a monkey living its life on the treetops.

Such knowledge is instinctive and is what we call the creation. If that knowledge is not given to a monkey and it has to be educated in order to know how to survive, then we can say that there is a defect in the creation.

Similarly, as a human being, I am born with a faculty of choice. Unlike a monkey, however, I can choose to live on treetops, or on the twentieth floor of a building in Manhattan, or in a cottage on some riverbank. I can choose to go to Alaska and keep only my nose out or I can live in the tropics. Because I have the faculty of choice, I can choose my course of action. I can choose various ends and various means to achieve those ends.

That a human being seeks securities and pleasures is a common fact that we have already analysed. And in seeking these ends, they have to follow certain means to achieve them. More often than not, upon analysis, we find that the problems lie only in the means and not in the ends. For example, the desire for money, an end, is not a sin. In fact, if we seek money, Lord Viṣṇu will be very happy about it, knowing that his wife, Lakṣmī, the Goddess of wealth, is so popular. The security that money represents is a natural need perceived by all human beings.

Seeking security is natural

People seek different forms of security. In itself, this seeking is neither good nor bad, only natural. The means alone is what is important here.

If you are controlled by a set of instincts, then you need not think about whether the means you employ is right or wrong. If you live in India and leave a couple of bananas on the window sill and a monkey comes along and takes them away, you cannot say the monkey is a thief. At the most, you can say that you were careless. When you know there are monkeys around, you have to keep certain things away from them.

Whatever a monkey does, that action cannot be labelled as wrong because it is controlled by its own instincts. So, the monkey is always right and is not responsible for what it does. This is what is meant by *svabhāva*, one's own nature. Only when there is a choice, is there right and wrong. Wherever choice is involved, you cannot avoid the concept of right and wrong. There can be proper choice and improper choice.

Now, if this knowledge of what is proper and improper is to be given to you by an educational institution, it will definitely be denied to a lot of people, thereby making it possible for them to destroy themselves.

Just as the monkey is given an instinctive knowledge of gravitation for its survival, so too, a human being is given a common sense knowledge with reference to what is good and not good for him or her. No institution is required to teach such knowledge. 'That I should not get hurt,' for example, is a piece of knowledge. A mother and father need not teach this common sense knowledge to their child because the child already knows it.

So, when I know 'I should not get hurt,' I also understand that, like me everyone else is aware of this fact. I also know exactly what is expected of me by others. I do not expect you to hurt me just as you do not expect me to hurt you. No one needs to be taught this knowledge. Because I have to choose, this knowledge is not left to education. It must be known to me. When I choose a means of action or perform an action, I must necessarily see whether it will hurt me or hurt anyone else or anything else. Knowledge of this moral order is what we mean when we say knowledge is born of common sense.

A moral order is known to you. That you do not want to be robbed and that no one else wants to be robbed is very well-known. You do not want to be cheated or deceived, nor does anyone else want to be cheated or deceived by you. You do not want to be the target of anyone's anger, hatred or jealousy. You also know very well that no one wants to be the target of yours. To put it positively, you want others to sympathise with you, to understand you, and others also want you to understand them. You want others to help you when you are in trouble. Others also want your help when they are in trouble.

There are many values involved in a moral order – non-injury, *ahiṁsā*, absence of deception, speaking the truth, compassion, sharing, absence of jealousy, absence of hatred and so on – all of which are connected to each other. With reference to the behaviour of others, we are very clear. So, this particular knowledge is with all of us and is gathered by common sense. No education is necessary to know what is right and wrong. Duryodhana had this knowledge and so did the Pāṇḍavas. However, problems arise because of our priorities, which is why we settle for compromises.

Universal, cultural and individual values

Values can be universal, cultural and individual. In the West, for instance, there are a lot of individual likes and dislikes. In fact, children are taught to develop them at a very young age. The mother asks, 'What do you want on your toast? Do you want honey or brown sugar?' From childhood on, you are asked, 'What do you want? This or that?' In this way, you have been taught to exercise your faculty of choice. In India it is not done. You are offered tea with the milk and sugar already in it. There is no choice in the matter, whereas in the West you are not only asked what you would like in it, but whether you would like tea, coffee, or something else.

Our choices are based on personal likes and dislikes, which we are not concerned with here. We are concerned with the fact that there is a common structure, a universal structure, wherein no one wants to be robbed, for example. Whether the person is a tribesman living in a remote desert or an urbanite living in a sophisticated society, it is the same. A person may be walking along in a street in Delhi, and a person may be walking in a forest; but both of them do not want to get hurt or robbed. No one says, 'Because New York city is such a wonderful city, I want to get mugged there.' No one wants to get mugged anywhere.

Therefore, there is a structure that we all commonly sense, a structure which is already there. This universal structure that is already there is a moral structure. It comes up in the *Gītā* itself later on, and I will talk about it more then. The word *dharma* refers to this structure, this order, which includes the ecological order. This *dharma* is known to me, to you and everybody else.

Money, power, name and influence are not universal values. You may seek money as a form of security and be prepared to destroy your name for it. There will also be another person who is ready to give up his or her money for the sake of power, name, or influence. Although name, influence, money and power are generally sought after, they are not universal.

Values are not absolute

Sympathy, love and compassion, on the other hand, are universal values, which does not mean that they are absolute. Values are never absolute; they are always relative, even though they may be universal. The point is that, you should not go against the universal values while pursuing individual or cultural values. For example, as long as your pursuit of money conforms to the universal values, you are living a life of *dharma*. Whereas if your pursuit, whether for money, power, or pleasure, comes into conflict with the universal values, then there is *adharma*.

The Pāṇḍavas also sought money, power and pleasure, but they tried to conform to *dharma* at the same time.

Duryodhana, on the other hand, represents a life of *adharma*, wherein power becomes so important that its pursuit comes into conflict with the order, *dharma*. For such people, however, this is not a problem because they do not think of it in these terms. Therefore, for them, the means can be anything, as long as the end is achieved. To say, 'For the sake of power, I can do anything,' is not due to ignorance, really speaking. There is some ignorance involved, as we shall see later, but the ignorance is not of the universal values.

Duryodhana definitely knew that he did not want to be cheated and that the Pāṇḍavas did not want to be cheated either. But power was so important to him that he did not mind cheating or destroying anyone, legitimately or illegitimately, who stood in his way. He simply did not think about the legitimacy or illegitimacy of what he was doing.

My understanding of the laws, reflected in my choice of the means, is what is meant by inner maturity. When I choose a means which is not proper for the sake of money, I go against the order, *dharma*, for the sake of money because I do not understand what I lose. I only know what I gain; money, which is very important to me. The difference between having the money and not having it is very clear to me.

One person may tell a lie for the sake of five thousand dollars while another person may tell a lie for a hundred thousand dollars, or for any amount in between, but not for five thousand dollars. There may also be those who would tell a lie for as little as a dollar. Everyone seems to have a price.

The value of a value

We even try to bribe the Lord in order to get to heaven. We are always ready to compromise if we can get something that is valuable enough to us. If a man sees the difference between having five thousand dollars and not having it, he may even deceive a friend who has offered to give him twenty percent over and above the value of the house he bought and renovated. All he has to do is to jack the price up by the amount of money that is so important to him. This man knows that the money can take him to Hawaii. It will definitely give him a good vacation somewhere. Thus, to have this five thousand dollars will definitely make a difference in his life. Therefore, he is ready to compromise.

Suppose you tell someone, 'You should not tell a lie,' and the person, being very pragmatic, questions you, 'What do I lose if I tell a lie?' What will you say? Or, if your child asks, 'Dad, If I can get some money so that we can have some more things, why should I not tell a lie?' Generally, you will say that, telling a lie is wrong, which is another way of saying, 'Do not do it.'

The general message the child gains is that, what is 'wrong' is what I should not do. But this does not explain anything. Therefore, the child will come back asking, 'Why is it wrong?' 'Well, because it is not right,' you say. Again the child argues, 'Why is it not right? Everybody else does it, and those who lie get money. I do not get it because I do not tell a lie, but if I tell a lie, I will get it. Why should I not tell a lie then?' A father who is little more intelligent will say, 'You see, my child, you will be detected.'

Now the whole question becomes, 'Is it all right to tell a lie if I do not get caught?' Someone might say 'So what? even if I get caught, so what?' 'You will lose your credibility,' the person is told. But if the person does not care about his or her credibility or anything else, then where is the problem? 'You will not be eligible for a credit card,' may be your response, to which the person replies, 'That is why I steal them. That way I get five cards at the same time!'

This line of argument is, of course, foolish and should not be pursued. What I should appreciate is this. If there is a universal value and I go against that value, I must lose something. But my focus is on the gain that results from such an action. Perhaps I gain money, which makes a difference to me because I see the value of it. But what do I lose? Since I do not care for credibility, I do not see that I lose anything.

Compromise and moral order

If you can see the immensity of the loss with reference to compromises made to gain such things as money, power and so on, you are mature. You will not go for the bargain because you see it as a bad bargain. You should see that what you lose is more than what you gain, which has nothing to do with the moral majority.

If there is a universal structure, and there is, then what you lose must definitely be much more than what you gain. Therefore, the education needed for maturity is to know what you lose. Suppose I say, 'You will go to hell' and you do not accept the idea of hell, then, that is the end of it. You will simply say, 'You go to your hell, if there is one. I am not going because I do not accept a hell.'

How do I know there is a hell other than where I am now? Hell is simply a belief. Suppose it is wrong? The threat of hell is certainly not a very convincing argument for telling the truth. Perhaps I do not believe in hell or do not care if there is a hell. If there is a hell, I will tackle it when I get there. It is not my problem right now. All that I want to do is get out of the hot water I am in right now. I will deal with the heat in hell later. It is a different thing. I am in hot water right here and now, and five thousand dollars will make a difference.

However, if the person knows that he will be the loser by gaining this five thousand dollars, he may not compromise for the sake of that money. If I were to ask him, 'Why do you want this five thousand dollars?' He would say, 'Because I can then buy certain things.' I then ask, 'Why do you want those things?' He replies, 'So that I can be happier, more secure.' But if I were to show him that, in the process of getting this five thousand dollars, he becomes incapable of being happy and hence the bargain is a bad one, then he will not compromise. Now he understands the price he may have to pay for the compromise. This is how one understands the value of a value.

No one wants money for money's sake. If that were the case, a cashier's job would be good enough because, by just feeling money, he or she would be happy. You want money for your sake, so that you can be happy. Money is very interesting. Without it certain things cannot happen, but there is a limit to what money can offer. It can buy a book, but it can never make you read unless the author offers you a thousand dollars to read it. Then, of course, you will read it overnight. But even then the money cannot make you understand what the book says. For that, you require something else, something other than money.

Money can buy music, but it can never make you understand music. You can hire the best musician to sing for you, but the money you pay to the musician cannot stop you from falling asleep during the performance, unless, again, you are offered money to stay awake! So, money can provide situations. That is all it can do. And money indeed does that, which nothing else can; a point to be remembered. But, then, the enjoyment is for the person. You are the one who is to enjoy the music. If you lose the enjoyer, in the process of acquiring the money that will provide the opportunities for you to enjoy, then, it is a bad bargain.

Therefore, the whole education or inner maturity of a human being is not in knowing what is right and wrong, which one knows, but in knowing what one loses when one does the wrong thing. One needs to know this – What will I lose? How much will I lose? If I know this very well, it is not possible for me to go for the bargain. This is what is to be understood here.

When you tell a lie, you are speaking and, therefore, you are a doer, a performer, an actor. You are doing the action of speaking and, as an actor, when you tell a lie you are saying something that is not true to what you think. Therefore, the thinker is one and the actor is quite another. You know one thing, and by the time it comes out of your mouth, it is entirely different because what you say and what you think are not the same. It means there is already a split in you. As a speaker, a doer, who is telling a lie, you behave in such a way that you create a split in yourself, like Dr. Jekyll and Mr. Hyde.

Split between the thinker and the doer

Once you create a split in yourself, then, as a doer you are different from the one who knows, who thinks. If this split has taken place, do you think that you can succeed in life? Even with money or anything else, you cannot. Because the person, you, is already split. As a thinker, you are entirely different from the performer, the one who does things, the doer. There is only one 'I' and when you see yourself as a split person, then, you cannot enjoy what money buys. You will be worried all the time.

You cannot do a wrong thing without a conflict and every conflict naturally creates a split in you. The conflict itself is the split and the split creates conflict. The more conflict there is, the more split the person is. It is not a conflict of choice. It is a conflict between you, the knower, and you, the doer. The split is in the very personality, the very person. So, the mind is unable to enjoy the pleasures that money has bought. If a person already has a split between what he or she thinks and does, how can there be enjoyment of anything, whether it be food or a beautiful house? Being in conflict, the person is also potentially moody. You have to determine whether someone is in a good mood before you can talk to the person. And good moods come only occasionally! When you say what you have to say, the person may feel so bombarded that he or she gets into yet another bad mood. So, the person is nothing but mood, potential mood, all due to split, the conflict between the thinker and the doer.

By analysing such situations, you find that this split, which is the basis of all psychological problems, has something to do with our rubbing against the law of *dharma*. Just look at yourself. When you are in conformity with the order, there is always freedom. There is harmony, joy and certain composure. Whereas, when you rub against the order, you get rubbed in the process.

No one can rub against something without getting rubbed. If you rub against a rough bark of a tree with your bare body for five minutes, you will see who gets rubbed – and this knowledge will stay with you for at least ten days. That you never rub against anything without getting rubbed in the process, needs to be well understood.

Every gain implies a loss

Having understood that you cannot rub against the moral order without being rubbed in the process, it takes even more understanding to know exactly how much you lose by performing some actions. It becomes a matter of self-esteem. What kind of self-esteem can there be when a division has been created between the thinker and the doer? Sooner than later, you will conclude that you are worthless.

This process can be seen when you make a very simple resolution such as, 'Tomorrow I am going to get up early in the morning, at six o'clock, and I am going to meditate for half an hour.' You have decided that to begin the day with some kind of meditation is good and this is what you want to do. Therefore, you are going to get up half an hour earlier than usual and meditate.

Whose decision is this? It is not someone else's; it is yours. You even set your alarm clock to ring at six o'clock, and it does. In fact, it never stops. It goes on beeping, beeping, beeping. Then what you do? Annoyed, you turn the alarm off and go back to sleep!

Do you know why? Because the one who made the decision last night to get up half an hour earlier did not consult the one who had to wake up the next morning. This is like a husband making a decision to go on a weekend family trip without informing or consulting his wife! The decision to wake up earlier was made by someone who thinks and figures things out, whereas, I am the one who has to get up. Therefore, you had better consult me before you decide anything!

Between husband and wife, there can be some consultation. But when I am thinking that I will get up half an hour earlier, the waker is not there to be consulted. Here is a real problem because the waker is also me. While this plight looks very simple, it is actually a very complex issue. The split between the one who thinks and knows and the one who does is a very self-detrimental split, one that eventually and naturally leads to self-condemnation.

If you tell me to do something and I decide not to do it, it is quite different from when I tell myself to do something and I cannot do it. Once, twice, or thrice is not a problem, but when

I cannot conform to my own decisions more times than not, what self-esteem will I have? If it happens only once, I can always justify not having done something. But if I do it consistently, then I cannot have any self-esteem. And, without self-esteem, no one can really help me. Even the Lord cannot boost me up because, intrinsically, I have a problem. Therefore, I am the loser.

If I am together as a person, I can enjoy sports and a variety of other situations that do not cost money. I can even enjoy myself, which also does not cost money. Whereas, if in the process of gaining money, I lose myself, the transaction is definitely a bad bargain. To know this about myself is education; it is growing up. Who, then, can afford not to have such knowledge?

Since I have a faculty of choice, I must necessarily exercise that choice. I must know the norms which are the basis upon which I choose. These norms are known to me by my own common sense. The only education needed with regard to them is an understanding of what I lose when I gain something. In a so-called gain, I should be able to see how much I lose. If I do not lose, then the gain is truly a gain, and is worthwhile. Whereas, if I lose, the gain is not worthwhile. Therefore, the means that one follows in gaining one's ends are very important.

Significance of battle in the Gītā

In the *Gītā* we have a conflict between two groups of people, based on a historical event. One group was ready to compromise the means and go against *dharma* even though *dharma* is so very important. The other group was committed to maintaining the moral order, *dharma*.

This conflict can also be looked upon as one between a person's common sense knowledge and what he or she wants to accomplish – an inner war, an inner Mahābhārata, so to speak. After all, every war takes place first in one's mind, and only later, outside.

The moral order is considered to be so important that a person will sacrifice everything for its sake. In the Mahābhārata there are many stories of such sacrifice. One story is about a man who gave up his kingdom and everything else he had in order to uphold the universal value of speaking truth.

Because India is a place where *dharma* is important, it is referred to in the *Gītā* as *dharmakṣetra*. The Veda rules the hearts of the people and everything subserves the order of *dharma*. In the country of Bhārata (India), in a place called Kurukṣetra, these two groups of people have assembled, prepared to fight; one group does not understand the value of values, while the other group does.

All eyes were upon Arjuna, considered to be the greatest archer. Arjuna's driver was none other than Lord Kṛṣṇa. The illustration of Arjuna, seated in his magnificent chariot drawn by white horses and driven by Lord Kṛṣṇa, is very beautiful in that it relates to one's own life. This illustration also appears elsewhere in the Veda, in the Kaṭhopaniṣad.

Body-chariot analogy

In this illustration, your body is likened to a chariot, your senses are the horses, the mind is the reins, and your intellect, *buddhi*, is the driver. You are the one who is seated in the chariot; in other words, you are the *svāmi*, the master. If your *buddhi* is loose, if your understanding is not very clear, you can end up anywhere because your chariot, your physical body, will not take you to the destination.

You can take the chariot to *artha*, *kāma*, *dharma* or *mokṣa*. It all depends on the driver and you, the *svāmi*. The driver, the *buddhi*, educates the swami, really speaking. You are as good as your driver. If the driver is uneducated, and drunk also, you have had it. If, however, your driver is informed, educated, then he or she can take you anywhere you want to go.

In the *Gītā*, Kṛṣṇa, the driver, became the one who educated Arjuna. He was a *guru* to Arjuna and Arjuna was the *svāmi*, the one seated in the chariot. Arjuna ordered Kṛṣṇa to station his chariot between the two forces so that he could see those in the enemy ranks with whom he would fight. Kṛṣṇa moved the chariot as directed. From the vantage point selected by Kṛṣṇa, Arjuna saw his own people in both camps and decided that nothing would be gained by fighting this battle.

Arjuna found himself facing Bhīṣma, who was his grandfather, and Droṇa, who was his teacher in archery. He saw uncles and cousins, friends and acquaintances, and other relatives. These were the people Arjuna would be destroying, the very people he needed with him in order to be happy about winning the war. Therefore, he said, 'I would rather not fight.' We will see his arguments for this thinking later.

The whole problem for Arjuna was one of, 'These are my own people.' We have this problem even today. For example, when we say 'my people' we mean that our people can get away with doing anything and other people, unknown people, cannot. But in Arjuna's case the people were not unknown. If the opposing army had been made up of men who were unknown to Arjuna, there would have been no *Gītā* at all. Kṛṣṇa would only have had to drive the chariot, nothing else, and Arjuna would have fought.

However, Arjuna happened to see people he knew, people with whom he was connected, with whom he had to settle accounts, and people who, in the process, might die. This is what bothered him, as it should have. It would bother any cultured person, any mature person. These were the people who really counted in Arjuna's life. Duryodhana also saw the same people, but it did not bother him as it did Arjuna because his value structure was different.

There are a few select people in everyone's life whose opinions count. You may not want to be seen by them on New York city's 42nd street, for instance. It may not be because you do not want to be there but, rather, because you are afraid of what these people will think of you. You do not want to fall short of the good opinion they have of you. These were the people who were standing in front of Arjuna against whom he was supposed to fight.

Arjuna's dilemma

Because Arjuna no longer wanted to fight, he had a problem. According to the code governing the war in those days, there was no such thing as a successful retreat. Either you won or you lost, the loss amounting to death since the fight was always to the end. Thus, Arjuna knew that in order to hoist the flag of victory, he had to destroy all the people in whose company he would be happy and in whose absence he would be unhappy.

Arjuna wept, not out of fear, but out of compassion, out of sympathy, out of care. His response was that of a mature person. He began to think that war was not the answer to the problem, which, of course was true, given that the loser always prepares for a comeback. The first and second world wars are recent examples. No one wants to accept the fact that he or she has lost.

Not only did Arjuna think war would not solve the problem, he also felt that its aftermath would create great confusion in the society. Since all the able-bodied people would be destroyed, the society would have no leadership and the very structure of the society would disappear because people would be confused as to their duties. Even *dharma*, for the sake of which Arjuna was supposed to win the war, would be in trouble for there would be no one to carry it forward to the next generation.

Dharma is both a discipline and a life of discipline. The values that govern that discipline are also *dharma*. The lifestyle, that is *dharma*, has to be handed over to the next generation by the present one and is not something that can simply be bottled and buried for the future. *Dharma* is something that has to be lived. Thus, when you protect a person who lives a life of *dharma*, you are protecting *dharma*.

You can protect libraries, but you can never protect scholarship unless you protect the scholars. Protection of the scholar is the respect you have if you value scholarship. When a society values scholarship, the people will sell their shirts to gain that scholarship because it commands their respect. This was the situation in India. A king would come to his knees when a scholar entered his court. When scholarship is valued, respected, in this way, the scholar will be protected and valued. Only then will scholarship continue.

Similarly, to protect *dharma*, you have to protect the one who lives the life of *dharma*, the *dharmī*. If the *dharmī* is protected, meaning that he or she is respected and valued, then everyone will want to be a *dharmī*. Arjuna naturally thought that by destroying these people there would be no one left to live a life of *dharma*, and that the *dharma* itself would thereby be destroyed – the very *dharma* he wanted to protect by waging the war. The battle was supposed to be one of *dharma*, but the very fighting of it, he thought, would endanger *dharma*.

Arjuna, therefore, felt that he would be incurring a great sin by causing confusion in the society. Naturally, he wanted to avoid this problem. At the same time, he did not run away from the battlefield. He did not jump out of the chariot and run towards Rishikesh, which was only a short distance away. Instead, he dropped his bow and arrows and sat back in the chariot, as we will see at the end of the first chapter of the *Gītā*.

Kṛṣṇa's rallying cry

Arjuna was so completely overwhelmed by compassion sympathy and consideration, that he could not fight. Addressing the sad Arjuna, Kṛṣṇa expressed his sense of surprise. To extend his actual words, he may have said, 'Arjuna, where did you get such a disposition? I never expected you to behave like this. This is not a time for talk; it is a time to act. To talk in the battlefield is not befitting your temperament at all. You are supposed to act. You are a prince, and the most respected prince at that. You are the greatest archer and you are someone who is supposed to protect *dharma*. If you, of all people, do not want to do this, what will happen? It is definitely the wrong time for you to be talking like this.'

'Had you told me a few years ago, while you were in the forest, that you did not want to return to the kingdom, that you wanted to study and contemplate, I could have appreciated it and we could have discussed it at length. But not here. You came to the battlefield. You even brought me along with you! Now you are making a right-about turn. It is making you look silly. And you are making me look silly, too. When I stake on a horse, I am ready to lose my bet, but I do expect the horse to run. That much satisfaction I should have. And now you are telling me that you will not even start!'

Kṛṣṇa then asked Arjuna to stand up and fight. It should be understood that not all of Kṛṣṇa's words are scriptural. Here, they were purely words of advice and not meant as an order. Only when he taught and dealt with the ultimate concerns in life, the universal problems, that belong to me, to you and to all and sundry, at any time and place, do his words assume the status of a scripture. Kṛṣṇa was just giving Arjuna a pep talk.

Recognising that Kṛṣṇa was talking to him as though he was afraid to fight, Arjuna exclaimed, 'How can I fight against Bhīṣma and Droṇa in this battle? They are men worthy of my respect! I would rather live the life of a mendicant and live on alms than destroy these people.' This was Arjuna's thinking.

Arjuna as a student

Arjuna also said, in so many words, 'I do not think this sorrow will go away just by gaining a kingdom, whether the kingdom be here or in the hereafter. Even if I go to heaven and become the ruler there, I would be the same wanting person. I would have the same problems.' Arjuna knew that to be the ruler of a kingdom brought only royal problems, that enemies abound, especially if the kingdom is prosperous or unrivalled. He, therefore, did not see himself as one who would be free from the problem of sorrow by gaining any kingdom.

The problem of sorrow, as Arjuna pointed out, is self non-acceptance. In fact, self non-acceptance is the original problem. 'If I do not see myself as an acceptable person, that self non-acceptance will always be there, with or without a kingdom.' Therefore, Arjuna saw no solution to the problem. He recognised that he had spent his time on immediate, empirical concerns and had never dealt with the ultimate concerns of life.

Because of his desire to solve the original problem, Arjuna offered himself as a student to Lord Kṛṣṇa and asked him to teach him what he needed to know. He considered himself to be qualified for this knowledge because he had enough experiences in life and had discovered the problem. All that now remained was for Kṛṣṇa to decide whether he would accept him as a student, a *śiṣya*. In other words, the ball was in Kṛṣṇa's court, Arjuna having done his part by saying, 'I am your *śiṣya*, please teach me.' All of this we will see in detail, later.

There are three very significant words that mean 'the student' in Sanskrit – *vidyārthī*, *antevāsī* and *śiṣya*. *Vidyārthī* means the one who wants to know, and can refer to the type of student who enrols in a college to get a degree, but spends very little time in the classroom. An *antevāsī* is a student who lives with the teacher. This type of student also wants to know but may not be able to grasp what is being taught.

A *śiṣya* is one who is truly qualified to study and therefore, deserves to be taught. He or she may also gain other experiences while studying, but these are by-products only. For the *śiṣya*, there is a certain direction and commitment that is necessary for him or her to really accomplish anything in life.

If I am happy that you are in my class, then you are a *śiṣya*, and if I miss you when you are not there, you are a *śiṣya*. If I wait for you, if you are delayed by a few minutes, you are a *śiṣya*. To be a *śiṣya* means you are qualified to be a student. The teacher looks for your presence and does not want you to be absent. When this is so, you are definitely a *śiṣya*.

When Arjuna told Kṛṣṇa, 'I am your *śiṣya*. Please teach me,' he was also saying that he had a commitment to this knowledge, that he saw the value of it and also that he looked upon Kṛṣṇa as a qualified teacher. He did not say he was a student, but he said, 'I am your student, *ahaṁ te śiṣyaḥ*,' meaning that he had chosen Kṛṣṇa as his teacher.

The *Gītā* began only because Kṛṣṇa took Arjuna seriously and chose to teach him. Therefore, we have seventeen chapters of dialogue between the teacher and the student; *kṛṣṇa-arjuna-saṁvāda*. Kṛṣṇa may have taught in prose, but Vyāsa chose to put it in the form of verses. Each chapter is a dialogue with a predominant subject matter, which is revealed by the title of the chapter. So, the first chapter is called *arjuna-viṣāda-yoga*, meaning that the topic discussed is Arjuna's sorrow.

A fundamental problem requires a fundamental solution

A problem can be solved topically or fundamentally, and Arjuna decided to solve it fundamentally. Because of the clarity it produces in one's thinking, a fundamental solution resolves the problem so completely that topical issues of right and wrong no longer arise.

In fact, in the second chapter of the *Gītā*, Kṛṣṇa told Arjuna that his sorrow was not legitimate, that no sorrow is legitimate, even though legitimate sorrow is commonly accepted. In other words, we acknowledge that it is legitimate to be sad in certain situations. When you have lost a loved one, for instance, it is wrong to tell yourself that you do not want to be sad or that it is not legitimate to be sad. If you are sad, you are sad. Therefore, it is best to acknowledge the sadness and that there is a reason to be sad.

Remember, however, that you become sad because you are already subject to sadness. In fact, only the sad become sad, just as the mad become mad and the bad become bad. All that is required is a particular situation. The sad person is already there and it may take no more than a change of weather for him or her to become sad. Certain plans may have been made based on a weather forecast of a 'good' weekend. A rainy weekend then becomes a 'bad' weekend.

There are vulnerable spots in everyone and, when these are touched, the person is touched to the quick, meaning that he or she suddenly becomes angry, frustrated, sad, hateful or desperate. A person does not suddenly become a desperate person; he or she is already desperate. The person is the despair. Psychologically speaking, there is sadness and there is some legitimacy for it. But, if you look into the matter dispassionately and realistically, you will find that there is no real reason to be sad.

When you go to a therapist, you are a seeker. The therapist analyses your past and arrives at a solution to your problem saying, for example, 'It is all due to your mother.' 'Yes, that is true,' you say. In this way, the therapist validates your feelings. Knowing there is a reason for your sadness, you have a sense of freedom. You had certain opinions about yourself that made you sad and now your reactions and responses have been validated properly. Your conclusions, based upon wrong notions about yourself, can now be looked at differently. By changing those opinions, you gain a freedom, as though you have thrown light upon yourself.

Accepting situations as they are

You begin, then, by acknowledging the situations and validating your responses. Later, you find there is no reason for sorrow. It does not mean you are suppressing the sorrow, only that you see the situation as it is. What we are doing is taking the sorrow one step further and asking, 'Is there a real reason for sorrow?' Lord Kṛṣṇa told Arjuna there was not. How could he say this? Was it merely because he had never experienced sorrow? After all, Kṛṣṇa was looked up to, everyone prostrated to him, and all the *gopīs* were after him. Did he not recognise Arjuna's limitations?

Lord Kṛṣṇa understood Arjuna's limitations very well. Everyone has limitations – physical, perceptual, intellectual, and others that are picked up while living one's life, due to the natural ageing process. Originally, you may have had 20/20 vision and now perhaps a vision of 20/60. Thereafter, you require glasses, a hearing aid, and perhaps a cane also.

In spite of all these limitations, Lord Kṛṣṇa said there is no room for sorrow. It is something to know and is what the teaching is about. Arjuna asked for the knowledge and Lord Kṛṣṇa taught him in the second chapter. He did not just make the statement and ask Arjuna to work on it. He made it very clear. Once Arjuna received the teaching, it became a matter of questioning and assimilating the knowledge given to him.

Thus, the second chapter ends with Arjuna's question, 'How do you describe a wise man?' Kṛṣṇa had told him that the person who is wise is different. He or she is one in whom, due to wisdom, there is no room for sorrow. Since the problem is to be solved by knowledge, Arjuna wanted to know how a wise man behaves while conducting the affairs of his life. He wanted to know how he walked, how he talked, whether he talked, and so on.

Kṛṣṇa did not answer the question literally, but instead, responded to the spirit of the question. Had he not done so, Arjuna may have thought that all he had to do to be wise was to walk, talk and sit in a certain way.

A wise person is one who is happy and secure with himself or herself, one who requires nothing else to become secure. It refers to one who looks at oneself as a totally acceptable person, the one who can say, 'I cannot be better than myself.' Because the acceptance is total, there is no area of non-acceptance. The self is essentially free from any sense of want or limitation; it is the whole, in spite of the limitations of the body-mind-sense complex.

You are the whole. I am the whole. If you understand this, then you do not need to prove yourself to anyone; to do so is no longer a necessity. Such a person may do a lot of things, but not to prove himself or herself. This is how Kṛṣṇa defined a wise man to Arjuna and he gave a few examples, as we will see later.

Two lifestyles for gaining self-knowledge

Kṛṣṇa also talked about *karma-yoga*, a life of activity, and about *sannyāsa*, a life of renunciation. Then he said that all you need in order to be free is to know yourself. 'Why, then,' Arjuna asked, 'do you ask me to engage myself in this war which will result only in destruction?' It was a very relevant question.

Arjuna thought that Kṛṣṇa was giving him two conflicting pieces of advice. Kṛṣṇa had said that knowledge liberates and, therefore, Arjuna felt that he was telling him to pursue knowledge, which was what he wanted to do. Not only had Kṛṣṇa said that knowledge liberates, he had also said that *karma* binds. Then, he had told Arjuna to do *karma*! What did this mean? Thus, Arjuna begged Kṛṣṇa, "Please do not say, '*sannyāsa* is good and *karma-yoga* is also good.' I cannot accept this. Tell me one or the other."

Knowing the difference between *karma-yoga* and *sannyāsa* is a matter of understanding and Arjuna was confused. Therefore, he asked Kṛṣṇa to tell him which one was right for him to follow. But Kṛṣṇa did not want to play the role of a consultant; he only wanted to teach Arjuna. To teach is to make the other person see as clearly as you see so that he or she does not need to come to you again. The person who is able to do this is a teacher. Kṛṣṇa, being a teacher, did not give Arjuna advice. Instead, he taught him the remaining chapters of the *Gītā*.

At the beginning of the fifth chapter, Arjuna had the same doubt and rephrased his question. Again, Kṛṣṇa told him that *sannyāsa* was good and *karma-yoga* was good. Then he told

Arjuna that it was not a matter for choice, that it was a matter for understanding.

How this teaching came about

We have two epics, the Rāmāyaṇa and the Mahābhārata. Both are historical and also have a literary value. I consider these historical, poetic works to be similar to those we have in English literature. Shakespeare's plays, for example, while based on certain historical figures, also have drama woven into them. Walter Scott's novels are especially historical in their mention of the names of particular kings. The description of the time, period and condition is all true, whereas the heroes and heroines are fictional.

Similarly, we see in the Rāmāyaṇa, authored by the poet Vālmīki, historical figures in Rāma, Sītā and Daśaratha. Also, Ayodhyā, the city in which they lived, did exist. So too, the island called Laṇkā and the demonic king, Rāvaṇa. But we can also see an underlying meaning conveyed by Vālmīki when he presented Rāvaṇa as having ten heads. If someone has ten heads and each head thinks in its own way, then you have a person who thinks as though he has ten heads, each one having its own way of thinking. He is, therefore, a person of great confusion.

Rāvaṇa was like that. He was a *brāhmaṇa* and a great devotee of Lord Śiva. However, he did not behave like a *brāhmaṇa*. A *brāhmaṇa* should not rule a kingdom and Rāvaṇa did. Furthermore, although he was a devotee, he was also demonic.

Thus, Rāvaṇa was an embodiment of contradictions. This may be why he was potrayed as having ten heads, an aspect that is purely poetic.

We also find, in these epics, a lot of poetry centred on certain historical events. That is why they are called *Itihāsa*, meaning 'this is how it was – *iti-ha-āsa*.' Thus, the Rāmāyaṇa, authored by Vālmīki, and later the Mahābhārata, authored by Vyāsa, are both considered to be historical poetry.

Mahābhārata – the fifth Veda

There are four Vedas and the Mahābhārata is referred to as the fifth Veda because it is so complete. There is not nearly the amount of information in the Rāmāyaṇa as there is in the Mahābhārata Any topic you could ask for is there – *dharma*, logistics, political acumen and so on. All of these are beautifully illustrated through the epic's excellent characterisations.

Various values are highlighted in the stories by presenting the same person in different moods and situations. Bhīma, for instance, stands out as a person with his own moods, proclivities, characteristics, inclinations, capacities, limitations, and points of vulnerablity. Each of these aspects is mentioned when characterising any given hero. In this way, the five Pāṇḍavas and the hundred sons of Dhṛtarāṣṭra, from Duryodhana downward, are all presented individually as characters in their own right.

Vyāsa – the author

Vyāsa is considered to be a principal link in the Vedic teaching tradition. He is, therefore, an important figure.

Beginning from Lord Nārāyaṇa, all the way down to my own teachers, there is a live tradition in which Vyāsa is the most important historical connecting link. The *paramparā*, lineage of the teachers of *brahma-vidyā* is presented in the following verse.

नारायणंपद्मभुवंवसिष्ठं शक्तिञ्च तत्पुत्रपराशरञ्च
व्यासं शुकं गौडपदं महान्तं गोविन्दयोगीन्द्रमथास्य शिष्यम् ।
श्रीशङ्कराचार्यमथास्य पद्मपादञ्च हस्तामलकञ्च शिष्यं
तं तोटकं वार्त्तिककारमन्यानस्मद्गुरून् सन्ततमानतोऽस्मि ॥

nārāyaṇaṁ padmabhuvaṁ vasiṣṭhaṁ śaktiñca tatputraparāśarañca
vyāsaṁ śukaṁ gauḍapadaṁ mahāntaṁ govindayogīndramathāsya śiṣyam
śrīśaṅkarācāryamathāsya padmapādañca hastāmalakañca śiṣyaṁ
taṁ toṭakaṁ vārttikakāramanyānasmadgurūn santatamānato'smi

I remain as one who always salutes Nārāyaṇa, Brahmā, Vasiṣṭha, Śakti, his son Parāśara, Vyāsa, Śuka, the great Gauḍapāda, Govinda (*govinda-bhagavatpāda*) the most exalted among the *yogī*s, his disciple Śaṅkarācārya, Śaṅkara's disciples Padmapāda, Hastāmalaka, Toṭaka, and the author of the *vārtika*s (Sureśvaracārya) and our other teachers.

Vyāsa is also called Veda-vyāsa because it was he who edited, classified and codified all the *mantra*s of the Vedas. He grouped them into four and made them available to the future generations by making one family responsible for maintaning one *śākhā*, branch. To commit all four Vedas to memory is not realistic. It requires twelve years and a bright mind to commit even one entire *śākhā*, branch, to memory. A young boy, in his eighth year, goes to a teacher and spends his next twelve years doing this. To memorise four Vedas, then, would mean becoming a grandfather by the time the work is completed.

Therefore, Vyāsa made it easy. A particular family maintains one branch of the Veda throughout the generations. In this way, the four Vedas have come down to us in their original form through an unbroken chain of oral tradition. Because Vyāsa was responsible for handing over the Vedas to posterity, he came to be known as Veda-vyāsa.

Gītā's prayer of invocation

Although the Bhagavadgītā is presented by Vyāsa in the middle of the Mahābhārata, it is an independent work. Every work begins with a prayer in recognition that any successful undertaking involves three important factors – effort, *prayatna*; time, *kāla*; and the unknown factor, *daiva*. We ourselves are capable of providing the effort and we can also wait out the time it takes for the result to come. Success or failure, however, is accounted for by the third factor, the unknown factor, *daiva*. Therefore, we cannot fail to take *daiva* into account.

Daiva is there whether you take it into account. In spite of all your efforts and waiting, you do not always get what you want. There seems, then, to be some unknown factor over which you have no control. You may call it chance or luck, but we call it *daiva*, grace.

Grace is nothing but *karma-phala*. It is a graceful way of referring to *karma-phala*. It is something you earn by prayer. It is not an arbitrary decision on the part of God. Otherwise, God would be just another autocrat who goes about distributing packets of grace every morning, and missing us more times than not.

We do not see the connection between grace and our actions because we do not know which action produces the grace. Although it is the result of prayer, we have no direct knowledge of whether it is cumulative or the result of one single prayer. All we know is that there is a plus factor as well as a minus factor with reference to the result of our actions. Thus we find that in spite of all our efforts, there is something else which makes the difference between success and failure. That is the *daiva*, the unknown factor.

Astrology tries to unfold a pattern in your life that can be projected from your horoscope. Your birth is an event, a visible event that inaugurates your life. An event occurs in a particular place, *deśa*, at a particular time, *kāla*, and is a link in the whole process. If there is a pattern, if there is destiny, then this event is the inaugural event from which the destiny would unfold itself. You do not know what the pattern of destiny is, but you do know that your birth, an event, took place at a given time.

Now suppose there is another pattern that is projectable. This projectable pattern and the pattern unknown to you are connected. How? When you are born, the constellations and planets are in a particular configuration. Because each planet has its own orbit and its own speed, you can find patterns of the horoscope which are projectable to any future time.

By observing people's lives, relationships can be seen between the heavenly patterns and the events in a person's life. Recurrences of specific events in the lives of people under certain planetary configurations give rise to rules of astrological prediction. The planets do not interfere with your life, your actions in the past and present do, according to the *śāstra*.

Astrology is only a predictive discipline. Indian astrology is useful in that, it gives you a basis for specific prayers to neutralise the negative *karma*s in terms of undesirable situations unfolding in this life and to enhance the results of positive *karma*s in terms of desirable situations.

Daiva, the third factor, a factor in which you can neutralise the results already created either in this life or previously is done through prayer. So, for any undertaking, the third factor, *daiva*, is invoked, which is why before beginning the study of any discipline of knowledge, we invoke the Lord through a prayer.

The *Gītā*, coming in the middle of the Mahābhārata, does not have a prayer as such, although Vyāsa did invoke the unknown factor in the form of a prayer at the beginning of the epic itself.

Because of the importance of the message of the *Gītā*, it is described as a pendant jewel in the midst of the Mahābhārata Therefore, there should be a prayer for the *Gītā* also. Prayer can be in different forms. It can be mental, it can be in so many words, or it can be suggested by one word. Here, we have a suggestive prayer in the narrator's sentence, *dhṛtarāṣṭra uvāca.*

The word, '*dhṛtarāṣṭra*' is much more than the name of the blind old man seated in his palace wanting to know what had happened in the battlefield. *Dhṛta* means 'is sustained' and *rāṣtra* means 'the entire world.' *Dhṛtarāṣṭra*, then, means the one by whom the entire world is sustained, *dhṛtaṁ rāṣṭraṁ yena* And who is that? The Lord – the entire world is sustained by Īśvara. By beginning the *Gītā* with the words *dhṛtarāṣṭra uvāca*, two purposes are served. The Lord is invoked by the word *dhṛtarāṣṭra*, which is a kind of prayer, and the word *uvāca* indicates that the narration of the *Gītā* was about to begin.

The *Gītā* opens with the blind king Dhṛtarāṣṭra, sitting in his palace with his companion, Sañjaya, a minister who was blessed by Vyāsa with an extraordinary audio-visual capacity. He could hear what was happening far away. He had a mind like a radio that could pick up sounds from a distance. He could also see situations and events beyond the frontiers of human eyesight. Knowing that Sañjaya had these psychic powers, the blind Dhṛtarāṣṭra asked, 'Sañjaya! What happened on the battlefield between my sons and the Pāṇḍavas?'

With this extensive introduction, we will now begin the *Gītā* verses. Chapter one and the first ten verses of chapter two are actually a continuation of the Mahābhārata and thereby provide the context in which the dialogue between Kṛṣṇa and Arjuna took place. Although we are only interested in

Kṛṣṇa's teaching, which does not begin until the eleventh verse of chapter two, it is important to understand the condition of Arjuna's mind that led him to ask Kṛṣṇa to teach him. Therefore, these contextual verses will be analysed in some detail.

Chapter 1

अर्जुन-विषाद्-योगः

Arjuna-viṣāda-yogaḥ

Topic of Arjuna's sorrow

Verse 1

Prayer

धृतराष्ट्र उवाच ।
धर्मक्षेत्रे कुरुक्षेत्रे समवेता युयुत्सवः ।
मामकाः पाण्डवाश्चैव किमकुर्वत सञ्जय ॥ १ ॥

dhṛtarāṣṭra uvāca
dharmakṣetre kurukṣetre samavetā yuyutsavaḥ
māmakāḥ pāṇḍavāścaiva kimakurvata sañjaya (1)

dhṛtarāṣṭraḥ – Dhṛtarāṣṭra; *uvāca* – said;
sañjaya – O Sañjaya!; *dharma-kṣetre* – at the abode of *dharma*; *kurukṣetre* – at Kurukṣetra; *samavetāḥ* – those who have assembled; *yuyutsavaḥ* – desiring to fight; *māmakāḥ* – my people; *pāṇḍavāḥ* – Pāṇḍu's sons; *ca* – and; *eva* –indeed; *kim* – what; *akurvata* – did they do

Dhṛtarāṣṭra said:
Sañjaya! Desiring to fight, what did my people and the Pāṇḍavas do, assembled at Kurukṣetra,[13] the abode of *dharma*?

---

[13] Kurukṣetra exists even today between Delhi and Ambala. The great King Kuru, the founder of the Kuru dynasty, performed big *tapas* here and established *dharma*. Therefore, it is Kurukṣetra and also called *dharmakṣetra*.

In the Indian tradition, any beginning begins with a prayer. Being in the middle of the Mahābhārata, the *Gītā* does not require a beginning prayer of its own. Yet, for this chain of eighteen chapters, for this pendant jewel placed against the background of the much larger epic, it seems that a prayer should be there, and it is implied in this first verse.

A prayer can be either expressed or implied. The first word of the *Gītā*, 'Dhṛtarāṣṭra' is a prayer by implication. It means the one who sustains a kingdom or the whole universe, *yena dhṛtaṁ rāṣṭram*. It is, therefore, an appropriate name for a king. Had Dhṛtarāṣṭra not been blind, he would have been the ruler of the kingdom.

Rāṣṭra also refers to the world, the entire universe. The Lord is the one who is the holder, the sustainer, of the order that is the world. Therefore, Dhṛtarāṣṭra is also the name of the Lord. By beginning the *Gītā* with the name of the Lord, the traditional opening prayer is implied.

The opening scene of the *Gītā* takes place in the palace in Hastināpura, the capital of the kingdom of the Kauravas. It was the kingdom that the Pāṇḍavas were supposed to rule, but which was now ruled by their cousin Duryodhana who had usurped the kingdom. As we have seen, the Pāṇḍavas were tricked into exile by Duryodhana. They had to spend twelve years in the forest plus one more year living incognito somewhere in the empire. The kingdom was to be returned to them after they had fulfilled these conditions.

The Pāṇḍavas served this term of thirteen years and came back to claim their kingdom. However, Duryodhana would not give it back to them and therefore, war was declared. They could choose to either go back to the forest or take the kingdom back in battle. All possible compromises were put forward, but Duryodhana would not give one needle-point of land to the Pāṇḍavas. It had, therefore, become a problem of justice – *dharma*.

Problem of justice – dharma

Dharma, here, means that which has to be done. Rulers also have their *dharma* in that there are certain things that must be done by them. The kingdom belonged to the Pāṇḍavas, and in fact, Yudhiṣṭhira was the ruler. Every minute that Duryodhana continued to occupy the throne confirmed *adharma*, for which the Pāṇḍavas were responsible. Therefore, there was no other way but to accept the challenge and fight it out.

Duryodhana had gathered the support of most of the important kings within the empire by bribing them in various ways. He had the power in his hands to do this. Some of the kings joined the Pāṇḍavas too. In this situation, Kṛṣṇa was another force to be reckoned with. His kingdom was Dvārakā, on the west coast in Gujarat; Kṛṣṇa had a well-known and very valorous army of Nārāyaṇas.

Duryodhana thought that Kṛṣṇa's support would tilt the balance. Although Duryodhana's army was bigger than that of the Pāṇḍavas, and he had great stalwarts like Bhīṣma and Droṇa in his ranks, he felt that Kṛṣṇa's army would make the difference between victory and defeat. Therefore, he went to Kṛṣṇa's palace to seek his help. Kṛṣṇa was resting at that time.

Duryodhana was the first one to arrive. He saw Kṛṣṇa was sleeping. He found a nice chair at the head end of the sleeping Kṛṣṇa and sat on it, waiting for Kṛṣṇa to wake up. Arjuna also arrived shortly who had come for the same reason. Since Kṛṣṇa was sleeping, he stood with folded hands at Kṛṣṇa's feet. To Arjuna, Kṛṣṇa was not just a king. Through his mother, Kuntī, they were related, but Arjuna knew Kṛṣṇa to be more than an ordinary mortal. He had not yet recognised him as his *guru*, but he did recognise him as a person of extraordinary powers, calibre and wisdom.

Rumour had it that Kṛṣṇa was an incarnation of the Lord, that he was an *avatāra*. In fact, many members of Arjuna's family worshipped him. Arjuna's uncle, Vidura, and his wife looked upon Kṛṣṇa as the Lord, as did Arjuna's brothers, their wife, Draupadī, and their mother Kuntī. Arjuna recognised him more or less in the same way and wanted his help. This recognition of Kṛṣṇa as an *avatāra* is an important aspect of the *Gītā*.

Duryodhana knew why Arjuna had come and Arjuna also knew why Duryodhana was there. As he opened his eyes, Kṛṣṇa saw Arjuna first. Duryodhana no doubt made his presence known, perhaps, by clearing his throat. Kṛṣṇa then turned to him and asked what he could do for him. He then put the same question to Arjuna. Duryodhana responded by saying, 'You know why we have come, why I have come. I seek your support.' He also added, 'I was the first to arrive and therefore, my request should be entertained first.' Arjuna also said, 'War has been declared and I am seeking your support.'

Kṛṣṇa's proposal

Kṛṣṇa was now in a great fix, but he was an adept at getting out of such tight situations. To both of them, he made a proposal. He said, 'If I join either of you, I will not fight. You have a choice between me, who will not lift a weapon on one hand, and my army on the other hand. If you choose me, you will be choosing the person Kṛṣṇa, mere Kṛṣṇa, who refuses to fight.' Kṛṣṇa was known to be a great fighter. Even as a child he had knocked out Kaṁsa and had dealt with hordes of demonic people. To have such a fighter on one's side would be a great asset, but this was not Kṛṣṇa's proposal. Instead, he said, 'Arjuna, I happened to see you first even though Duryodhana claims to have arrived first. However, because you are the younger of the two, you have the chance to choose first. The younger ones are entitled to this privilege. Therefore, I am proposing this to you and ask you to choose one of the two options – that is, Kṛṣṇa who will not fight on one side and the army of the Nārāyaṇas on the other side. If you choose me, I am not going to fight. I will come to your side and perhaps give some advice. But the army will go to Duryodhana. If you choose the army instead of me, then Duryodhana must take me.'

Kṛṣṇa issued this proposal to Arjuna knowing what his choice would be. He also knew what Duryodhana would prefer. As he expected, Arjuna chose Kṛṣṇa's services, whatever they would be and in whichever form they would be available. This was what Arjuna wanted and so he said, 'Kṛṣṇa, Please come to me.'

If Duryodhana ever prayed in his life, this was surely the time he prayed and his prayers were answered; because he thought the Pāṇḍavas to be sentimental and born losers. Duryodhana expected Arjuna to ask for Kṛṣṇa. He certainly did not want Kṛṣṇa for himself. He would only be another mouth to feed during wartime when food was necessarily rationed. In addition, Kṛṣṇa being a respected person, Duryodhana would have to take good care of him. Duryodhana did not want to be continually torn between taking care of Kṛṣṇa and thinking about the war. A fighting Kṛṣṇa would have been something to think over, but a mere non-fighting Kṛṣṇa would be useless to him, he thought. Duryodhana wanted Arjuna to ask for Kṛṣṇa so that he would get Kṛṣṇa's army and this was exactly how it worked out. He returned to his camp rejoicing. Duryodhana had made his day! He was sure that he would win the war. Kṛṣṇa's army meant crack divisions with men who were fit to fight, adding greatly to his already enormous strength.

Arjuna was equally happy. He knew Duryodhana was ecstatic and he also knew what Duryodhana thought of him. Duryodhana's attitude and value structure was such that he would definitely look down on Arjuna and his preference. But Arjuna knew that with Kṛṣṇa by his side, he would win the war. Sañjaya expresses the same idea in the last verse of the *Gītā*:

यत्र योगेश्वरः कृष्णो यत्र पार्थो धनुर्धरः ।
तत्र श्रीर्विजयो भूतिर्ध्रुवा नीतिर्मतिर्मम ॥

yatra yogeśvaraḥ kṛṣṇo yatra pārtho dhanurdharaḥ
tatra śrīrvijayo bhūtirdhruvā nītirmatirmama

Wherever Lord Kṛṣṇa is, wherever Arjuna is, with his bow in hand, ready to fight, there, all wealth, victory, glory and justice will be.

The unknown factor – Daiva

In Arjuna's mind this was very clear. He knew he had all the weapons and skill that he required. Nevertheless, he also knew he had to allow for one more thing, the unknown factor, *daiva*. A *dhārmika*, one who is committed to a life of *dharma*, appreciates his or her limitations and then takes this one step beyond – recognising that success is ultimately possible only because of this unknown factor, *daiva*. Later in the *Gītā*, Bhagavān himself talks about it.

Daiva is a factor over which you have no control at all, a factor that makes the difference between success and failure, between victory and defeat. We often call this unknown factor 'luck'– good luck and bad luck. In all cultures, I suppose, there are equivalents for these two words because people have to account for a factor that seems to work favourably or otherwise. Even a hard-boiled dialectical materialist has to miss a bus occasionally and is constrained to say, 'I was unlucky.' Catching the bus earlier than expected is also not an uncommon event.

This unknown factor is viewed here as a divine factor, the unknown invisible *adṛṣṭa*, explained earlier in the introduction.

It represents an order and is called the law of *karma*, the law of *dharma*. The factor is not visible, but the results that are reaped by us are seen very clearly. The results are *dṛṣṭa*, whereas the causes are *adṛṣṭa*.

Qualities of a mature person

The one who does not leave *adṛṣṭa* to the hands of chance, the one who does something to change the *adṛṣṭa*, is considered to be a *bhakta* and is religiously mature. You may call such a person a religious person, but I would refer to him or her as a mature person who recognises unseen hands that shape, and are behind these known hands. Such hands are not the hands of chance. They are the hands of the law, hands that are the law, and are looked upon as the Lord. The law is not separate from the Lord and the wielder of the laws is also the Lord.

Throughout the *Gītā*, Kṛṣṇa describes the person who recognises this factor, and at the same time recognises the necessity of his or her own effort, as a mature person, a *yogī*. A mature person is one who has a fear of *adharma*, one who tries to conform to *dharma*. Dharmaputra, his four brothers, and his entire family, underwent many privations for a long period of time only because of their commitment to *dharma*.

Having such a commitment, Arjuna naturally recognised his own prowess and believed in his skills. He had self-confidence and was a person who knew the importance of effort. He did not keep beseeching the Lord, 'Please give me, give me, give me.' He knew that would not work.

Qualities for success

In order to be successful, six qualities[14] are required – *udyama*, proper effort; *sāhasa*, perseverance; *dhairya*, courage; *buddhi*, knowledge; *śakti*, skill and resources; and *parākrama*, the capacity to overcome obstacles. You may have courage and enthusiasm, but no proper effort at the right time. On the other hand, you may have right effort, but no enthusiasm. You may also have the necessary enthusiasm to persevere but if, after some time, you have not accomplished what you set out to accomplish, you may give up due to lack of courage.

In warfare, the knowledge of logistics is very important. You need to know how to approach the enemy, how to enter the opponent's ranks and how to get out again. Skill and resources are also required. Without resources, what is the use of planning? Such effort is useless. If something requires manpower, you must have that. If raw material or skill is required, you must also have that. Finally, you must have the capacity to tide over an obstruction, *parākrama*, to be able to encounter and deal with forces that are inimical to you.

You must be like a flowing river, unmindful of all obstructions. If a huge mountain is there, the river simply flows around it. It does not stop. If the obstruction is a simple rock, the river jumps over it. If it is a bigger rock, it simply goes around or swallows

---

[14] उद्यमः साहसं धैर्यं बुद्धि-शक्ति-पराक्रमाः । षडेते यत्र वर्तन्ते तत्र देवः सहायकृत् ॥
udyamaḥ sāhasaṁ dhairyaṁ buddhi-śakti-parākramāḥ, ṣaḍete yatra vartante tatra devaḥ sahāyakṛt

it and flows over it. If it comes to a valley, the river fills the valley first and then continues flowing. That is the nature of a river. It does not see an obstruction as an obstruction.

Even if these six qualities are present, we cannot say with any degree of certainty that a person will meet with success. There is still that unknown factor to be recognised, *daiva*, that extended helping hand to be sought. Dharmaputra and Arjuna recognised it. They did not go to the forest because they were afraid of Duryodhana or of a fight. They went only to conform to *dharma* because they recognised *daiva*. They knew that one cannot get away with what one does.

Kṛṣṇa as the unknown factor

Arjuna, being a mature person, knew the necessity of recognising the unknown factor, which for him was *daiva*, Īśvara, the Lord. He recognised it in Kṛṣṇa. Kṛṣṇa was there and he told Arjuna he was available. Arjuna recognised him as grace in flesh and blood. Grace does not fight; it is not a weapon, a bow or arrow, a place or time. It is something that is not visible.

Here, however, grace was visible in the form of Kṛṣṇa, with hands and legs, always wearing a smile as though he knew nothing. This was Kṛṣṇa and for Arjuna, mere Kṛṣṇa was enough.

One can always fight if one has to. With the six qualities required for success, one can take care of the obstructions. However, the seventh factor is in Bhagavān, the Lord. Arjuna recognised this factor in the Lord, and he knew it made the difference between victory and defeat. He wanted only grace. Therefore, he wanted Kṛṣṇa with him.

Duryodhana viewed things differently. He was happy with the outcome and thought Arjuna was an idiot because Duryodhana's belief was only in strength. He knew that strength required effort. He was also a great believer in effort, which was why he went to Kṛṣṇa to seek his help. Duryodhana was a man of great effort and had planned well for this day. He was continually scheming. He saw to it that Bhīṣma, Droṇa, Karṇa, Jayadratha, and the others felt obliged to him only because he felt they were very important to his strength. Naturally, then, Duryodhana believed only in the strength of Kṛṣṇa's army, and not in Kṛṣṇa's grace. In addition, he got the army he wanted.

Thus, Duryodhana and Arjuna felt equally victorious. What a proposition! Because they were two such different people, they could both be happy with the outcome. No judgement would make both the affected parties feel victorious; but, here, Duryodhana thought he was the victor and so did Arjuna. How could this be? It is because these two men had two types of thinking, two different commitments, and two different attitudes. Arjuna was happy that Kṛṣṇa would be with him and Duryodhana was happy that Kṛṣṇa's army would be with him. So, they represented two forces.

Kṛṣṇa, then, was going to be with the Pāṇḍavas. Where would he be during the war? Arjuna wanted him to be nearby, but where would he put him? His chariot had only two seats, one at the back for himself and the other in front, for his driver. Given the arrangement, Arjuna could not ask Kṛṣṇa to sit beside him. However, a double-seater could have been arranged. When you are preparing for war, it does not take much time to create a new chariot with two back seats. But, if Kṛṣṇa were to sit on one side or the other of Arjuna, how could Arjuna draw inspirations from Kṛṣṇa during the battle? As soon as he turned his head towards Kṛṣṇa he could lose the battle.

Arjuna's opponents were Bhīṣma, Droṇa, and Karṇa, among others, none of whom was a mediocre fighter. One blink of the eye and Arjuna would be opening his eyes in heaven! Because his opponents were not ordinary men, Arjuna knew that the only way to win the war was to keep Kṛṣṇa in mind and fight, which meant that Kṛṣṇa would have to be in front of him. He, therefore, asked Kṛṣṇa to be his charioteer. He said, 'You told me you would not fight. However, driving a chariot is not fighting. Will you drive my chariot, Kṛṣṇa?' Kṛṣṇa agreed, thinking it would be fun to see the show. He would have a front-row seat, so to speak.

Kṛṣṇa as Arjuna's charioteer

Arjuna thus handed over his chariot, horses, and himself into Kṛṣṇa's hands. Every arrow had to pass through Kṛṣṇa before it reached Arjuna. When you keep Kṛṣṇa, the divine factor, in front of you and do what you have to do, fighting or whatever, the arrows that come to you will have already been blunted. This is exactly what happened when Arjuna fought with Karṇa.

Karṇa was considered to be the answer for Arjuna. Duryodhana had cultivated him only for that purpose alone. That, there would be finally, a dual between the two was a foregone conclusion. Again, except Arjuna and Kṛṣṇa, nobody else was a match for Karṇa. Kṛṣṇa, knowing all this, had very intelligently planned for that day. At first, when he knew that war was inevitable, he himself met Karṇa and tried to convince Karṇa that he should join the Pāṇḍavas by revealing to him the truth of his birth. He told Karṇa that he was in fact a Kaunteya, son of Kuntī, like Arjuna, born of Lord Sūrya. However, being the noble person that he was, Karṇa refused to ditch Duryodhana at the last moment.

Kṛṣṇa made sure that Karṇa made a vow that he would not kill any Pāṇḍava other than Arjuna. To extract this vow from Karṇa, Kṛṣṇa had tutored Kuntī very well. Kuntī at the behest of Kṛṣṇa went to Karṇa and told him the story of his birth and requested him to join the Pāṇḍavas. Again, he refused; but he promised her that he would spare all her other sons except Arjuna. He told her that he would not kill any of the others. And if it came to a combat between him and Arjuna, one of them would live and she still would have five sons. He wanted nothing more than to kill Arjuna in order to show his gratitude to Duryodhana. Giving one's word was very important and was upheld even at the cost of one's life. The two epics, Mahābhārata and Rāmāyaṇa are filled with situations based on someone having given his or her word.

Karṇa had been born with *kuṇḍala*s, earrings, in his ears and a *kavaca*, armour, on his chest. It meant that he was gifted, that he was a very brilliant person and had the blessings of Lord Sun.

However, he had one complex. He could not accept the fact that he was not a *kṣatriya*. 'After all, I am only the son of a chariot driver,' he would say. Because he did not know who his real parents were, he always thought that he was a charioteer's son. His entire lot in life, however, was with the *kṣatriya*s because he was brilliant in archery, having acquired this expertise from Paraśurāma, who was like an *avatāra*.

Paraśurāma's curse on Karṇa

Paraśurāma had made a vow that he would never teach a *kṣatriya* because of some problems he had with them as a child. In fact, he had made a vow to destroy them and he did destroy a lot of *kṣatriya*s. A man of great powers, he lived even at the time of Rāma, with whom he had a verbal battle. Karṇa went to Paraśurāma as a *brāhmaṇa*, and learned archery from him.

One day, Paraśurāma was sleeping with his head on Karṇa's lap. A big insect came along and bit Karṇa. Although the wound was bleeding profusely, Karṇa would not disturb his *guru*'s rest. Feeling the wetness of blood, Paraśurāma woke up. Seeing the blood, he knew that Karṇa could not be a *brāhmaṇa*. Had he been, he would have made a great hue and cry over the sight of his own blood. Because Karṇa was able to stand the pain and the sight of the blood, Paraśurāma was prompted to ask, 'Who are you? Tell me the truth.'

Paraśurāma had vowed to teach no one other than a *brāhmaṇa*, and now Karṇa was forced to admit that he was not a *brāhmaṇa*. Having been deceived by Karṇa in this way, Paraśurāma cursed him, 'All that I have taught you will not be available to you at the time of need. You will forget all the *mantras*.' These *mantras* were, in fact, the guided missiles Karṇa needed in battle.

Karṇa later obtained another missile, by the name *śakti*, for a one-time use, from Lord Indra in return for the *kavaca* and the *Kuṇḍalas* when Lord Indra came in the disguise of a *brāhmaṇa* and asked for them. True to his reputation, he would not deny anything that any one asked as *dāna* and he had gifted them away. But he had obtained this *astra* called *śakti* from Lord Indra which he had reserved it to be used on Arjuna. So, even Arjuna would have been powerless against this *astra*. Kṛṣṇa knew this and all the time carefully avoided the dual between Arjuna and Karṇa as long as Karṇa had it with him. He arranged for a situation where Karṇa had to use it against Ghaṭotkaca, Bhīma's son. Thus, by careful planning Kṛṣṇa saved Arjuna from the *śakti*.

Karṇa still had the serpent missile, *nāga-astra*, which he had also reserved to use against Arjuna. And use it, he did! When finally Karṇa faced Arjuna in the dual, he used it. It was coming right for Arjuna's head. Because Arjuna had no answer for Karṇa's *nāga-astra*, it looked as though he would surely die. For a *nāga-astra*, a *garuḍa-astra*, an eagle missile, is required. Only an eagle can take care of a serpent. What did Kṛṣṇa do? He pressed the chariot so that it went down a few inches needed for the arrow to hit Arjuna's crown and not his head.

To lose his crown was a great shame for Arjuna because he was no mean fighter, but at least his head was saved by

Kṛṣṇa's intervention. Kṛṣṇa did not fight; he only pressed the chariot down. Stories such as these show the play of *daiva*, the unknown factor, in any situation. During the war Arjuna kept this factor in front of him, in the form of Kṛṣṇa, his driver, and thereby saved himself.

Everyone's life is a battle. With the awareness that Kṛṣṇa, in other words, the Lord, is always with you, everything becomes easier. Arjuna did this and it saved him all the way. There were many occasions like this, either before, during or after the war, when Kṛṣṇa's presence as the unknown factor made significant difference in the lives of the Pāṇḍavas.

The blind Dhṛtarāṣṭra knew that war had been declared. Sañjaya had just returned from the warfront carrying the news that Bhīṣma had fallen on the tenth day of the war. Dhṛtarāṣṭra was shocked at the news and after lamenting the fall of Bhīṣma, requested Sañjaya to tell him everything in detail that had happened after the war had been started. This request forms the first verse of the Bhagavadgītā, the dialogue between Lord Kṛṣṇa and Arjuna. This dialogue called the Bhagavadgītā occurred at the beginning, before the war actually started. And this dialogue was reported verbatim by Sañjaya. Dhṛtarāṣṭra was not only visually blind, but he was blind in his thinking also, as can be seen in the first verse itself.

Dhṛtarāṣṭra's question

Sañjaya was sitting in the palace in Hastināpura in front of Dhṛtarāṣṭra who asked the question, 'What happened between the Pāṇḍavas and my people at Kurukṣetra?' As the narrator of the *Gītā*, Sañjaya had been given the power by Vyāsa to see and hear what was taking place elsewhere.[15] Although Dhṛtarāṣṭra was the oldest, most revered person in the family, he was nursing a jealousy towards the Pāṇḍavas because they were the sons of his younger brother, Pāṇḍu, who ruled the kingdom instead of himself due to his blindness. Such complexes do not easily disappear.

It is important to note that the word *dharma* is the first word of the *Gītā*. If you protect *dharma*, *dharma* will protect you, *dharmo rakṣati rakṣitaḥ*. But this is not the case with things like money. The money you protect may protect you in a time of need, but it can also attract bandits and muggers. But when *dharma* is protected, it does protect you.

To protect *dharma* is to live *dharma*, and for a *kṣatriya* to live *dharma*, he must do what is to be done. To do what is to be done leads to *mokṣa*. That is why *dharma* is placed first among the four *puruṣārthas*, human ends or pursuits, *dharma*, *artha*, *kāma*, and *mokṣa*. In fact, the order is more accurately reflected as – *artha*, *kāma*, *dharma* and *mokṣa*, in keeping with a person's

---

[15] Just before the war, Vyāsa had gone to Dhṛtarāṣṭra to talk to him. He had tried to convince him to bear upon Duryodhana to make peace with the Pāṇḍavas and avoid the war. But Dhṛtarāṣṭra was not convinced. He then offered Dhṛtarāṣṭra a divine eyesight, so that he could witness the happenings at the warfront sitting in his palace. Dhṛtarāṣṭra refused, saying that it was very painful for him to witness the destruction of his own people. He requested Vyāsa to bestow that power on Sañjaya. Vyāsa then gave a boon to Sañjaya that he would witness everything that happened in every nook and corner of the battlefield, from wherever he was. He said that nothing would be *parokṣa* to him, that is, he would know everything as if he was a direct witness. He would know everything including what was spoken and thought of by those in the battlefield. Using this, Sañjaya faithfully reported everything to Dhṛtarāṣṭra.

natural tendency to go for security and pleasure, *artha* and *kāma* first. But *dharma* is placed first because of its importance.

Law of dharma

Because the *Gītā* begins with the word *dharma* in the compound '*dharma-kṣetre*,' the importance of *dharma* is evident. *Kṣetra* means a place. A place of pilgrimage is called *kṣetra*. It can be a country or your physical body. The whole Bhārata, India, was a place where the Vedas once ruled the hearts of the people and, therefore, it is a *dharma-pradhāna kṣetra*, meaning that the predominant ruling factor of all human activity is the law of *dharma – veda-ukta-dharma*. *Dharma* is important and everything else, power, wealth and so on, should be in conformity with it. Power without *dharma* is not power at all and is not considered proper. Money without *dharma* is not true wealth. Any form of pleasure should be gathered legitimately.

According to *dharma*, a ruler is to be respected, which is why you do not seek a king's audience with empty hands. Similarly, when you go to a temple or to a teacher, you always carry something. No one should approach these three, *devatā*, *guru*, and *rājā*, empty-handed. This is why the citizens of India always greet a new king with flowers or some other offering in their hands. They even did this for Alexander, the Great. Until he actually won the war, they fought against him. Once he won, they all lined up and offered flowers to him.

The entire country was ruled by the Vedas, which is why it was referred to as *dharma-kṣetra*. Because *dharma* prevailed, the Indian people always respected the king. The British knew this very well, which was why they retained the local kings. These kings ruled the people, who worshipped them and the British ruled the kings, extracting annual tributes from them. Although there were rumblings, they allowed the small kingdoms to exist. The Moslems also were able to rule the majority of people only because of this particular *dharma*.

Every New World country, previously colonised and subsequently independent, has a history of bloody coups. India, on the other hand, has never had such coups because, even today, *dharma* is in the very blood of the people. This is *vaidika-dharma*. You cannot change it completely; it is still there. India is a peace-loving country. Because there is a Vedic genius there, the whole country is a *dharma-kṣetra*. It is a place where even in the courtyards of people's homes, one can hear talk of the timeless, the all-knowledge, and the limitless.

What a culture it is! Classes on the *Upaniṣad*s are conducted under a tree for large groups of people. A mountain may be in view and the river Gaṅgā may be flowing by. Here, the teacher, a hermit, says, 'All that is there is one. All the dividing factors are but a myth.' This is India, *Bhāratabhūmi*. This particular *bhūmi*, earth, or land, has something amazing about it. It has survived thousands of years of deliberate exploitation and destruction only because of the intrinsic worth of the Vedic wisdom. Therefore, it is called *dharma-kṣetra*.

Looking at the words in the first verse, then, *Kuru-kṣetra* is the name of the place from where the Kuru clan ruled, a place named after the head of this clan, whereas *dharma-kṣetra* refers to the entire country. Those who wanted to fight, who had gathered to fight, are called *yuyutsus*, meaning the ones who have a desire to fight.

Dhṛtarāṣṭra's weakness

The words '*māmakāḥ*' and '*pāṇḍavāḥ*' in this verse are significant. Pāṇḍu's sons were not unknown to Dhṛtarāṣṭra and yet he did not include them among his own people here. Dhṛtarāṣṭra was the eldest in the family and should have looked upon Pāṇḍu's children as his own. Yet he used the words, *pāṇḍavāḥ* and *māmakāḥ*, thus creating a division, when he asked, 'What happened between my people and the Pāṇḍavas?'– revealing where his heart lay.

This information was important to Dhṛtarāṣṭra because his son's victory would be his own. Therefore, he wanted to know, 'Did Duryodhana win?' Impelled by *dharma*, out of fear of destroying his own people, 'Did Dharmaputra decide to go back to the forest so that my Duryodhana could retain the kingdom?' His question reflected his wishful thinking. Otherwise, the question would have been irrelevant. He would not have asked, '*kim akurvata*, what did they do?' Everyone had obviously come to fight. They were armed to the molars. They had not assembled there to have fun. Dhṛtarāṣṭra himself knew that. Moreover, he was very eager to know everything that had happened in detail.

Dhṛtarāṣṭra knew he did not have *dharma* with him. He also knew very well that his sons had no *dharma* either. He did not stop the war. He did not tell Duryodhana that what he was doing was wrong, and withdraw his support. Had he done so,

Bhīṣma and Droṇa would not have joined Duryodhana because what he was doing would have been against his father's mandate. None of this happened, however. All Dhṛtarāṣṭra had to do was to speak one sentence to Duryodhana, but he did not do it. This was Dhṛtarāṣṭra. He was very jealous of the Pāṇḍavas. His jealousy and his blind love for Duryodhana led him to support all the schemes that Duryodhana hatched against the Pāṇḍavas. Thus he was indirectly responsible for the war and its outcome.

War in one's mind

This verse can also be looked at subjectively. *Kuru-kṣetra* would then mean *karma-kṣetra,* the physical body. Because the human body is a place where, backed by free will, *karma* is done, it is called *karma-kṣetra.* The same *karma-kṣetra* is also called *dharma-kṣetra* because it is born of *dharma,* meaning *puṇya.* According to the law of *karma,* a human incarnation is due to a mixture of both *puṇya* and *pāpa,* with *puṇya* being the predominant factor. Therefore, it is called *puṇya-pradhāna-kṣetra.*

Here, then, in this human physical body called *puṇya-pradhāna-dharma-kṣetra* and *kuru-kṣetra,* two forces have assembled – *dharma* represented by the Pāṇḍavas, and *adharma,* represented by Dhṛtarāṣṭra's sons. Dhṛtarāṣṭra was blind but, more than that, his mind was blind to *dharma* and *adharma,* right and wrong. Therefore, his sons, the Kauravas, are considered to be the brood of ignorance. In other words they were born of the lack of discrimination between right and wrong, *aviveka.*

Blindness is ignorance and *aviveka* is the lack of discriminative knowledge. The *Gītā* deals with two types of *aviveka*. One is with reference to *dharma* and *adharma*, right and wrong, and the other is with reference to *ātmā* and *anātmā*, which is why the *Gītā* is called both *yoga-śāstra* and *brahma-vidyā*. The blind man here stands for ignorance, *ajñāna*. In blindness you do not see and in ignorance also you do not see.

Fight between dharma and adharma

Confusion is born out of ignorance. No one, however, can say, 'I am ignorant of what is right and wrong.' Whatever one expects from others in terms of behaviour, attitudes and so on, is right if the same behaviour and attitudes are expected of oneself by others. It means that everyone understands the values, but the value of the values is not.

Here, the Kauravas represent the many confusions caused by ignorance, which is why they are greater in number than the Pāṇḍavas. Pāṇḍu stands for discriminative knowledge. In the Mahābhārata, he was presented as being very white in appearance. White always stands for knowledge. The Pāṇḍavas, then, were born of this discriminative knowledge, with reference to *dharma* and *adharma*. They were only a handful and represent our inclinations towards *dharma*. There are also inclinations towards *adharma*. These are born out of *aviveka*, lack of discrimination, with reference to the value of values, whereas inclinations towards *dharma* are born out one's general knowledge of right and wrong.

Since there is a confusion surrounding the values, there is a fight between the inclination towards *dharma* and those towards *adharma*. Only in a human body, or in its equivalent, is this fight possible. No human being can avoid this conflict unless he or she understands everything properly. Dhṛtarāṣṭra's question – 'What did they do?' – reflects confusion related to values, born of ignorance.

Any external problem can come from an internal problem. All wars are first fought in the mind; are they not? The Second World War was first fought in the mind of Hitler. The conflict that began in the mind was actualised on the battlefield. All problems start in the mind and later find their expression outside. Without conflict in the mind, there would be no external conflict.

Imagery of the chariot

Arjuna's chariot, with Arjuna and Kṛṣṇa in it, can be seen in terms of self-knowledge unfolded by the *Upaniṣad*s and the *Gītā*. The significance of this scenario is explained in the Kaṭhopaniṣad. The physical body is the chariot, *ratha*, the intellect, *buddhi* is its driver, *sārathi*. The self, *ātmā*, is the master seated in the back seat. The mind is likened to the reins that control the horses and the horses represent the sense organs. The sense objects become the roads, as it were, because the sense organs naturally go towards them. These horses are held in check by the *sārathi*, the driver. He or she may let go of the reins, but the horses are still kept under control.

Thus, with your body as your chariot and your intellect as your driver, seated in the back seat, you are out in the world. If your *viveka*, discrimination, is not available to you, it is because your driver is confused and what happens to the chariot under such circumstances becomes quite understandable.

Buddhi as guru

Now we can bring in this imagery into the opening scene of the *Gītā*. Here the charioteer is Lord Kṛṣṇa, the *guru*. He keeps the horses under control thereby keeping the chariot under control. Kṛṣṇa being a *jñanī*, his mind and senses are under his control. He has absolute mastery over them. The student who is a *karma-yogī* too, has a *buddhi* that has the mind and senses under its control. Now, the student's *buddhi* is not different from the *guru*'s *buddhi*, when such a *buddhi* is exposed to the *pramāṇa* taught by the *guru*. And, such a *buddhi* that is exposed to the teaching can itself be likened to the *guru*.

Although we say that the *pramāṇa* is Vedanta, it is really a thought, a *vṛtti*, that is the *pramāṇa*. *Pramāṇa* is that which gives rise to knowledge. For example, the eyes are not the final *pramāṇa* for seeing. The *vṛtti* is the final *pramāṇa* inasmuch as it is the final cause for knowledge. To see a flower, you must have a flower-*vṛtti*. It is this flower-*vṛtti* that gives rise to the knowledge of the flower seen. This is what is meant by *pramāṇa*. A *vṛtti* is born out of certain situation and becomes the *pramāṇa*. We say that ears and eyes are the *pramāṇa* but, in the final analysis, *vṛtti* alone is the *pramāṇa*.

The mind, being the place where the *vṛtti* occurs, is called *antaḥ-karaṇa,* meaning, inner instrument. When you are exposed to a teacher or the teaching, your *buddhi,* the intellect, assumes the very form of the *pramāṇa,* the teaching. Therefore, the *guru*'s *buddhi* or the teaching, and your *buddhi* become one and the same.

This *guru-buddhi* tells us, 'You are that, *tat tvam asi.*' Here, the *guru-buddhi* is turned towards Arjuna, who represents the confused *antaḥ-karaṇa,* the ego, or one's notion of 'I'. Arjuna was definitely confused. He had great sorrow and he was being told, '*tat tvam asi.*' That is why he asked so many questions in the seventeen chapters that followed. Exposed to the teaching, one's own *buddhi* assumes the very meaning of the teaching and thereby becomes the *guru* to oneself.

If your *buddhi* does not know this fact, *tat tvam asi,* it cannot tell you. It cannot tell you anything more than what it knows. This is why continually asking, 'Who am I?' does not work. Nothing can happen because you do not know what you do not know. Someone has to teach you. You cannot simply ask, 'Who am I,' and expect to get an answer, because, the 'I' that is always present is the one asking the question. How will the answer to such a question come? You cannot hope to stumble upon the fact. The fact is you; therefore, you are not going to stumble upon an answer that is anything more than what you already know.

The only way an answer can be obtained is by the *buddhi,* meaning the *śāstra* pointing towards the confused *jīva* and saying, 'You are the whole, *paraṁ-brahma,*' as we shall see.

Thus, the whole *Gītā* can be presented through the Kṛṣṇa-Arjuna chariot scene.

Verses 2-11

Sañjaya narrates Duryodhana's words to Droṇa

सञ्जय उवाच ।
दृष्ट्वा तु पाण्डवानीकं व्यूढं दुर्योधनस्तदा ।
आचार्यमुपसङ्गम्य राजा वचनमब्रवीत् ॥ २ ॥

sañjaya uvāca
dṛṣṭvā tu pāṇḍavānīkaṁ vyūḍhaṁ duryodhanastadā
ācāryamupasaṅgamya rājā vacanamabravīt (2)

sañjayaḥ – Sañjaya; *uvāca* – said
tadā tu – then; *pāṇḍava-anīkam* – army of the Pāṇḍavas; *vyūḍham* – in battle formation; *dṛṣṭvā* – seeing; *rājā duryodhanaḥ* – King Duryodhana; *ācāryam* – the teacher (Droṇa); *upasaṅgamya* – approaching; *vacanam* – these words; *abravīt* – spoke

Sañjaya said:
Then, seeing the army of the Pāṇḍavas in battle formation, King Duryodhana approaching his teacher, Droṇa, spoke these words.

Sañjaya[16] referred to Dhṛtarāṣṭra's son, Duryodhana, as king, *rājā*, when responding to Dhṛtarāṣṭra's question. *Rājā* means the one who shines in his own glory – in other words, a king. Sañjaya was now in the employ of these Kauravas and,

[16] Sañjaya was a minister and a constant companion of Dhṛtarāṣṭra.

therefore, he had to refer to Duryodhana as the king, because even though Dhṛtarāṣṭra was on the throne of Hastināpura, it was Duryodhana who held all the power. He told Dhṛtarāṣṭra that his son, the king, had inspected both the armies. Duryodhana might have done this to see who had actually come to fight because there was still a lot of mystery surrounding who was going to join whom. He had gathered a lot of support, but there may have been people whom he had omitted and who may have joined the Pāṇḍavas. In addition, he may have wanted to know if those who had refused to join him were neutral or whether they were going to support the other side. All this he would have seen as he inspected both the armies.

After surveying the army of the Pāṇḍavas, Duryodhana approached Droṇa, the teacher, and spoke to him. According to the style used in the Mahābhārata, the next verse should begin with, '*duryodhana uvāca*, Duryodhana said.' However here, in the *Gītā* we do not see this being done. Since the *Gītā* is a dialogue between Kṛṣṇa as Bhagavān and Arjuna, we do find '*śrībhagavān uvāca*' and '*arjuna uvāca*' throughout the text. Also, the first words of the *Gītā* are, '*dhṛtarāṣṭra uvāca,*' which serve as an introduction to the context and as an implied prayer, as we have seen. Throughout the text, '*sañjaya uvāca*' is mentioned a few times to indicate the presence of a narrator.

Although the words, '*duryodhana uvāca,*' are not mentioned here, they are to be understood. The next verse, then, is within quotes, as it were, since Duryodhana, approaching Droṇa in the battlefield, spoke these words to him.

पश्यैतां पाण्डुपुत्राणामाचार्य महतीं चमूम् ।
व्यूढां द्रुपदपुत्रेण तव शिष्येण धीमता ॥ ३ ॥

paśyaitāṁ pāṇḍuputrāṇāmācārya mahatīṁ camūm
vyūḍhāṁ drupadaputreṇa tava śiṣyeṇa dhīmatā (3)

ācārya – O teacher!; *tava śiṣyeṇa* – by your disciple; *dhīmatā* – by the brilliant; *drupada-putreṇa* – by the son of Drupada; *vyūḍhām* – formed (and led); *pāṇḍu-putrāṇām* – of the sons of Pāṇḍu; *etām* – this; *mahatīm* – great; *camūm* – army; *paśya* – please look at

> O Teacher! Please look at this great army of the sons of Pāṇḍu, formed and led by your brilliant disciple (Dhṛṣṭadyumna), the son of Drupada.

Why does Duryodhana go to Droṇa first? Droṇa is not his commander-in-chief. Duryodhana had chosen Bhīṣma for this post. Given that the war is about to begin, he should only be talking to Bhīṣma. However, he approached Droṇa first because he was certain that Bhīṣma was on his side, whereas he was unsure of Droṇa. Droṇa had come to the battlefield to join Duryodhana, but many of his dearest disciples were in the opposite camp. Therefore, he gave Droṇa extra status by going to him first.

Also, Droṇa had been Duryodhana's teacher of archery, his *ācārya*. He therefore went to him first as a sign of respect. He asked Droṇa to look upon the great army of the Pāṇḍavas arranged in formation in front of them – so many elephants, horses, men, and chariots, all surging forward to the line of battle. This great army of the Pāṇḍavas was led by Dhṛṣṭadyumna, Drupada's son. He was also one of Droṇa's disciples, but Droṇa had life long enmity with Drupada, the king of Pāñcāla. Duryodhana did not miss the opportunity to point out to Droṇa that his own disciple, the brilliant son of Drupada, had formed and was leading the opposing army. In other words, Duryodhana was as much as saying, 'Everything *drupada-putra* knows, he learned from you, Droṇa, and now he is going to use it against you.'[17]

Duryodhana introduced to the *ācārya* all the important people in the opposite camp and also presented to him the great men-at-arms in his own army. He did this because he considered Droṇa to be very important to his winning the war and retaining the kingdom.

Describing the army of the Pāṇḍavas, Duryodhana continued.

---

[17] Droṇa and Drupada went to the same *gurukula* and were very close friends. At that time Drupada impulsively promised Droṇa that he would give half of his kingdom to him when he became the king. Droṇa, at a later day, went to claim that promise. But Drupada refused. Droṇa vowed to avenge his humiliation. When he became the *ācārya* of the princes of Hastināpura, he had his chance. Arjuna defeated Drupada and brought him as prisoner to Droṇa. Droṇa had his revenge and took away half of Drupada's kingdom and released him. Now it was Drupada's turn to seek revenge! He did a *yāga* praying for a daughter and son to avenge his humiliation at the hands of Droṇa. Dhṛṣṭadyumna was the son who came out of that *yāga* and he was destined to kill Droṇa. Yet Droṇa took him as his disciple and taught him everything. He was the commander-in-chief of the Pāṇḍava-army.

अत्र शूरा महेष्वासा भीमार्जुनसमा युधि ।
युयुधानो विराटश्च द्रुपदश्च महारथः ॥ ४ ॥

atra śūrā maheṣvāsā bhīmārjunasamā yudhi
yuyudhāno virāṭaśca drupadaśca mahārathaḥ (4)

धृष्टकेतुश्चेकितानः काशिराजश्च वीर्यवान् ।
पुरुजित्कुन्तिभोजश्च शैब्यश्च नरपुङ्गवः ॥ ५ ॥

dhṛṣṭaketuścekitānaḥ kāśirājaśca vīryavān
purujitkuntibhojaśca śaibyaśca narapuṅgavaḥ (5)

युधामन्युश्च विक्रान्त उत्तमौजाश्च वीर्यवान् ।
सौभद्रो द्रौपदेयाश्च सर्व एव महारथाः ॥ ६ ॥

yudhāmanyuśca vikrānta uttamaujāśca vīryavān
saubhadro draupadeyāśca sarva eva mahārathāḥ (6)

atra – here (in the army of Pāṇḍavas); *yudhi* – in battle; *bhīma-arjuna-samāḥ* – equal to Bhīmā and Arjuna; *śūrāḥ* – unrivalled experts; *maheṣvāsāḥ* – men of great archers; (*santi* – there are); *yuyudhānaḥ* – Yuyudhāna (Sātyaki); *virāṭaḥ* – the king of Virāṭa; *ca* – and; *drupadaḥ* – King Drupada (father of Draupadī); *ca* – and; *mahārathaḥ* – man of great valour…

dhṛṣṭaketuḥ – Dhṛṣṭaketu; *cekitānaḥ* – Cekitāna; *ca* – and; *vīryavān* – the valiant; *kāśirājaḥ* – the king of Kāśi; *purujit* – Purujit; *kuntibhojaḥ* – Kuntibhoja; *ca* – and; *śaibyaḥ* – Śaibya; *ca* – and; *narapuṅgavaḥ* – the one who is the most exalted among men; *ca* – and…

vikrāntaḥ – the one who is very powerful; *yudhāmanyuḥ* – Yudhāmanyu; *ca* – and; *vīryavān* – warrior of great strength; *uttamaujāḥ* – Uttamaujas; *ca* – and; *saubhadraḥ* – son of Subhadrā (Abhimanyu); *draupadeyāḥ* – the sons of Draupadī; *ca* – and; *sarve* – all (these); *eva* – indeed; *mahārathāḥ* – men of great valour

> Here are unrivalled experts, equal to Bhīma and Arjuna in battle, great archers (each one of them)—Sātyaki,[18] the king of Virāṭa,[19] and King Drupada, a man of great valour...
>
> ...Dhṛṣṭaketu,[20] Cekitāna,[21] the valiant king of Kāśī, Purujit,[22] Kuntibhoja[23] and Śaibya,[24] the most exalted among men...
>
> ...the powerful Yudhāmanyu, Uttamaujas,[25] a warrior of great strength, the son of Subhadrā (Abhimanyu),[26] and the sons of Draupadī, all valorous warriors.

---

[18] Sātyaki was the son of Śini, a *yādava* chieftain. He was a disciple of Arjuna and was totally devoted to Kṛṣṇa. He was counted as an *atiratha*.

[19] King Virāṭa of Matsya-deśa (also known as Virāṭa-deśa) was the father of Uttarā who was given in marriage to Abhimanyu. It was in his country that the Pāṇḍavas spent their *ajñāta-vāsa*.

[20] Dhṛṣṭaketu was the son of Śiśupāla, the king of Cedi.

[21] Cekitāna was a *yādava* chieftain belonging to the *vṛṣṇi* clan and was the commander of one of the seven *akṣauhiṇī*s of the Pāṇḍava-army.

[22] One of the brothers of Kuntī.

[23] King of Kunti-deśa, who adopted Kuntī as his daughter.

[24] Father of Devikā, another wife of Yudhiṣṭhira.

[25] Yudhāmanyu and Uttamaujas were brothers and they were princes under the king of Pāñcāla. They fought valiantly for all the eighteen days of the war, but were killed, while asleep, by Aśvatthāmā in the end.

[26] Abhimanyu was the son of Arjuna and Subhadrā, sister of Kṛṣṇa. He was a great warrior who was mercilessly killed by the ganging up of all the *mahāratha*s of the Kaurava-army.

Duryodhana told Droṇa that there were unrivalled experts in fighting and logistics in the army of the Pāṇḍavas. In the war that was about to take place, it was not enough to be able to send arrows. Logistics were also required. Therefore, all of them were top-notch fighters in battle, equal to Bhīma and Arjuna in their knowledge of warfare. Duryodhana mentioned their names to Droṇa because he knew he had a soft corner in his heart for these people.

Maheṣvāsa was a name given to people who wielded bows of great fame. Arjuna's bow, for example, was known as Gāṇḍīva. There are many stories about these bows. Each person had a special conch, *śaṅkha*, also as a part of his equipment. Before a warrior started fighting, he would work himself up by blowing his own trumpet, which may be where the expression, 'blowing your own horn,' originated. It was done as a warming-up exercise. These conches also had names, as we shall see later.

Thus, these were all people of famous bows. It was not that the bows had made a big name for themselves, but that the men who wielded them were considered to be great. They were experts in warfare, equal to Bhīma and Arjuna. The king of Virāṭa was there, along with Drupada, the father of Draupadī, and a man of great valour, *mahāratha*. A *mahāratha* was one who was able to continue fighting, while protecting himself, his driver, and his horses. Because he needed his horses to pull his chariot, he could not allow them to get hurt. He also had to protect his driver because, if he allowed him to be hit, no one would want to drive for him. A great charioteer, then, was one who was able to neutralise all of the arrows that came to his horses, his driver, or to himself. Such men were called *mahāratha*s. They were not ordinary soldiers. Everyone named here by Duryodhana was a *mahāratha* without question.

Next, Duryodhana pointed out six more unrivalled archers who would be fighting against them. Dhṛṣṭaketu was the name of an important warrior who was well-known at that time. Cekitāna also enjoyed a great reputation. Although not specifically mentioned by name, the king of Kāśī[27] was presented by Duryodhana as a man of great valour. Purujit and Kuntibhoja were also acknowledged by Duryodhana and Śaibya was described by him as the most exalted of men.

Yudhāmanyu is described as a powerful chieftain and Uttamaujas is also known to be very mighty. Everyone mentioned thus far in Duryodhana's introduction was a great chieftain. Also mentioned was Arjuna's son Saubhadra, Abhimanyu, born of Subhadrā, one of Arjuna's wives. The five sons of Draupadī born to each of the five Pāṇḍavas were also there.

All these people were great warriors, *mahāratha*s, as was said earlier. The various levels of expertise have been defined elsewhere and are given below.

एको दशसहस्राणि योधयेद्यस्तु धन्विनाम् ।
शास्त्रशास्त्रप्रवीणश्च महारथ इति स्मृतः ॥

eko daśasahasrāṇi yodhayedyastu dhanvinām
śastraśāstrapravīṇaśca mahāratha iti smṛtaḥ

---

[27] His name was Abhibhū.

He who can, by himself, fight with ten thousand bowmen and who is an expert in using weapons and in the science of war is said to be *mahāratha*.

अमितान् योधयेद्यस्तु सम्प्रोक्तोऽतिरथस्तु सः ।
रथस्त्वेकेन यो योद्धा तन्न्यूनोऽर्धरथः स्मृतः ॥

amitān yodhayedyastu samprokto'tirathastu saḥ
rathastvekena yo yoddhā tannyūno'rdharathaḥ smṛtaḥ

He who can fight with a thousand to ten thousand bowmen simultaneously is called an *atiratha*. He who can fight with one thousand bowmen is called a *ratha* and the one who is little less than that in capacity is called an *ardharatha*.

Before continuing with this descriptive verses, it is important to understand their purpose. They provide the context necessary for us to come to know Arjuna's condition. The story that is unfolding is not an illustrative story. Illustrative stories are useful tools for communication, no doubt, but here the story is to tell us how the teaching came about.

This information is also given in the *Upaniṣad*s, where we are told that a given person went to another person in order to be taught, and that person had gone to yet another person, and so on. Thus, a story is told. For example, in the sixth chapter of the Chāndogyopaniṣad, there is a story about a great teacher, Uddālaka, and his son Śvetaketu. When this boy was twelve years of age, Uddālaka decided to send him to a *gurukula* because he did not think his son could learn any more at home.

Śvetaketu spent twelve years in the *gurukula* and came home when he was twenty-four. All this is mentioned in the *Upaniṣad.*

The young man returned home very proud and seeing this, his father asked, 'Did you ask your teacher for that knowledge, gaining which everything is as well-known?' The son replied, 'I do not think my teacher had such a knowledge. Otherwise, he would have taught it to me.' Śvetaketu later asked his father if there was such a knowledge. His father proved to him that there was.

By the knowledge of the cause, *kāraṇa*, everything else is as well-known. If you know the clay, you know the pot. The word, 'pot' is only with reference to a name and form, *nāma* and *rūpa*, for the substance clay. There is no substance in the pot, other than clay, for you to know. Similarly, once you know the cause of this entire creation, if there is such a cause, then everything is as well-known. It is not that everything is known, but that everything is as well-known. Just as you know the substance, clay, in terms of reality, you also know what *satya* is, what *mithyā* is. You know the real and the unreal. This is all there is to know.

Uddālaka established the possibility of such a knowledge and, in time, Śvetaketu wanted to know. That is how we get *mahāvākya-upadeśa*, the teaching of 'that thou art, *tat-tvam-asi*.' This kind of story, then, reveals the context and tells us about the urge to know, how it has to be known, and so on. In other words, the whole teaching methodology, *sampradāya*, is brought out through these stories.

It is important, therefore, to know how Arjuna, a great warrior and a man of culture and compassion, became a seeker, *jijñāsu*, the one who wanted to have this knowledge. In the process, we understand how a person discovers a quest in himself or herself to know the meaning of all the struggles in life. Although Kṛṣṇa sometimes spoke to Arjuna strictly within the context of the Mahābhārata, the context can be changed to apply to anyone. For example, when Kṛṣṇa told Arjuna to fight, he was speaking only to Arjuna and to no one else.Yet, there is something relevant to everyone, and that is – what is to be done in a given situation must be done.

This context is naturally still a part of the Mahābhārata and the actual *Gītā* is yet to begin, which it does in the second chapter. Only with the words, '*śrī bhagavān uvāca*' does it become Bhagavadgītā. The first chapter is only the context, leading to the *Gītā*. Although the previous chapters of the Mahābhārata have no direct connection to the Bhagavadgītā, there is a link with reference to Arjuna's lot. Therefore, even though these first few verses of the *Gītā* have no real relevance to what we want to know, they do give us the context and for this reason, we look into them.

Having talked to Droṇa about the important people in the army of Pāṇḍavas, he then, changed the topic to those in his own army.

अस्माकं तु विशिष्टा ये तान्निबोध द्विजोत्तम ।
नायका मम सैन्यस्य संज्ञार्थं तान्ब्रवीमि ते ॥ ७ ॥

asmākaṁ tu viśiṣṭā ye tānnibodha dvijottama
nāyakā mama sainyasya sañjñārthaṁ tānbravīmi te (7)

dvija-uttama – O learned among the twice-born! (*brāhmaṇas*); *asmākam* – of us; *tu* – whereas; *ye* – those who; *viśiṣṭāḥ* – are important; *mama sainyasya* – of my army; *nāyakāḥ* – leaders; *tān* – them; *nibodha* – please take note; *te* – to you; *sañjñārtham* – in order to introduce; *tān* – them; *bravīmi* – I mention

Whereas, the learned among the twice-born (*brāhmaṇas*)! Please take note of those who are important amongst ourselves, the leaders of my army. I mention them in order to introduce them to you.

The people who had joined Duryodhana were also not just ordinary soldiers. They too were leaders, *mahārathas*. Wanting to point this out to Droṇa, Duryodhana again said, 'In order to introduce them to you, I will mention them by name.'

In this verse, he addressed Droṇa as *dvija-uttama*, the best among the twice-born, *dvija*. A *brāhmaṇa*, a *kṣatriya* and a *vaiśya* are considered to be born again when they are initiated into the *gāyatrī-mantra*. Droṇa was described by Duryodhana as *uttama*, the best, because he was a learned teacher of archery.

Describing his own army, Duryodhana said:

भवान्भीष्मश्च कर्णश्च कृपश्च समितिञ्जयः ।
अश्वत्थामा विकर्णश्च सौमदत्तिर्जयद्रथः ॥ ८ ॥

bhavān bhīṣmaśca karṇaśca kṛpaśca samitiñjayaḥ
aśvatthāmā vikarṇaśca saumadattirjayadrathaḥ (8)

अन्ये च बहवः शूरा मदर्थे त्यक्तजीविताः ।
नानाशस्त्रप्रहरणाः सर्वे युद्धविशारदाः ॥ ९ ॥

anye ca bahavaḥ śūrā madarthe tyaktajīvitāḥ
nānāśastrapraharaṇāḥ sarve yuddhaviśāradāḥ (9)

bhavān – Your Honour; *bhīṣmaḥ* – Bhīṣma; *ca* – and; *karṇaḥ* – Karṇa; *ca* – and; *kṛpaḥ* – Kṛpa; *ca* – and; *samitiñjayaḥ* – one who is always victorious; *aśvatthāmā* – Aśvatthāmā; *vikarṇaḥ* – Vikarṇa; *ca* – and; *saumadattiḥ* – Saumadatti, son of Somadatta (Bhūriśravā); *jayadrathaḥ* – Jayadratha; *anye ca* – and others; *bahavaḥ* – many; *śūrāḥ* – warriors; *madarthe* – for my sake; *tyakta-jīvitāḥ* – who are determined to give up their lives; *nānā-śastra-praharaṇāḥ* – having many kinds of weapons; *sarve* – all; *yuddha-viśāradāḥ* – experts in warfare

Your Honour, Bhīṣma, Karṇa, Kṛpa,[28] who is always victorious in war, Aśvatthāmā,[29] Vikarṇa,[30]

---

[28] He was the brother of Droṇa's wife Kṛpī. He taught archery to the Kaurava and the Pāṇḍava princes before Droṇa became their master. He is counted among the *cirañjīvī*s, those who live forever.

[29] He was the son of Droṇa and is also one of the *cirañjīvī*s. He was so fiercely devoted to Duryodhana that on the last day when he was sure there was no more hope for Duryodhana, he went to the Pāṇḍavas' camp at night and killed all the men there when they were asleep.

[30] A son of Dhṛtarāṣṭra, an exception among the Dhārtarāṣṭras, he was noted for his sense of justice and righteousness. He was the only one who protested against the humiliation of Draupadī in the Kaurava-sabhā.

Saumadatti,[31] son of Somadatta (Bhūriśravā), and Jayadratha[32]...

...and many other warriors, all experts in warfare, armed with many kinds of weapons, who are determined to give up their lives for my sake (are present on our side).

Instead of calling him by name, Duryodhana addressed Droṇa as *bhavān*, meaning 'Your Honour or You, Sir.' Because Droṇa's dearest disciples were on the other side, Duryodhana was afraid that his heart would not be in the fight. He was, therefore, always trying to win Droṇa over. Later in the battle, he began taunting him, saying that the reason he was not fighting his best was because his heart was with the Pāṇḍavas.

When Duryodhana was losing and Bhīṣma was on his deathbed, Droṇa became Duryodhana's commander-in-chief. He became so inflamed by Duryodhana's taunts that he was determined to take Yudhiṣṭhira, dead or alive.

---

[31] Bhūriśravā—he was the grandson of Bāhlika, older brother of Śantanu.

[32] He was the husband of Duśśalā, Duryodhana's sister and the king of Sindhu-deśa. He was instrumental in the killing of Abhimanyu by stopping the Pāṇḍavas from going to Abhimanyu's help when he was caught up inside the *cakra-vyūha*. He could do this because, earlier he had obtained a boon from Lord Śiva that he would defeat all the Pāṇḍavas together except Arjuna, single-handedly for one day. The killing of Abhimanyu by several *mahāratha*s together, led Arjuna to make a vow that, if he did not kill Jayadratha by sunset of the next day he would kill himself. The next day, Duryodhana did all he could to protect Jayadratha so that Arjuna would be forced to put an end to his own life. Again, Kṛṣṇa saved the situation by creating an artificial sunset and forcing Jayadratha come out of his hiding so that Arjuna could kill him and fulfil his vow.

In this verse, Duryodhana acknowledged Droṇa's importance by using the term *bhavān*. Only then did he point out the invincible Bhīṣma, the oldest in the family and the strongest. There was no one to equal Bhīṣma at that time. When he fought, no one could stand against him. He had the boon that death would come to him only when he chose it. Even Kṛṣṇa, who had promised not to fight, became so impressed with Bhīṣma's strength that he actually took up his *cakra*. Only then did he remember that he had promised not to fight. That Kṛṣṇa had been moved to pick up his *cakra* was enough for Bhīṣma, and that caused him to give up in the end.

The others described in this verse are Karṇa, Duryodhana's answer for Arjuna, and Kṛpa, presented here as one who was always victorious in any conflict and who could defeat an army single-handedly. Duryodhana also remembered to mention Droṇa's son Aśvatthāmā, along with his own brother, Vikarṇa, who was the youngest and of the same age as Aśvatthāmā. Jayadratha, a very important person who caused the death of Arjuna's son, Abhimanyu, and Saumadatti were also presented to Droṇa by Duryodhana.

Having mentioned these people by name, Duryodhana then pointed out that there were many other warriors who had come to join him on the battlefield.

Duryodhana's words, 'Other warriors... who have given up their lives for my sake, *anye ca bahavaḥ śūrāḥ madarthe tyakta-jīvitāḥ*,' can be taken here as a divine omen of what was to come.

Had they given up their lives, as he had said, he would have had a dead army on his hands! He meant that they were ready to give up their lives, but what he said was an example of *daiva*, certain words that indicate what is to come. Such words are not deliberately spoken. The speaker means one thing, but the words themselves mean something else. In fact, these warriors had already given up their lives for Duryodhana's sake. They were all going to die. This *daiva* is very uncanny; it comes out! Here, it came out in Duryodhana's speech. His defeat was indicated by his own words.

Who were these people? They were people who had a variety of weapons with them. Weapons can be either *praharaṇa*s, those that can be aimed and released like an arrow or spear, or *śastra*s, weapons that are held in one's hand, like a mace or sword. Not only did these people come with all of these weapons, but also they were experts in using them. They had a thorough knowledge of weaponry and warfare, some having expertise in more than one particular martial art. In the next verse, Duryodhana, assessing the overall strength of the two armies, continued his attempt to arouse Droṇa's enthusiasm:

अपर्याप्तं तदस्माकं बलं भीष्माभिरक्षितम् ।
पर्याप्तं त्विदमेतेषां बलं भीमाभिरक्षितम् ॥ १० ॥

aparyāptaṁ tadasmākaṁ balaṁ bhīṣmābhirakṣitam
paryāptaṁ tvidameteṣāṁ balaṁ
bhīmābhirakṣitam (10)

bhīṣma-abhirakṣitam – well-protected by Bhīṣma; *asmākam* – our; *tat* – that; *balam* – army; *aparyāptam* – cannot be overwhelmed; *tu* – whereas; *bhīma-abhirakṣitam* - even though protected by Bhīma; *eteṣām* – of these people in front of us; *idam* – this; *balam* – army; *paryāptam* – can be overwhelmed

> Our army (being larger), well protected by Bhīṣma, cannot be overwhelmed, whereas the army of these people in front of us, even though protected by Bhīma, can be overwhelmed.

Here, Duryodhana pointed out to Droṇa that the Pāṇḍavas could not overwhelm his army because it was well protected by Bhīṣma. Also it consisted of eleven *akṣauhiṇis*, divisions, whereas the Pāṇḍavas had only seven *akṣauhiṇis*.[33] He therefore considered his army to be in no danger, not only because it had more divisions, but because it had such great leaders. Even though the mighty Bhīma would protect the Pāṇḍavas' army, Duryodhana was sure that his army could easily overwhelm them and that he would win the war.

There is another meaning sometimes given for this verse that does not hold. In this version, Duryodhana told Droṇa that the strength of his army was not adequate, but at least it was protected by Bhīṣma, whereas the Pāṇḍavas' army was adequate, but was protected only by Bhīma. This meaning is not correct. Since Duryodhana had eleven divisions, he naturally thought

---

[33] An *akṣauhiṇi* is a division of army consisting of 21870 chariots, 21870 elephants, 65610 horses, 109350 foot-soldiers.

that his army could not be overwhelmed by the seven divisions of his opponents.

Given the numbers involved, he concluded that there was no way that the Pāṇḍavas could defeat them. It would be a walkover! The contention surrounding these two interpretations centres on the meanings given to the words, *aparyāptam* and *paryāptam*. This, then, was Duryodhana's thinking. His words were meant merely to generate some enthusiasm in Droṇa so that Duryodhana would gain Droṇa's whole-hearted support in this battle.

In the next verse, Bhīṣma's importance to the outcome of the war was mentioned to Droṇa by Duryodhana.

अयनेषु च सर्वेषु यथाभागमवस्थिताः ।
भीष्ममेवाभिरक्षन्तु भवन्तः सर्व एव हि ॥ ११ ॥

ayaneṣu ca sarveṣu yathābhāgamavasthitāḥ
bhīṣmamevābhirakṣantu bhavantaḥ sarva eva hi (11)

sarveṣu ayaneṣu ca – in all divisions (of the army); *yathābhāgam* – in (your) respective positions; *avasthitāḥ* – stationed; *bhavantaḥ sarve eva hi* – all of you indeed; *bhīṣmam eva* – Bhīṣma in particular; *abhirakṣantu* – should protect

Stationed in your respective positions, in all the divisions of the army, all of you should indeed protect Bhīṣma in particular.

Bhīṣma was not just a commander-in-chief appointed according to seniority. Although he was the oldest person in Duryodhana's ranks, he was the one who really counted in this battle. As we know, Bhīṣma was not an ordinary person. He was invincible. No one can kill him. He would die only when he chose to die. And as long as he had his bow in his hand, no one can approach him. Therefore, Duryodhana said that they must all protect Bhīṣma. If Bhīṣma were to be protected, then the army would be protected and victory would be certain, 'I do not want Bhīṣma to get hurt in any way,' he said.

In fact, Duryodhana had organised the entire army into formations that would ensure the protection of his commander-in-chief. There was no way for the Pāṇḍavas to penetrate his ranks and get at Bhīṣma, he thought. Confirming his plans, he asked Droṇa to make sure that everyone remained in their assigned places so that Bhīṣma would be well-protected. As long as Bhīṣma was there, they were safe. Because Duryodhana had to shout in order to be heard over the din of the battlefield, Bhīṣma might have overheard him telling Droṇa, 'Everyone should protect Bhīṣma.' However, Bhīṣma knew that he needed no one to protect him, and that, not only could he protect himself but everyone else too, including Duryodhana. Duryodhana's concern was evidently silly. Therefore wanting to reassure and encourage Duryodhana, he let out a huge war cry, as described in the next verse.

Verses 12-20

Conches are blown

तस्य सञ्जनयन्हर्षं कुरुवृद्धः पितामहः ।
सिंहनादं विनद्योच्चैः शङ्खं दध्मौ प्रतापवान् ॥ १२ ॥

tasya sañjayanayanharṣaṁ kuruvṛddhaḥ pitāmahaḥ
siṁhanādaṁ vinadyoccaiḥ śaṅkhaṁ dadhmau
pratāpavān (12)

pratāpavān – one who is known for his valour; *kuruvṛddhaḥ pitāmahaḥ* – the grandfather of the Kuru family; *tasya* – his; *harṣam* – happiness; *sañjanayan* – intending to produce; *uccaiḥ* – loudly; *siṁhanādam* – a lion's roar; *vinadya* – making; *śaṅkham* – conch; *dadhmau* – he blew

Bhīṣma, the grandfather of the Kuru family, known for his valour, loudly let out a lion's roar and blew his conch in order to make Duryodhana happy.

Just to produce some kind of joy in the hearts of Duryodhana and the others, Bhīṣma, the old man of the Kuru family, the grandfather, roared loudly like a lion. In this verse, Bhīṣma is described as one who had a number of titles denoting valour, having had many exploits in his life. Bhīṣma sounded the beginning of the war by blowing his conch.

Bhīṣma had backed Duryodhana's challenge to the Pāṇḍavas. Being the commander-in-chief of Duryodhana's army, he was the one who had to give the command that would alert everyone to be ready. To do this, then, he blew his conch.

Once Bhīṣma's conch had sounded, everyone else in Duryodhana's army blew his conch too, as described in the next verse.

ततः शङ्खाश्च भेर्यश्च पणवानकगोमुखाः ।
सहसैवाभ्यहन्यन्त स शब्दस्तुमुलोऽभवत् ॥ १३ ॥

tataḥ śaṅkhāśca bheryaśca paṇavānakagomukhāḥ
sahasaivābhyahanyanta sa śabdastumulo'bhavat (13)

tataḥ – then; *śaṅkhāḥ* – conches; *ca* – and; *bheryaḥ* – kettledrums; *ca* – and; *paṇava-ānāka-gomukhāḥ* – tabors, trumpets and cow-horns; *sahasā eva* – suddenly; *abhyahanyanta* – were blasted forth; *saḥ* – that; *śabdaḥ* – sound; *tumulaḥ abhavat* – was earth shaking

Then, suddenly, conches, kettledrums, tabors, trumpets and cow-horns were blasted forth and the sound was indeed earth shaking.

All the various instruments of sound are described here. There was no music in these sounds, just loud noises coming from a variety of sound-making instruments – kettledrums, varieties of other drums, bugles, and so on.

First, there were the conches. Bhīṣma had to start off because he was the commander-in-chief and also the eldest. Everyone respected him. Thus, he started and everyone else followed. Then came the kettledrums, tabors, trumpets, and cow-horns. All varieties of sounds coming from this array of instruments burst forth immediately. Even those people who had no instruments might have produced their own sounds by imitating various instruments. The effect was tremendous, earth-shaking, frightening, and something unimaginable.

When Duryodhana's entire army, with its many divisions, simultaneously began blowing their conches and other instruments, the whole sky was rent with this enormous noise. Given this situation, what did the Pāṇḍavas do? Of course, they too followed suit, a description of which appears in the next six verses.

ततः श्वेतैर्हयैर्युक्ते महति स्यन्दने स्थितौ ।
माधवः पाण्डवश्चैव दिव्यौ शङ्खौ प्रदध्मतुः ॥ १४ ॥

tataḥ śvetairhayairyukte mahati syandane sthitau
mādhavaḥ pāṇḍavaścaiva divyau śaṅkhau
pradadhmatuḥ(14)

tataḥ – then; *śvetaiḥ hayaiḥ* – by white horses; *yukte* – yoked (drawn); *mahati syandane* – in the great chariot; *sthitau* – seated; *mādhavaḥ* – Kṛṣṇa; *pāṇḍavaḥ* – Arjuna; *ca* – and; *eva* – also; *divyau* – divine; *śaṅkhau* – conches; *pradadhmatuḥ* – blew

Then, Kṛṣṇa and Arjuna, seated in the great chariot drawn by white horses, blew their divine conches.

Having described the war cry of the Kauravas, Sañjaya, the narrator, then turned his attention to Arjuna, referred to here as Pāṇḍava, meaning Pāṇḍu's son. The name given to Kṛṣṇa in this verse is Mādhava, meaning the Lord of wealth (Lakṣmī). Throughout the *Gītā*, Kṛṣṇa is addressed or mentioned by different names – Hṛṣīkeśa, Acyuta, Keśava, Janārdana and so on.

Kṛṣṇa and Arjuna were seated in Arjuna's magnificent chariot that was drawn by white horses, white being a colour that could not be missed amidst horses of different colours. In response to the war cry of Duryodhana's army, Arjuna and Kṛṣṇa sounded their conches, described here as *divyau*, celestial, because they were not gathered in the ordinary way.

पाञ्चजन्यं हृषीकेशो देवदत्तं धनञ्जयः ।
पौण्ड्रं दध्मौ महाशङ्खं भीमकर्मा वृकोदरः ॥ १५ ॥

pāñcajanyaṁ hṛṣīkeśo devadattaṁ dhanañjayaḥ
pauṇḍraṁ dadhmau mahāśaṅkhaṁ bhīmakarmā
vṛkodaraḥ (15)

hṛṣīkeśaḥ – Lord of all the senses, Kṛṣṇa; *pāñcajanyam* – Pāñcajanya; *dhanañjayaḥ* – Arjuna; *devadattam* – Devadatta; *bhīmakarmā* – the one of fierce deeds (Bhīma); *vṛkodaraḥ* – Bhīma, one with the stomach of a wolf; *mahāśaṅkham* – (his) huge conch; *pauṇḍram* – Pauṇḍra; *dadhmau* – blew

Kṛṣṇa (blew) the Pāñcajanya and Arjuna the Devadatta. Bhīma, the man of fierce deeds and one with the stomach of a wolf, blew his huge conch, Pauṇḍra.

Lord Kṛṣṇa's conch was called Pāñcajanya. As we have seen, the bows also had names. Arjuna's bow was known as Gāṇḍīva. Dhanañjaya was another name for Arjuna and Devadatta was the name of his conch, meaning that it was a gift from a god.

Bhīmakarmā was another name for Bhīma, because he was able to do the most frightening jobs, both in war and in peacetime. Bhīma never undertook ordinary work. For instance, when Pāṇḍavas were living incognito for one year, Bhīma was employed in the palace as a cook. In fact, he appointed himself because he wanted to be able to eat a lot of food. He excelled at cooking in large quantities, the kindof cooking wherein whole pumpkins were dropped into huge cauldrons.

There are two types of cooking mentioned in Sanskrit literature. One type is called Bhīmapāka, cooking for thousands of people at a time, and the other is called *nalapāka* named after King Nala who was also a great cook, but for small numbers of people.

We might think that Bhīma must have been very flabby, with a huge stomach and all that goes with it. However, that was not the case. He did not resemble a Sumo wrestler at all. Here, Bhīma was described as one who had the stomach of a wolf – it was so hollowed out that it almost touched the spine. A wolf is always hungry, which may be where the expression, 'keeping the wolf away from the door,' came from. This analogy is a good example of what is meant by the word *lakṣaṇa*. The implied meaning for wolf is hunger. Although a wolf is always hungry and eats a lot, its stomach remains the same, ever trim. By the description of Bhīma's stomach being like that of a wolf, we understand that he was a huge man. Therefore, keeping hunger away was always a concern for him. Bhīma also had very large lungs and, therefore, did not have an ordinary conch. Known as Pauṇḍra, his conch is described here as huge.

The conches of the other three Pāṇḍavas, Yudhiṣṭhira, Nakula and Sahadeva, are mentioned in the next verse.

अनन्तविजयं राजा कुन्तीपुत्रो युधिष्ठिरः ।
नकुलः सहदेवश्च सुघोषमणिपुष्पकौ ॥ १६ ॥

anantavijayaṁ rājā kuntīputro yudhiṣṭhiraḥ
nakulaḥ sahadevaśca sughoṣamaṇipuṣpakau (16)

kuntīputraḥ – son of Kuntī; *rājā yudhiṣṭhiraḥ* – King Yudhiṣṭhira; *anantavijayam* – Anantavijaya, the name of Yudhiṣṭhira's conch; *nakulaḥ sahadevaḥ ca* – Nakula and Sahadeva; *sughoṣa-maṇipuṣpakau* – Sughoṣa and Maṇipuṣpaka (the name of Nakula's and Sahadeva's conches)

King Yudhiṣṭhira, the son of Kuntī, blew Anantavijaya and Nakula and Sahadeva blew Sughoṣa and Maṇipuṣpaka respectively.

Although he was no longer the king, Sañjaya called Dharmaputra as 'King Yudhiṣṭhira' here. It is because, in Sañjaya's mind, even though Duryodhana ruled the kingdom,

Yudhiṣṭhira was the real king, albeit in exile. Because Sañjaya never agreed to this war and knew Duryodhana was making a mistake, he never missed an opportunity to point this out to Dhṛtarāṣṭra.

Ananta-vijaya, meaning that which produces countless victories was the name of Dharmaputra's conch. Nakula's conch was called Sughoṣa, meaning that which produces a pleasant sound. Maṇipuṣpaka, that which is decorated with precious gems, was the name give to Sahadeva's conch.

काश्यश्च परमेष्वासः शिखण्डी च महारथः ।
धृष्टद्युम्नो विराटश्च सात्यकिश्चापराजितः ॥ १७ ॥

kāśyaśca parameṣvāsaḥ śikhaṇḍī ca mahārathaḥ
dhṛṣṭadyumno virāṭaśca sātyakiścāparājitaḥ (17)

द्रुपदो द्रौपदेयाश्च सर्वशः पृथिवीपते ।
सौभद्रश्च महाबाहुः शङ्खान्दध्मुः पृथक्पृथक् ॥ १८ ॥

drupado draupadeyāśca sarvaśaḥ pṛthivīpate
saubhadraśca mahābāhuḥ śaṅkhāndadhmuḥ
pṛthakpṛthak (18)

pṛthivīpate – O king!; *kāśyaḥ ca parama-iṣvāsaḥ* – the king of Kāśī, an expert archer; *mahārathaḥ śikhaṇḍī* – Śikhaṇḍī, the man of great valour; *ca* – and; *dhṛṣṭadyumnaḥ* – Dhṛṣṭadyumna; *virāṭaḥ* – Virāṭa; *ca* – and; *aparājitaḥ* – unsurpassed; *sātyakiḥ* –

Sātyaki; *ca* – and; *drupadaḥ* – Drupada; *draupadeyāḥ ca* – and sons of Draupadī; *mahābāhuḥ saubhadraḥ ca* – and the mighty-armed son of Subhadrā (Abhimanyu); *sarvaśaḥ* – on all sides; *pṛthak pṛthak* – separately; *śaṅkhān dadhmuḥ* – blew their conches

> O The ruler of earth (Dhṛtarāṣṭra)! The king of Kāśī, an expert archer, Śikhaṇḍī of great valour, Dhṛṣṭadyumna and Virāṭa, and the unsurpassed Sātyaki...
>
> ...King Drupada, the sons of Draupadī and the mighty armed son of Subhadrā (Abhimanyu), all blew their own conches.

The king of Kāśī was described here as one having a huge bow. Śikhaṇḍī was also mentioned as being another great warrior in Arjuna's camp. Dhṛṣṭadyumna, the first commander-in-chief of the Pāṇḍava-army, King Virāṭa and Sātyaki, another king, were also mentioned by name.

In these two verses, Sañjaya concluded his account of those who had sounded their conches in the Pāṇḍavas' camp. Addressing Dhṛtarāṣṭra as '*pṛthivīpate*, O the ruler of earth!' Sañjaya then pointed out Drupada, the father of Draupadī, the sons of Draupadī and Abhimanyu, the son of Subhadrā, Saubhadra, whom he described as, 'one of mighty arms,' which is a description of Abhimanyu's valour, not the size of his biceps.

Together, these mighty warriors blew their conches. This sound is described in the next verse.

स घोषो धार्तराष्ट्राणां हृदयानि व्यदारयत्।
नभश्च पृथिवीं चैव तुमुलो व्यनुनादयन्॥ १९॥

sa ghoṣo dhārtarāṣṭrāṇāṁ hṛdayāni vyadārayat
nabhaśca pṛthivīṁ caiva tumulo vyanunādayan (19)

saḥ – that; *tumulaḥ* – terrible; *ghoṣaḥ* – sound; *nabhaḥ* – sky; *ca* – and; *pṛthivīm* – earth; *ca* – and; *eva* – indeed; *vyanunādayan* – reverberating; *dhārtarāṣṭrāṇām* – of the sons of Dhṛtarāṣṭra; *hṛdayāni* – the hearts; *vyadārayat* – pierced

That terrible sound, reverberating throughout the earth and sky, pierced the very hearts of the sons of Dhṛtarāṣṭra.

The sound made by the Pāṇḍavas in response to that made by Duryodhana's army was so tremendous that it pierced the very hearts of the sons of Dhṛtarāṣṭra. The simultaneous sound reverberated and echoed, wave after wave, bouncing from the earth to the sky and back again. The magnificence of the Pāṇḍava war cry pervaded the entire atmosphere, creating panic in those of the opposing side. Again, Sañjaya drove home his point that Dhṛtarāṣṭra's sons were no match for the Pāṇḍavas.

अथ व्यवस्थितान्दृष्ट्वा धार्तराष्ट्रान् कपिध्वजः।
प्रवृत्ते शस्त्रसम्पाते धनुरुद्यम्य पाण्डवः॥ २०॥

atha vyavasthitāndṛṣṭvā dhārtarāṣṭrān kapidhvajaḥ
pravṛtte śastrasampāte dhanurudyamya pāṇḍavaḥ (20)

हृषीकेशं तदा वाक्यमिदमाह महीपते ।

hṛṣīkeśaṁ tadā vākyamidamāha mahīpate

mahīpate – O king!; *atha* - then; *vyavasthitān* – standing assembled; *dhārtarāṣṭrān* – the sons of Dhṛtarāṣṭra; *dṛṣṭvā* – seeing; *kapidhvajaḥ pāṇḍavaḥ* – Arjuna, one who has Hanumān on his banner; *śastra-sampāte pravṛtte* – with the battle ready to begin; *dhanuḥ* – bow; *udyamya* – having lifted; *tadā* – then; *hṛṣīkeśam* – to Lord Kṛṣṇa; *idam* – these; *vākyam* – words; *uvāca* – said

> Then, with the battle ready to begin, O the ruler of earth! seeing the sons of Dhṛtarāṣṭra assembled (on the battlefield), Arjuna, who had Hanumān on his banner, lifting his bow, said these words to Kṛṣṇa.

In this verse, Arjuna was called Kapidhvaja, the one who had a monkey on his banner. Every chariot had a flag and each important person had a flag of his own; Arjuna's flag had Hanumān, the great devotee of Rāma. It had come about in this manner – During their *vanavāsa*, the Pāṇḍavas went on a pilgrimage to the Himalayas. There on the *gandhamādana* mountain, Draupadī came across a very beautiful lotus with thousand petals and great fragrance. It was the Saugandhika flower. She was so enamoured by it that she asked Bhīma to go and get more of them. He went searching for them and on the way encountered Lord Hanumān. Hanumān, being the elder brother to Bhīma, tested and advised him on *dharma*, etc. He also blessed and promised him that he would be present during the war to bless them. He offered to sit as a *dhvaja*, a flag or symbol, on top of Arjuna's chariot. Thus, Arjuna got the name of Kapidhvaja. He said that he would lend his voice to Bhīma whenever Bhīma roared in the battlefield and make Bhīma's roar more frightening to the enemies.

There is also another story not found in the Mahābhārata. It is said that Arjuna once went on a pilgrimage to Rāmeśvaram. When he saw the bridge that the monkeys had built for Rāma he thought to himself that Rāma need not have taken the help of the monkeys and could have built the bridge of arrows by himself. Hanumān, who was present there, read his mind and presenting himself as a small monkey before Arjuna, challenged him to build such a bridge. Arjuna built one. But it could not take the weight of the small monkey and collapsed. By the grace of Kṛṣṇa, Arjuna recognised Hanumān. He then asked for his blessing and Hanumān promised to be present on his flag during the war.

It is said that Hanumān slept through most of the war. Only when Kṛṣṇa talked to Arjuna did Hanumān choose to listen. He found the war itself very boring, something like baseball when no one is hitting. However, when Bhīṣma came to fight, he would open his eyes until it was over. Then he would close them again until there was some other skirmish that interested him. This would last for a few minutes and, again, he would go back to sleep. At the end of the war, when Bhīma asked him how he enjoyed the battle, Hanumān replied that it had been nothing compared to those he had seen earlier – the fight between Rāma and the ten-headed

Rāvaṇa, for example. After such episodes, watching arrows flying back and forth was like watching a game rather than a life-and-death battle! For Hanumān, sitting on top of Arjuna's chariot in the form of a small monkey, it was nothing.

In his chariot, then, with Hanumān on his banner and Kṛṣṇa as his driver, seeing Dhṛtarāṣṭra's sons in front of him, Arjuna picked up his bow. At the same time, he spoke to Lord Kṛṣṇa.

Verses 21-23

Arjuna commands Lord Kṛṣṇa

अर्जुन उवाच ।
सेनयोरुभयोर्मध्ये रथं स्थापय मेऽच्युत ॥ २१ ॥

arjuna uvāca
senayorubhayormadhye rathaṁ sthāpaya me'cyuta (21)

यावदेतान्निरीक्षेऽहं योद्धुकामानवस्थितान् ।
कैर्मया सह योद्धव्यमस्मिन् रणसमुद्यमे ॥ २२ ॥

yāvadetānnirīkṣe'haṁ yoddhukāmānavasthitān
kairmayā saha yoddhavyamasmin raṇasamudyame (22)

arjunaḥ – Arjuna; *uvāca* - said;
acyuta – O Kṛṣṇa!; *senayoḥ ubhayoḥ madhye* – between the two armies; *me* – my; *ratham* - chariot; *sthāpaya* – (you) place; *yāvat* – so that; *aham* – I; *yoddhukāmān avasthitān* – assembled (here) desirous to fight; *etān* – these people; *nirīkṣe* – can view; *asmin raṇa-samudyame* – at the onset of this battle; *kaiḥ saha* – with whom; *mayā yoddhavyam* – I should fight

Arjuna said:

> Place my chariot, Acyuta[34] (Kṛṣṇa)! Between the two armies so that I can view these people who have assembled here desirous of fighting, (and also view) with whom I should fight at the onset of this war.

Arjuna had been waiting for this day, his D-Day, for what seemed like ages. From childhood, his cousin Duryodhana had done so much injustice. The sinful actions he had been piling up were directed towards the Pāṇḍavas, especially Arjuna. Arjuna was the object of Duryodhana's jealousy and hatred because he was the most beloved disciple of Droṇa. They had all been Droṇa's disciples, but Arjuna was the best archer. Droṇa naturally had a soft corner in his heart for him. Arjuna had not attracted this jealousy because of his boasting or pride. He was considered a most pleasant person, but Duryodhana had his own problems. His father was blind and was, therefore, not the king. Because of this, all the one hundred brothers grew up nursing a jealousy and Arjuna was always its target.

Therefore, Arjuna had been waiting for the day when his pent-up anger could be released. Seeing these Dhārtarāṣṭras before him, his fury knew no bounds. He even forgot that Kṛṣṇa was with him, not by appointment but because of his prayerful request. Kṛṣṇa was seated in the front of his chariot as a driver by his own grace alone. Forgetting this, Arjuna

---

[34] *Sat-cid-ānanda-lakṣaṇa-svarūpād na kadāpi cyavate iti acyutaḥ* – the one who never falls from his nature of absolute existence, knowledge and limitlessness is Acyuta.

commanded him to place the chariot between the two forces so that he could see who was in each camp.

Thus, Arjuna told Kṛṣṇa exactly where he wanted his chariot placed. He said, 'Place my chariot in between the two armies in such a way that I can examine these people.' Who are they, who have come to the battlefield with a desire to fight on one side or the other? Arjuna especially wanted to see the army of his opponent in order to know with whom he should fight, once the war began.

योत्स्यमानानवेक्षेऽहं य एतेऽत्र समागताः ।
धार्तराष्ट्रस्य दुर्बुद्धेर्युद्धे प्रियचिकीर्षवः ॥ २३ ॥

yotsyamānānavekṣe'haṁ ya ete'tra samāgatāḥ
dhārtarāṣṭrasya durbuddheryuddhe
priyacikīrṣavaḥ (23)

dur-buddheḥ – of the one whose thinking is distorted; *dhārtarāṣṭrasya* – of the son of Dhṛtarāṣṭra; *yuddhe* – in the battle; *priya-cikīrṣavaḥ* – those who want to carry out in the war what is pleasing; *ye ete* – those who; *samāgatāḥ* – have gathered; *atra* – here; *yotsyamānān* – with the intention of fighting; *aham* – I; *avekṣe* – wish to see

> I wish to see those who have gathered here with the intention of fighting, who want to carry out in the war what is pleasing to the son of Dhṛtarāṣṭra (Duryodhana), the one whose thinking is distorted.

Arjuna wanted to see all those who had gathered there for the sake of pleasing Duryodhana. Therefore, he asked Kṛṣṇa to place his chariot in such a spot that he could do so. Kṛṣṇa, of course, being a good driver, did as he was told. Arjuna's use of the word 'my' with reference to the chariot indicated his frame of mind. He was a flame of fury. Kṛṣṇa was only a driver of his chariot.

Verses 24&25

Sañjaya's summary to Dhṛtarāṣṭra

सञ्जय उवाच ।
एवमुक्तो हृषीकेशो गुडाकेशेन भारत ।
सेनयोरुभयोर्मध्ये स्थापयित्वा रथोत्तमम् ॥ २४ ॥

sañjaya uvāca
evamukto hṛṣīkeśo guḍākeśena bhārata
senayorubhayormadhye sthāpayitvā rathottamam (24)

भीष्मद्रोणप्रमुखतः सर्वेषां च महीक्षिताम् ।
उवाच पार्थ पश्यैतान्समवेतान्कुरूनिति ॥ २५ ॥

bhīṣmadroṇapramukhataḥ sarveṣāṁ ca mahīkṣitām
uvāca pārtha paśyaitānsamavetānkurūniti (25)

sañjayaḥ – Sañjaya; *uvāca* – said

bhārata – O king of the Bharata lineage, Dhṛtarāṣṭra!; *guḍākeśena* – by Arjuna; *evam uktaḥ* – thus commanded; *hṛṣīkeśaḥ* – Lord Kṛṣṇa; *senayoḥ ubhayoḥ madhye* – in the middle of the two armies; *bhīṣma-droṇa-pramukhataḥ* – right in front of Bhīṣma and Droṇa; *ca* – and; *sarveṣām* – of all; *mahīkṣitām* – (of the) rulers; *ratha-uttamam* – the great chariot; *sthāpayitvā* – having placed; *pārtha* – O Arjuna!; *samavetān* – who have gathered here; *etān* –these; *kurūn* – the Kauravas; *paśya* – please look at; *iti* – thus; *uvāca* - said

Sañjaya said:

Bhārata[35] (Dhṛtarāṣṭra)! Commanded thus by Guḍākeśa[36] (Arjuna), Lord Hṛṣīkeśa[37] (Kṛṣṇa) placed the great chariot in the middle of the two armies, right in front of Bhīṣma, Droṇa and all the rulers and spoke thus: 'Pārtha[38] (Arjuna)! Please look at these Kauravas who have gathered here.'

Addressing Dhṛtarāṣṭra as Bhārata, Sañjaya told him that Kṛṣṇa thus, ordered by Arjuna, placed the great chariot between the two armies. Bhīṣma and Droṇa were the people with whom Arjuna would have to fight. So, naturally, Kṛṣṇa placed the chariot so that Arjuna could see them. These two men were not only important for the opposing army and for Duryodhana, but being respected by the Pāṇḍavas, they were important to them, also.

Droṇa was Arjuna's most revered teacher. Bhīṣma was the grand old man of the family and the most respected person. Arjuna and Bhīṣma shared a very special relationship.

---

35 *Bharatasya gotrāpatyam* – descendant of Bharata.

36 *Guḍākā nidrā tasyāḥ iśaḥ* – one who has mastery over sleep.

37 *Hṛṣīkāṇām indriyāṇām īśaḥ* – the lord of the senses.

38 *Pṛthāyāḥ apatyam* – son of Pṛthā (Kuntī).

Therefore, both of them were important, for people on both the sides of this war. Both were considered invincible. Thus, when Kṛṣṇa drove the chariot between the two armies, he placed it in front of Bhīṣma, Droṇa, and the other important kings, so that Arjuna could see these warriors. The place chosen by Kṛṣṇa was the best vantage point possible, a place from where Arjuna could see everyone on both sides. Arjuna was able to see everyone, just as he had asked.

It is the first time that Kṛṣṇa spoke in the *Gītā*. Although the verse does not begin with '*śrī bhagavān uvāca*, the Lord said,' the '*iti*' at the end of the verse indicates a quotation. 'Arjuna, please look at these Kurus who have gathered here,' Kṛṣṇa said.

Now that Arjuna could see those who had come to fight on both sides clearly, we shall see what happened to him.

Verses 26-31

Arjuna sees his kith and kin and is overwhelmed

तत्रापश्यत् स्थितान्पार्थः पितॄनथ पितामहान् ।
आचार्यान्मातुलान्भ्रातॄन्पुत्रान्पौत्रान्सखींस्तथा ॥ २६ ॥

tatrāpaśyat sthitānpārthaḥ pitṝnatha pitāmahān
ācāryānmātulānbhrātṝnputrānpautrānsakhīṁstathā (26)

श्वशुरान्सुहृदश्चैव सेनयोरुभयोरपि ।

śvaśurānsuhṛdaścaiva senayorubhayorapi

atha – then; *senayoḥ ubhayoḥ api* – on both sides of the two armies; *sthitān* – standing; *pitṝn* – paternal elders; *pitāmahān* – grandfathers; *ācāryān* – teachers; *mātulān* – uncles; *bhrātṝn* –

brothers; *putrān* – sons; *pautrān* – grandsons; *sakhīn* – friends; *tathā* – and also; *śvaśurān* – fathers-in-law; *suhṛdaḥ ca eva* – and well-wishers too; *pārthaḥ* – Arjuna; *tatra* – there; *apaśyat* – saw

> There, Arjuna saw paternal elders, grandfathers, teachers, uncles, brothers, sons, grandsons, friends, fathers-in-law and well-wishers too, assembled in the two armies.

The word '*kurūn*' in the previous verse covered the Kauravas on both sides, all of whom were members of the Kuru clan. Looking around him, Arjuna saw everyone of them – the elders connected to him from his paternal and maternal sides, parents, uncles, brothers, sons, and grandsons – all directly or indirectly related. In addition to these blood relatives, there were others too, such as fathers-in-law and friends. Arjuna also saw friends, in-laws on both sides, and those well-wishers, *suhṛd*s, who help others without having been introduced or being connected in any way. Everywhere he looked, he saw only relatives, friends and good people.

Generally, such people would be on your side and those against whom you are fighting would be enemies, invaders, and outsiders. Here, however, Arjuna found on both sides only his own people. This was his problem, which was not an ordinary one. Whichever way he turned, he saw only his own brothers, uncles, and cousins. This problem represented an important situation for Arjuna and was the reason for the *Gītā* to come about. Recognising that everyone who had come to fight was related to him Arjuna was overwhelmed with compassion.

तान्समीक्ष्य स कौन्तेयः सर्वान्बन्धूनवस्थितान् ॥ २७ ॥

tānsamīkṣya sa kaunteyaḥ
sarvānbandhūnavasthitān (27)

कृपया परयाविष्टो विषीदन्निदमब्रवीत् ।

kṛpayā parayāviṣṭo viṣīdannidamabravīt

saḥ kaunteyaḥ – son of Kuntī (Arjuna); *avasthitān tān sarvān* – all those who had assembled; *bandhūn* – relatives; *samīkṣya* – seeing clearly; *parayā kṛpayā* – by deep compassion; *āviṣṭaḥ* – (being) seized; *viṣīdan* – being sorrowful; *idam* – this; *abravīt* – said

Seeing clearly all the assembled relatives, Kaunteya[39] (Arjuna) was seized by deep compassion, said this,[40] sorrowfully.

Arjuna's compassion was too much for him. It was not some small matter that could be dismissed in the interests of practicality, simply because war had been declared.

When such thoughts of compassion come, they are generally dismissed by people. If we know something is not proper, we can usually say, 'What has to be done has to be done.' The battlefield was not the place for compassion. Arjuna could

---

[39] *Kuntyāḥ apatyam* – son of Kuntī.

[40] Arjuna's compassion was born of distress because what was going to happen was destruction and all the people who would be involved were his own people.

not afford to be compassionate here. He had to fight, like even a boxer cannot afford to be compassionate towards his opponent. If, because his opponent is bleeding, the boxer's compassion prevents him from hitting him, the boxer himself will be knocked down. Certainly, seeing his opponent's blood, the thought will come that it is not the proper time or place to hit him. But, then, another thought comes –'It is exactly the right time and place to strike.' Instinct will tell him this, some killer instinct. Any mercy or compassion is quickly dismissed in such situations. This is what is meant by *kṛpā*, a compassion that is dismissible. However when you cannot dismiss it, it becomes *parā kṛpā*, overwhelming compassion. Arjuna could not do anything about his compassion, which was born of distress because of the impending destruction about to befall all of his people.

अर्जुन उवाच ।
दृष्ट्वेमं स्वजनं कृष्ण युयुत्सुं समुपस्थितम् ॥ २८ ॥

arjuna uvāca
dṛṣṭvemaṁ svajanaṁ kṛṣṇa yuyutsuṁ samupasthitam (28)

सीदन्ति मम गात्राणि मुखं च परिशुष्यति ।
वेपथुश्च शरीरे मे रोमहर्षश्च जायते ॥ २९ ॥

sīdanti mama gātrāṇi mukhaṁ ca pariśuṣyati
vepathuśca śarīre me romaharṣaśca jāyate(29)

arjunaḥ – Arjuna; *uvāca* - said;
kṛṣṇa – O Kṛṣṇa!; *yuyutsum* – desirous to fight; *samupasthitam* – well stationed in battle positions; *imam* – this; *svajanam* – my own people; *dṛṣṭvā* – seeing; *sīdanti* – lose all their strength; *mama* – my; *gātrāṇi* – limbs; *mukham* – mouth; *ca* – and; *pariśuṣyati* – dries up; *me* – my; *śarīre* – in the body; *vepathuḥ* – trembling; *roma-harṣaḥ ca jāyate* – and the hair (on my body) is standing on its end

> Arjuna said:
>
> Kṛṣṇa! Looking at these people, who are my own people, well stationed in battle positions and desirous to fight, my limbs are losing all their strength, my mouth is drying up, my body is trembling, and the hair (on my body) is standing on its end.

Thus, under the spell of such a deep compassion, Arjuna said to Kṛṣṇa, 'Looking at my own people who have come with a desire to fight, each one very well prepared and well stationed, my limbs have lost their strength.'

Arjuna was so overwhelmed by the sight of his own people in both armies that his limbs gave in. They seemed to have lost interest in performing their functions. His hands did not want to lift or move in any way. It was the same with his legs. His mouth went dry and his whole body was trembling. His arms and legs were shaking and the hairs on his body were standing on their ends.

Any intense emotion can trigger these physical reactions. By their description, we can understand Arjuna's condition.

He himself explained it to Kṛṣṇa in this verse. Kṛṣṇa, still holding the chariot steady, looked over his shoulder at Arjuna, listening to him. Later, in the *Gītā*, when the real dialogue between them began, he altered his position and turned around completely to face Arjuna.

In the next verse, Arjuna continued describing his physical symptoms, telling Kṛṣṇa that it was not possible for him to stand, let alone fight.

गाण्डीवं स्रंसते हस्तात्त्वक् चैव परिदह्यते ।
न च शक्नोम्यवस्थातुं भ्रमतीव च मे मनः ॥ ३० ॥

gāṇḍīvaṁ sraṁsate hastāttvak caiva paridahyate
na ca śaknomyavasthātuṁ bhramatīva ca me
manaḥ (30)

hastāt – from (my) hand; *gāṇḍīvam* – Gāṇḍīva (the bow of Arjuna); *sraṁsate* – slips; *tvak* – skin; *ca* – and; *eva* – indeed; *paridahyate* – burns; *na ca śaknomi avasthātum* – I am not able to stand up; *me* – my; *manaḥ* – mind; *ca* – and; *bhramati iva* – totally confused, as it were

> The bow, Gāṇḍīva, is slipping from my hand and (my) skin also is burning. I am not able to stand up and my mind is totally confused as it were.

Arjuna's condition was such that his bow, known as Gāṇḍīva, was about to slip out of his hand. His entire body felt as though it was burning and it was not even possible for him to stand properly in the chariot. He said to Kṛṣṇa, 'It is not possible for me to stand, let alone fight.' He also thought he was losing his mind.

As though this was not enough, he saw ill omens everywhere:

निमित्तानि च पश्यामि विपरीतानि केशव ।
न च श्रेयोऽनुपश्यामि हत्वा स्वजनमाहवे ॥ ३१ ॥

nimittani ca paśyāmi viparītāni keśava
na ca śreyo'nupaśyāmi hatvā svajanamāhave (31)

keśava – O Keśava!; *viparītāni* - bad; *nimittāni* – omens; *ca* – and; *paśyāmi* – I see; *āhave* – in the battle; *svajanam* – one's own people; *hatvā* – killing; *śreyaḥ* – any good; *ca* – and; *na* – not; *anupaśyāmi* – I see

Keśava[41] (Kṛṣṇa)! I see bad omens and I do not see any good in killing one's own people in this battle.

Seeing his own people standing there on both sides, Arjuna could see nothing good coming out of this battle. His own people would be destroyed, like Bhīṣma and Droṇa. Even Duryodhana was his cousin, after all. All the omens he saw, both psychological and physical, indicated to him an unpleasant outcome.

---

[41] *Keśi-nāmānaṁ daityaṁ vāti hinasti iti keśavaḥ* – the one who is the destroyer of the demon Keśi is Keśava.

Verses 32-39

Arjuna loses Interest in war

न काङ्क्षे विजयं कृष्ण न च राज्यं सुखानि च ।
किं नो राज्येन गोविन्द किं भोगैर्जीवितेन वा ॥ ३२ ॥

na kāṅkṣe vijayaṁ kṛṣṇa na ca rājyaṁ sukhāni ca
kiṁ no rājyena govinda kiṁ bhogairjīvitena vā (32)

kṛṣṇa – O Kṛṣṇa!; *vijayam* – victory; *na kāṅkṣe* – I do not want; *na ca rājyam* – and not even the kingdom; *sukhāni ca* – nor comforts; *govinda* – O Kṛṣṇa!; *naḥ* – for us; *rājyena* – with a kingdom; *kim* – what is (the use); *bhogaiḥ* – with pleasures; *jīvitena* – by living; *vā* – even; *kim* – what is (the use)

> Kṛṣṇa! I want neither victory, nor the kingdom, nor comforts. Govinda[42] (Kṛṣṇa)! What is the use of a kingdom or of pleasures, or of life itself to us?

Because he knew he would not be happy when this battle was over, Arjuna had no more desire for victory. Since Arjuna did not want victory, he would not get the kingdom back from Duryodhana. If he wanted the kingdom, victory was important. But Arjuna said he did not want the kingdom also. Not having the kingdom meant that he would have to suffer. He would have to go back to the forest and perhaps live a life of an ascetic, living on roots and so on. Duryodhana would never allow him

---

[42] *Gobhiḥ vāṇibhiḥ vedānta-vākyaiḥ vindate iti govindaḥ* – the one who is gained (known) through the words of Vedanta is Govinda.

to stay in his kingdom. He had already made that clear by refusing to give him even a house.

Was Arjuna ready to return to a life of deprivation without the comforts the kingdom would provide? He had just said he did not want victory, kingdom, or comforts either. If there were no victory, there would be no kingdom, neither of which Arjuna wanted now. Without a kingdom, there would be no comfort, which also he no longer wanted. What did he want? He no longer cared. He asked, 'What do we get out of a kingdom? What do we get from all these enjoyments? Even by living, what do we get? Nothing.'

By destroying his own people, what would he get? If destroying them would give him a kingdom, what kind of a kingdom would it be? Arjuna did not think it would be a sane bargain at all. Even if he commanded enjoyments, how could he enjoy them with the nightmares he would have because of having destroyed all of these people?

In this way, Arjuna argued that victory, a kingdom, and even life itself were useless because:

येषामर्थे काङ्क्षितं नो राज्यं भोगाः सुखानि च ।
त इमेऽवस्थिता युद्धे प्राणांस्त्यक्त्वा धनानि च ॥ ३३ ॥

yeṣāmarthe kāṅkṣitaṁ no rājyaṁ bhogāḥ sukhāni ca
ta ime'vasthitā yuddhe prāṇāṁstyaktvā
dhanāni ca (33)

yeṣām arthe – for whose sake; *naḥ* – by us; *rājyam* – kingdom; *kāṅkṣitam* – was desired; *bhogāḥ* – objects of enjoyments; *sukhāni* – pleasures; *ca* – and; *te ime* – those same people; *prāṇān* – life; *dhanāni* – wealth; *ca* – and; *tyaktvā* – having given up; *yuddhe* – in the battle; *avasthitāḥ* – have assembled

> Those for whose sake (alone) the kingdom, objects of enjoyments and pleasures were desired by us, have assembled in (this) battle, having given up their wealth and their lives.

Arjuna's thinking was that a kingdom and the enjoyments that go with it, had only been desired by him for the sake of the very people whom he would be destroying – those who had come ready to die in the battle. To win the battle, he would have to destroy Duryodhana's entire army. There was no such thing in those days as retreat in a battle. Even if it were possible, Duryodhana would never have done so. He was a king and a despot at that. He would never give up. If anyone else ran away, he would have shot him from behind. Therefore, there was no way for these people to survive this battle.

Many of those who were going to fight on Arjuna's side would definitely have to die. When Bhīṣma fought, he did not throw flowers. Nor would there be garlands strewn about when Droṇa was fighting. People would die by the thousands and, thus, the battle became meaningless for Arjuna. All these people had given up their wealth, including their wives and children, to come and fight. Arjuna could make no sense of it all.

आचार्याः पितरः पुत्रास्तथैव च पितामहाः ।
मातुलाः श्वशुराः पौत्राः श्यालाः सम्बन्धिनस्तथा ॥ ३४ ॥

ācāryāḥ pitaraḥ putrāstathaiva ca pitāmahāḥ
mātulāḥ śvaśurāḥ pautrāḥ śyālāḥ
sambandhinastathā (34)

te ime – these same people are; *ācāryāḥ* – teachers; *pitaraḥ* – paternal uncles; *putrāḥ* – sons; *tathā eva ca* – and so too; *pitāmahāḥ* – the grandfathers (like Bhīṣma); *mātulāḥ* - maternal uncles; *śvaśurāḥ* – fathers-in-law; *pautrāḥ* – grandsons; *śyālāḥ* – brothers-in-law; *tathā* – so too; *sambandhinaḥ* – other relatives, friends and so on

These are (our) teachers, paternal uncles, sons, grandfathers, maternal uncles, in-laws, grandsons, cousins, friends and other relatives.

Wherever Arjuna looked, he saw only people known to him – his teachers, grandfathers, sons, uncles, cousins, in-laws, and friends. These were the people for whose sake he had desired the kingdom. If they were destroyed, what use would the kingdom be to him?

एतान्न हन्तुमिच्छामि घ्नतोऽपि मधुसूदन ।
अपि त्रैलोक्यराज्यस्य हेतोः किं नु महीकृते ॥ ३५ ॥

etānna hantumicchāmi ghnato'pi madhusūdana
api trailokyarājyasya hetoḥ kiṁ nu mahīkṛte (35)

madhusūdana – O Kṛṣṇa! the one who destroyed the demon named Madhu; *etān* – these; *ghnataḥ* – they are going to kill (me); *api* – even if; *na icchāmi* – I do not desire; *hantum* – to kill; *api* – even; *trailokya-rājyasya hetoḥ* – for the sake of ruling over the three worlds; *kim nu* – much less; *mahīkṛte* – for this kingdom on earth

> Madhusūdana[43] (Kṛṣṇa)! Even for the sake of ruling over the three worlds, much less for this kingdom on earth, I do not desire to kill these (people), even if they are going to kill me.

'I do not want to destroy them, even if they kill me,' Arjuna told Kṛṣṇa, addressing him as Madhusūdana, meaning the one who destroyed the demon Madhu. Even to rule over the three worlds, even if heaven were to come to him because of this battle, Arjuna did not want to see his people slain. How, then, could he justify their destruction for this small kingdom, which could be crossed on horseback in a matter of days?

Arjuna was convinced that it would serve no useful purpose to continue this fight because he saw all the people involved on both sides were his own people. Because they were dear to him, their destruction was not going to make him happy. Even from the standpoint of *dṛṣṭa-phala* – the immediate results such as gaining the kingdom, the pleasures and comforts that went with it – he did not consider the cost to be worthwhile.

---

[43] *Madhu-nāmānam asuraṁ sūditavān iti Madhusūdanaḥ* – the one who is the slayer of the demon Madhu, is Madhusūdana.

We have seen that he no longer cared for victory, much less for the kingdom. Nor did he care about the privations he would have to undergo not having the kingdom. What kind of happiness would he have, Arjuna argued, if he destroyed the very people he cared for? For him, then, there would be no *dṛṣṭa-phala*. Nor did he see any *adṛṣṭa*.

The Pāṇḍavas were supposed to be the protectors of law and order. In a battle based on *dharma*, they naturally had to see that Duryodhana paid for what he had done. According to this law, if a man who was supposed to protect *dharma* was derelict in his duty, *pāpa* would definitely come to him. *Pāpa* has the sense of sin, as we understand it. Any unbecoming action, an action which is not proper, will incur sin.

Arjuna thought that by destroying his own people, he would incur only sin. Such an action would bring no *puṇya* to him, only *pāpa*. Therefore, no good would possibly come of it. So far, his argument had been based on *dṛṣṭa-phala*, seen results. He, then, began to argue on the basis of *adṛṣṭa-phala*, unseen results.

निहत्य धार्तराष्ट्रान्नः का प्रीतिः स्याज्जनार्दन ।
पापमेवाश्रयेदस्मान्हत्वैतानाततायिनः ॥ ३६ ॥

nihatya dhārtarāṣṭrānnaḥ kā prītiḥ syājjanārdana
pāpamevāśrayedasmān hatvaitān ātatāyinaḥ (36)

janārdana – O Kṛṣṇa! (So called because he chastised those given to improper ways); *dhārtarāṣṭrān* – sons of Dhṛtarāṣṭra;

nihatya – destroying; *naḥ* – for us; *kā* – what kind of; *prītiḥ* – satisfaction; *syāt* – would there be; *etān* – these; *ātatāyinaḥ* – wrongdoers; *hatvā* – destroying; *pāpam* – sin; *eva* – only; *asmān āśrayet* – would come to us

> Janārdana[44] (Kṛṣṇa)! What kind of satisfaction would be there for us by destroying these sons of Dhṛtarāṣṭra? Sin alone would come to us by destroying these wrongdoers.

Here, Kṛṣṇa was addressed as *jana-ardana*, the one who chastises those given to improper ways. Previously, Arjuna addressed Kṛṣṇa as *madhu-sūdana*, the destroyer of Madhu. Both names indicate that Kṛṣṇa is one who did not allow anything wrong to happen in his presence.

Arjuna was making his case to Kṛṣṇa. 'What kind of satisfaction will we have? None at all.' The people in whose presence the victors would be happy were the very people who would be fighting against each other. There would be no positive *dṛṣṭa-phala*, with all of them dead. No visible result would accrue to the victors. On the other hand, he believed that there would definitely be *pāpa*, the invisible result accrued to the doer of an improper action.

Any action produces a two-fold result, *dṛṣṭa-phala* and *adṛṣṭa-phala*, as we have seen. With reference to a meritorious action, *dṛṣṭa-phala* is any satisfaction you receive now and

---

44 *asurāṇāṁ janānāṁ narakādi-gamayitṛtvād janārdanaḥ* – the one who chastises those given to improper ways is Janārdana.

adṛṣṭa-phala is the *puṇya* that you receive, which will later yield comfortable situations. For instance, when you have saved a person's life, the *dṛṣṭa-phala* is his or her thankfulness and gratitude to you, and the satisfaction of having done something good. For the same action, there is also some *adṛṣṭa-phala, puṇya*, accrued to you. On the other hand, a wrong action such as destroying someone, produces uncomfortable situations now due to *dṛṣṭa-phala*, and later *pāpa* due to *adṛṣṭa-phala*.

Arjuna said here, '*pāpa* will certainly come to us if we destroy these people.' In his mind, there would be no *puṇya* and no satisfaction either, even though the Dhārtarāṣṭrās were *ātatāyī*s, wrongdoers.

An *ātatāyī* is one who has committed any or all of the six kinds of wrongdoing.[45] An arsonist, one that sets fires, is called an *agnida*. One who commits the crime of poisoning someone is called *garada*. A person who comes after you with a weapon in hand, when you are unarmed, is a *śastronmatta*. A *dhanāpaha* is one who robs others of their wealth. A *kṣetrahara* is one who encroaches upon or occupies someone else's land. In spite of calling them by a respectable word like pioneer, such people are, in fact, *kṣetrahara*s. And one who kidnaps or grabs another man's wife is called a *dārahara*.

Duryodhana had committed all six kinds of crime. He had set fire to the wax house in which the Pāṇḍavas were staying.

---

[45] अग्निदो गरदश्चैव शस्त्रोन्मत्तो धनापहः । क्षेत्रदारहरश्चैतान् षड् विद्यादाततायिनः ॥

agnido garadaścaiva śastronmatto dhanāpahaḥ, kṣetradāraharaścaitān ṣaḍ vidyādātatāyinaḥ.

Only because of some timely inside information, were the Pāṇḍavas able to escape. He had also poisoned Bhīma when he was young. He had robbed the Pāṇḍavas of their wealth, had occupied their kingdom, and would not give them so much as a small piece of land. He had tried to take away their wife, Draupadī.

Those who have committed any of these crimes are all called *ātatāyī*s. The law of the land gives them capital punishment. For these types of crimes, then, there is no court of appeal. Duryodhana, being an *ātatāyī*, deserved punishment, according to the *dharma-śāstra*.

In the empirical world, *dharma-śāstra* rules. Anyone going against this code incurs sin and is necessarily punishable. Even so, knowing all of this, Arjuna did not think that they would gain *puṇya* by destroying these wrongdoers. He was certain that only *pāpa* would be the result for reasons that he would explain to Kṛṣṇa later. Arjuna thought that by destroying his own people, he would be creating great confusion in the society. Because they would be the perpetrators, and would be the cause of this confusion, no law of *dharma* would excuse them. They would incur only *pāpa* in the end although Duryodhana was an *ātatāyī*. This was Arjuna's thinking. It was not correct, but that was how he saw it. His affection for these people caused confusion in his own mind and, he concluded:

तस्मान्नार्हा वयं हन्तुं धार्तराष्ट्रान् स्वबान्धवान् ।
स्वजनं हि कथं हत्वा सुखिनः स्याम माधव ॥ ३७ ॥

tasmānnārhā vayaṁ hantuṁ dhārtarāṣṭrān svabāndhavān
svajanaṁ hi kathaṁ hatvā sukhinaḥ syāma mādhava (37)

tasmāt – therefore; *svabāndhavān* – one's own relatives; *dhārtarāṣṭrān* – the sons of Dhṛtarāṣṭra; *vayam* – we; *hantuṁ na arhāḥ* – should not kill; *mādhava* – O Kṛṣṇa!; *svajanam* – one's own people; *hatvā* – having destroyed; *kathaṁ hi* – how indeed; *sukhinaḥ* – happy people; *syāma* – we would become

Therefore, we should not kill our own relatives, the sons of Dhṛtarāṣṭra. Destroying our own people, Mādhava[46] (Kṛṣṇa)! how would we be happy?

Because they would incur only *pāpa* by destroying their own relatives, Arjuna concluded that they were not qualified to kill the sons of Dhṛtarāṣṭra and the others. 'O Kṛṣṇa!' he asked, 'How can we be happy by destroying our own people? Happiness under such circumstances would be impossible. With our own people gone, there will not be anyone with whom we can celebrate our victory.'

Calling him Madhusūdana and Janārdana, Arjuna told Kṛṣṇa that these were all people whom he did not want to kill. 'You are Madhusūdana and Janārdana; you chastise those who are wrongdoers and you destroy demons, all of whom are people unknown to you. My situation is different. These are all my own people.' Arjuna thereby expressed that the kind of problem he had to deal with was entirely different from the ones Kṛṣṇa had faced.

---

[46] *Māyāḥ śriyo dhavaḥ patiḥ mādhavaḥ* – the consort of Goddess Lakṣmī is Mādhava.

Then he continued:

यद्यप्येते न पश्यन्ति लोभोपहतचेतसः ।
कुलक्षयकृतं दोषं मित्रद्रोहे च पातकम् ॥ ३८ ॥

कथं न ज्ञेयमस्माभिः पापादस्मान्निवर्तितुम् ।
कुलक्षयकृतं दोषं प्रपश्यद्भिर्जनार्दन ॥ ३९ ॥

yadyapyete na paśyanti lobhopahatacetasaḥ
kulakṣayakṛtaṁ doṣaṁ mitradrohe ca pātakam (38)
kathaṁ na jñeyamasmābhiḥ pāpādasmānnivartitum
kulakṣayakṛtaṁ doṣaṁ prapaśyadbhirjanārdana (39)

yadi api – although; *ete* – these; *lobha-upahata-cetasaḥ* – people whose minds are overpowered by greed; *kula-kṣaya-kṛtam* – born of the destruction of one's family; *doṣam* – defect (sin); *mitra-drohe* – in the betrayal of one's friends; *ca* – and; *pātakam* – sin; *na paśyanti* – do not see; *janārdana* – O Kṛṣṇa!; *kula-kṣaya-kṛtam* – born of the destruction of the family; *doṣam* – sin; *prapaśyadbhiḥ* – by those who see very clearly; *asmābhiḥ* – by us; *asmāt pāpāt* – from this sin; *nivartitum* – to withdraw; *kathaṁ na jñeyam* – how is it not considered

Although these people, whose minds are overpowered by greed, do not see the defect in the destruction of (one's) family and the sins of betraying one's friends, Janārdana (Kṛṣṇa)! how come it is not considered by us, who know that sin is born of the destruction of the family, to withdraw from this sin?

Here, Kṛṣṇa may have said, "Arjuna, this *svajana*-argument, that is, 'how can I fight against my own people'– is applicable to Duryodhana also, is it not? You are not the only one with this problem. Duryodhana, however, does not consider you one of his people. He considers you an enemy. He will not even give you a square inch of land in this kingdom. He does not look upon you as a *svajana*, as someone who is related to him. He looks upon you as someone who has come from another planet as it were, as an invader. Given the situation, what is this *svajana*-argument really all about? It is meaningless because Duryodhana does not feel the same way. If he did, there would be no war. You gave him every chance. You were ready to accept even a village, but he was not willing to give you one. Therefore, where is the problem? It is a simple question of *dharma* and *adharma*, right and wrong. You are supposed to be the protector of what is right, the protector of law and order, and if you allow *adharma* to continue, then it is a dereliction of duty on your part."

This could very well have been Kṛṣṇa's argument. Arjuna expected it and this verse was his answer for it. He told Kṛṣṇa that these people were unable to tell the difference between right and wrong because their minds had been destroyed by greed. Duryodhana was not a bad man; greed was the problem. Because of greed, his discrimination, his commitment to right and wrong, was lost. He was, therefore, unable to see what great destruction would be wrought by this war and what a crime it would be to destroy one's own family. Nor could he see the sin he would incur by *droha*, cheating and deceiving his own friends. The word *mitra*, here, means one's cousins and other relatives, as well as friends. An example of *droha* is this. You ask a friend, whom you trust, to keep some money for you. And, when you claim it back, if he or she says, 'What money?' then, that is betrayal. The betrayal of Christ by Judas is also an example of *droha*.

The reason these people did not see was not because they were uneducated. In fact, they were all educated people. However, education is not required in order to differentiate right from wrong. Even uneducated people know the difference. The people Arjuna was referring to, have been well brought up. They were not raised in criminal colonies. As children, they had lived in palaces with tutors. Yet, they did not see this because they were possessed by greed. Their faculty of discrimination, their minds, had been robbed away by greed.

Greed is capable of anything. You may be highly educated, but greed overpowers all education. It robs away one's understanding of right and wrong and one's capacity to interpret them. That being the case, the education only helps you justify your actions with cogent arguments. Here, too, the Dhārtarāṣṭras used every argument they knew to justify what they wanted to do because of greed. This was why they could not see the destruction they were bringing about.

'But we do see the *pāpa* that is going to be incurred by us,' Arjuna told Kṛṣṇa. 'Recognising this, how can we not turn away from this great sin?' Arjuna wanted to know. How would they possibly consider this particular situation as anything other than one they should withdraw from?

Anticipating yet another argument from Kṛṣṇa – that, if the family had to be sacrificed, in order to protect *dharma*, then it should be done – Arjuna continued:

Verses 40&41

Arjuna feels that war would destroy dharma

कुलक्षये प्रणश्यन्ति कुलधर्माः सनातनाः ।
धर्मे नष्टे कुलं कृत्स्नमधर्मोऽभिभवत्युत ॥ ४० ॥

kulakṣaye praṇaśyanti kuladharmāḥ sanātanāḥ
dharme naṣṭe kulaṁ
kṛtsnamadharmo'bhibhavatyuta (40)

kulakṣaye – when the family is destroyed; *sanātanāḥ* – the ancient; *kuladharmāḥ* – the *dharma*s of the family; *praṇaśyanti* – they die; *dharme naṣṭe* – when the *dharma* is lost; *adharmaḥ* – *adharma*; *kulaṁ kṛtsnam* – the entire family; *abhibhavati uta* – will it not overwhelm?

When the family is destroyed, the ancient *dharma*s of the family perish. When the *dharma* is lost, will not *adharma* overwhelm the entire family?

Arjuna felt that if the destruction of the clan were to be looked at in this way, the problem would always remain because there would be no one to establish *dharma* and *adharma*. Therefore, Arjuna did not agree with the argument that *dharma* was to be protected at the cost of destroying one's relatives. This verse reveals how he further substantiated his argument.

When important members of a family are destroyed, everything to be done by that particular family will also be destroyed. It is because *dharma* cannot be protected unless the *dharmī*, the one who follows the *dharma*, is protected. *Dharma* cannot be protected in a bottle! *Dharma* is not like historical scrolls that can be stored for posterity so that, even if a whole civilisation is destroyed, a future generation can find the scrolls and know the history. *Dharma* cannot be preserved by writing it up and keeping it somewhere. Only when the person following the *dharma* is protected, is *dharma* itself protected. Just as the 'pot-ness' of a pot cannot be retained if a pot is destroyed, so too, *dharma* cannot be retained if the *dharmī*, the one who follows the *dharma*, is destroyed.

Flowing from time immemorial, from one generation to the next, this ancient family *dharma*, *kula-dharma*, is perennial. Because, *dharma* – what is to be done and what is not to be done – runs in the family, it will be destroyed if the family is destroyed. Moreover, when the *dharma* is destroyed, those who survived because they were not in the battlefield will definitely succumb to *adharma*. It was Arjuna's argument here, one that was quite convincing.

He then went on to say:

अधर्माभिभवात्कृष्ण प्रदुष्यन्ति कुलस्त्रियः ।
स्त्रीषु दुष्टासु वार्ष्णेय जायते वर्णसङ्करः ॥ ४१ ॥

adharmābhibhavātkṛṣṇa praduṣyanti kulastriyaḥ
strīṣu duṣṭāsu vārṣṇeya jāyate varṇasaṅkaraḥ (41)

kṛṣṇa – O Kṛṣṇa!; *adharma-abhibhavāt* – due to the increase of *adharma; kulastriyaḥ* – the women in the family; *praduṣyanti* – will be given to improper ways; *vārṣṇeya* – O Vārṣṇeya! *strīṣu duṣṭāsu* – when the women become corrupt; *varṇasaṅkaraḥ* – the confusion of *varṇa* (societal groups); *jāyate* – is born

> Kṛṣṇa! Due to the increase of *adharma*, the women in the family will be given to improper ways. Vārṣṇeya[47] (Kṛṣṇa)! When the women become corrupt, confusion is born in the society.

In this verse, Arjuna tells Kṛṣṇa that *adharma* would only increase. It would be everywhere. Because of the increase of *adharma* in the ruling clan, it would pervade all other clans as well. The Kuru clan was not the only ruling clan at that time. There were many other clans ruling different parts of this country. And all the other clans had come to fight on one side or the other in this war. Every one of them was going to be destroyed.

Kings and soldiers alike would all be just a fodder for the arrows of Arjuna, Karṇa, and the others. There was a huge infantry on both sides that had been given a crash training course and sent to the front only to exhaust their weapons, to become the victims of flying arrows. Since all the able-bodied men were here, and would be destroyed, how would *dharma* be protected in their families?

---

[47] *Vṛṣṇi-kula-prasūtaḥ vārṣṇeyaḥ* – the one who is born in the dynasty of Vṛṣṇi is Vārṣṇeya.

Arjuna could not understand how such destruction could be sanctioned. Strictly speaking, it was the women who protected the *dharma* in any society and they, in turn, were protected by the men. It was the societal condition at that time. If all the men who had been recruited, trained, and sent to the battle, and all the great kings, princes, soldiers and leaders were destroyed, the women would not be protected and thus would be unable to follow *dharma* and thereby protect it.

Since a particular atmosphere is required to follow *dharma*, Arjuna's argument was that, in the absence of the order that governs a well-structured society, the women would be given to ways that were not proper. When those people who form the framework of a society's structure are destroyed, the structure itself is naturally destroyed.

Arjuna told Kṛṣṇa how the structure of society would fall apart. Each family had its own *dharma*, called *kula-dharma*. For example, there was a *dharma* for marriage, which states the exact way it has to be done. In the performance of rituals, each family had its own *sūtra*s and the methods that governed them; in other words, the know-how required. There were *dharma*s relating to different groups, *kula-dharma*, *varṇa-dharma*, *āśrama-dharma*, and so on. *Varṇa* means group – *brāhmaṇa*, *kṣatriya*, *vaiśya* and *śūdra*, which we shall discuss later. *Āśrama* refers to the stages of life – the student stage, *brahmacarya*; the married stage, *gārhasthya*; preparation for *sannyāsa*, *vānaprastha*; and renunciation, *sannyāsa* – all of which had their own *dharma*s.

Who would be left to protect all the *dharma* that was handed over from one generation to the next? *Dharma* was not a system with built-in lateral controls; it was a tradition. There was no central organisation from which everything flowed down such as exists in the form of papacy, diocese and parish. Here, the form was purely a structure, handed over by the family. The parents passed it along to their children. The *dharma*, being an individual pursuit, would be destroyed. 'What will happen then?' Arjuna asked.

A society is strong only when its women are strong. When the women themselves are given to certain weaknesses, to ways that are not becoming, then you will find confusion. If the family is destroyed, one's parentage becomes a problem and an enormous confusion is thereby created. Arjuna argued from the standpoint of his society's social structure. He was convinced that the confusion would not only be within the *varṇa*s, but also in the *āśrama*s, once the women could no longer maintain the *dharma*.

One may then ask, 'So what if the *varṇa*s are destroyed?' The question 'so what?' can always be asked at any stage. So you will die; so what? You will not be here; so what? Your family will miss you; so what? Therefore, let there be confusion, one may say. In anticipation of such a response, Arjuna continued:

Verses 42-45

Dharma would be lost without dharmī

सङ्करो नरकायैव कुलघ्नानां कुलस्य च ।
पतन्ति पितरो ह्येषां लुप्तपिण्डोदकक्रियाः ॥ ४२ ॥

saṅkaro narakāyaiva kulaghnānāṁ kulasya ca
patanti pitaro hyeṣāṁ luptapiṇḍodakakriyāḥ (42)

saṅkaraḥ – confusion; *kulaghnānām* – of the destroyers of the family; *kulasya ca* – and of the family; *narakāya* – for the world of pain; *eva* – only; *eṣām* – their; *pitaraḥ* – ancestors; *lupta-piṇḍa-udaka-kriyāḥ* – denied of their post death rituals; *patanti* – fall; *hi* – indeed

Confusion, indeed, leads the family and the destroyers of the family to the world of pain. Their ancestors, denied of their post death rituals, indeed fall.

Here, Arjuna included the very family itself because, after the heads of these families die, the others would not follow *dharma*. For both the destroyers of the families, then, as well as those who survived the destruction of their famileis, there would be *naraka*. *Naraka* is the Vedic equivalent to hell, with the difference that, *naraka* is a place you go to and come back, unlike the concept of hell in Christianity. There is no concept of eternal damnation here because people who incur *pāpa* would go to *naraka*, a place of pain, after death for a period of time. Therefore, *saṅkara*, confusion, can only lead to *naraka*.

Thus, for those who destroy the family and for the survivors of the family, the outcome is nothing but *naraka* when there is *saṅkara*. Many people would survive, but they would have no role models. Therefore, confusion would result. They would do things that are not to be done. Hence, there would be more *pāpa*s accrued. People would be doing things that are not proper and would end up in *naraka*.

In Arjuna's mind, the situation was even more serious than that. His ancestors would also be affected. The wrong doings of the ancestors of the three preceding generations were traditionally neutralised by prayers performed month after month by the survivors in the next generations. Those for whose sake these oblations were made may have committed many *pāpa-karma*s. Those *karma*s would be neutralised by the rituals performed by their children.

The ritual performed for the sake of one's departed ancestors is called *piṇḍa-udaka-kriyā*. In this ritual, water is religiously offered with chants, along with a *piṇḍa*, a ball of cooked rice. If the families were destroyed, no one would perform this ritual and the ancestors would be deprived of having their wrong doings neutralised by their children. Because of their children's prayers, they have all been protected somewhere. If, however, they were denied these rituals, they would fall from there.

Who would perform these rituals if the people who were to do them were destroyed? Even those who destroyed the families would also be destroyed in the process and would not be able to do the rituals. Nor would those who were left, protect the ancestors in this way because they would not have grown up respecting the need to perform these rituals. Instead, they would choose to spend their time in other kinds of activities. It means, the rituals for the ancestors would be left undone.

There would be no role models, no family, and no home either. Therefore, those who were left would not know who was who and what was what. Without roots, what self-identity would they have? Without self-identity, they could not perform rituals. Arjuna's point was that they should not think that if they destroyed all these people and were destroyed in the process, their children would save them; they would not. They would all be rock stars, punk artists, and the like! What would they possibly do for their ancestors? Therefore, there would be no one to help.

By saying what he did, Arjuna was citing the *dharma-śāstra*; but Kṛṣṇa had an answer for it all, as we shall see in the next chapter. Arjuna continues in the same vein.

दोषैरेतैः कुलघ्नानां वर्णसङ्करकारकैः ।
उत्साद्यन्ते जातिधर्माः कुलधर्माश्च शाश्वताः ॥ ४३ ॥

doṣairetaiḥ kulaghnānāṁ varṇasaṅkarakārakaiḥ
utsādyante jātidharmāḥ kuladharmāśca śāśvatāḥ (43)

kulaghnānām – of those who destroy the family; *varṇa-saṅkara-kārakaiḥ* – by that which creates confusion about *varṇa-dharma*, etc; *etaiḥ* – by these; *doṣaiḥ* – by wrong actions; *śāśvatāḥ* – perennial; *jāti-dharmāḥ* – the *dharma*s of the community; *kula-dharmāḥ* – the *dharma*s pursued by the family; *ca* – and; *utsādyante* – are destroyed

By these wrong actions of those who destroy the family, creating confusion in the society, the perennial *dharmas* pursued by the community and the family are destroyed.

Here, Arjuna concluded that all the *dharma* perennially handed over by one generation to the next, from time immemorial, would be destroyed by wrong actions producing confusion with reference to *kula-dharma*, *varṇa-dharma*, *āśrama-dharma*, and so on. Therefore, to destroy all these people would be wrong because the *dharma* would also be destroyed. Arjuna was trying to tell Kṛṣṇa that the battle was not going to work. In addition, the entire society would be destroyed by these acts of destruction. Therefore, he was not going to fight.

Dharma is to be seen here as three-fold – *sādhāraṇa-dharma*, *varṇa-āśrama-dharma* and *kula-dharma*. *Sādhāraṇa-dharma* or *sāmānya-dharma* is universal ethics, applicable to all and sundry. Whether the person is of the age or of any other age, from this country and culture or from any other country and culture, he or she has a code of *dharma* in common.

Universal values, universal law and order, are a part of the creation and are something that we all sense commonly. In other words, they are universal. Whether you are educated in this *dharma*, you do know what is right and wrong. What you want and do not want others do to you, become right and wrong, respectively.

Being endowed with common sense, a human being is able to appreciate right and wrong without any education whatsoever. I need not be taught that I should not be hurt, that I should not be robbed and so on. These values are commonly sensed by everyone, and thus govern all human interactions, although other non-universal values may override them. This causes people to compromise. Compromises, therefore, are not born out of total ignorance of universal values.

Varṇa-āśrama-dharma, and *kula-dharma,* together, are called *viśeṣa-dharma,* which can be divided in many ways. *Viśeṣa-dharma* means peculiar or particular *dharma,* governing certain situations, whereas *sāmānya-dharma* applies to all human beings whether a person is a student, a householder, or in any other stage of one's life. A particular *dharma* is one that is governed by the structure of a society. For instance, in the Vedic society, the society envisioned by the Vedas, there was a structure called *varṇa* and another called *āśrama.*

The structure, consisting of the *varṇa*s, made it possible to assign particular jobs to particular groups of people. A broad division was thereby created, along with a concept of duty. Because I belong to this *varṇa,* this is to be done by me. It is all an integral part of *karma-yoga,* as we will see later. This structure of assigning specific duties to particular groups of people is called *varṇa-dharma.* It is a *viśeṣa-dharma.*

Then there is *āśrama-dharma,* defining that which has to be done, given one's stage in life. For example, a *brāhmaṇa,* as a student, had to follow a certain order. When he or she married, some changes occurred and additional *dharma* was included. As a student, one was not supposed to pursue certain activities. One could follow politics, but one did not participate in politics. If one did, one ceased to be a student. One became a politician, instead. Thus, there was a structure with reference to one's *āśrama.*

Āśrama-dharma – what was expected of you, depending on the stage of life you were in – is also *viśeṣa-dharma.*

Another example of *viśeṣa-dharma* was *strī-dharma* or *puruṣa-dharma,* based on whether a person was a female or a male. There was also *kula-dharma, dharma* applicable to a particular family or clan. The Kuru clan, for instance, had its own *dharma.* Because it included all of these *viśeṣa-dharmas, kula-dharma* was used in this verse to cover all of them.

Arjuna argued that by destroying the *dharmī,* they would be destroying all these *dharmas* because an attribute cannot exist by itself without a locus, a substantive. In the expression, 'a white cow,' for example, the substantive 'cow' is qualified by the adjective 'white.' If you destroy the cow, the white also goes. Similarly, *dharma* being what it is, must be lived by the *dharmī,* the person who is supposed to follow it.

Here, all these people had come to fight against and kill each other. For the sake of what? 'You cannot tell me,' Arjuna said, 'that it is for the sake of protecting *dharma.*' When the people who were supposed to follow *dharma* were destroyed, how could *dharma* be protected? With the *dharmī* gone, *dharma* would only be in the books. There would be no *dharmī* for the others to follow. This *dharma* had always been handed over to the next generation, but after the war, the role models would be gone, creating a lot of confusion in the society.

Arjuna argued that, by going on with the war, he would be the cause of all this confusion and, therefore, he wanted to be no part of it. Further, he said:

उत्सन्नकुलधर्माणां मनुष्याणां जनार्दन ।
नरके नियतं वासो भवतीत्यनुशुश्रुम ॥ ४४ ॥

utsannakuladharmāṇāṁ manuṣyāṇāṁ janārdana
narake niyataṁ vāso bhavatītyanuśuśruma (44)

janārdana – O Kṛṣṇa!; *utsanna-kula-dharmāṇām* – for those who have destroyed the *dharma* of the family; *manuṣyāṇām* – for those men; *niyatam* – inevitable; *narake* – in the world of pain; *vāsaḥ* – a life; *bhavati* – is; *iti* – thus; *anuśuśruma* – we have heard

> We have heard, Janārdana (Kṛṣṇa)! that a life in the world of pain is inevitable for those people who destroy the *dharma* of the family.

Here, Arjuna reminded Kṛṣṇa of what he had learned from the religious teachers – that those who destroy the *kula-dharma* must necessarily go to *naraka*, a place of pain, after death. Therefore he concluded, if the Pāṇḍavas were to destroy the family, they would gain nothing but *pāpa* and would have to live in *naraka*, for a certain length of time. They had heard this from their elders who knew the *dharma-śāstra*. Believing this to be the case, Arjuna could see neither *dṛṣṭa-phala* nor *adṛṣṭa-phala* as a result of this war. In his mind, there would be no immediate or future gain, here or in the hereafter. It was the basis for Arjuna's argument.

Duryodhana, on the other hand, was not concerned about *adṛṣṭa-phala* at all. He cared only for *dṛṣṭa-phala*, immediate gain.

He did not think about *pāpa* and all that went with it. Had he done so, he would not have been an *ātatāyī*, a wrongdoer. He had no respect for the *adṛṣṭa-phala*, which meant that he was not an *āstika*. He was therefore a *nāstika*, a disbeliever. The word *adṛṣṭa-phala* is known to us only through the scripture, the *śāstra*. Being a disbeliever Duryodhana had no faith in *puṇya* and *pāpa*; he was interested only in what was available to him here, in this world.

He wanted to rule a kingdom. The power that went with the kingdom made him feel big. He had enjoyed absolute power, without any contention, for thirteen years. As we know, power has a knack of corrupting. Power corrupts and absolute power corrupts absolutely. Duryodhana had been absolutely corrupted by power and he did not care. He enjoyed absolute power and did not want to lose it. Although others thought of it as corruption, he did not. In fact, he thought those who thought this way, were idiots and deserved only to live in the forest, nothing more; this was Duryodhana's thinking.

Arjuna's thinking was in keeping with what he had learned about *dṛṣṭa-phala* and *adṛṣṭa-phala*. He believed in *dharma* and was very clear that the fight was between *dharma* and *adharma*. Arjuna knew this, but still he thought that by destroying his own people, there would be no happiness for him, either then or later.

Therefore, he lamented:

अहो बत महत्पापं कर्तुं व्यवसिता वयम् ।
यद्राज्यसुखलोभेन हन्तुं स्वजनमुद्यताः ॥ ४५ ॥

aho bata mahatpāpaṁ kartuṁ vyavasitā vayam
yadrājyasukhalobhena hantuṁ svajanamudyatāḥ (45)

aho bata – alas!; *yat* – that; *rājya-sukha-lobhena* – due to greed for a kingdom and its pleasures; *svajanam* – our own people; *hantum udyatāḥ* – ready to kill; *vayam* – we; *mahat-pāpam* – grave sin; *kartuṁ vyavasitāḥ* – are determined to commit

> Alas! Ready to kill our own people due to greed for a kingdom and its pleasures, we are determined to commit a grave sin!

Up until this verse, Arjuna's lamentation focused on what he was about to do. Here, however, although the first arrow had yet to be shot, we see that Arjuna was bothered by all these people having come to fight. He asks himself, 'What were we thinking of when we gathered all these armies to declare war and to come to Kurukṣetra? What happened to that thinking, that *viveka* that I now have? Where was it? Because it was not there, we are here in the battlefield right now! Why did I not figure this all out before? Fie upon us! What kind of *pāpa* caused us to decide to come here, determined to commit this great universal sin, the destruction of *dharma*?' Running away with his own train of thoughts, Arjuna had now come to this conclusion.

Lobha is greed or longing. When you have a kingdom, *rājya*, you have all the pleasures, *sukha*, that go with it – the best music, dancers, poets who praise you daily, titles and salutations, all of which boost your ego. This is what is meant by a power trip. For a mortal, this power is very enticing. 'Is it not greed for the kingdom and pleasures that has made us come with our stockpiles of weapons, prepared to fight and kill our own people,' Arjuna mused. Since they would be destroying their own people, Arjuna became ill at ease at the very thought that they could ever have considered doing such a thing.

Verse 46

Arjuna concludes – being killed would be better

यदि मामप्रतीकारमशस्त्रं शस्त्रपाणयः ।
धार्तराष्ट्रा रणे हन्युस्तन्मे क्षेमतरं भवेत् ॥ ४६ ॥

yadi māmapratikāramaśastraṁ śastrapāṇayaḥ
dhārtarāṣṭrā raṇe hanyustanme kṣemataraṁ
bhavet (46)

yadi – if; *apratīkāram* – who does not retaliate; *aśastram* – who is unarmed; *mām* – me; *śastra-pāṇayaḥ* – who are with weapons in hand; *dhārtarāṣṭrāh* – the sons of Dhṛtarāstra; *raṇe* – in battle; *hanyuḥ* – were to kill; *me* – for me; *kṣemataram* – better; *bhavet* – will be

> It will be better for me if the sons of Dhṛtarāṣṭra, with weapons in hand, were to kill me, who is unarmed and who does not retaliate, in the battle.

Kṛṣṇa must have looked at Arjuna in wonderment. He had been going on and on, and now he was telling him that, if they gave up the fight, they may all be killed; but he did not care. Arjuna was determined not to fight back. However, this kind of thinking was not shared by those in the other camp.

It was only in Arjuna's mind. Therefore, if Arjuna was not going to fight, either he would have to run away from the battlefield or stand there unarmed and be killed.

Arjuna would be unarmed but not disarmed. He would have voluntarily given up all his arms. Moreover, he thought that it was better if he were to be killed. 'Let it be for my good,' he said. 'Myself not being killed but destroying all these people would definitely not be for my good. I am going to suffer from the pains that I caused by destroying all these people. It will always haunt me, even if I am killed in the process. Alive, I am going to be haunted; and dead I will haunt this battlefield where my arrows destroyed my own people. It is even worse,' said Arjuna.

Having decided not to fight, Arjuna concluded that being killed would be better. What Arjuna then did was recounted to Dhṛtarāṣṭra by Sañjaya in the last verse of this first chapter:

Verse 47

Arjuna's action recounted by Sañjaya to Dhṛtarāṣṭra

सञ्जय उवाच ।
एवमुक्त्वार्जुनः सङ्ख्ये रथोपस्थ उपाविशत् ।
विसृज्य सशरं चापं शोकसंविग्नमानसः ॥ ४७ ॥

sañjaya uvāca
evamuktvārjunaḥ saṅkhye rathopastha upāviśat
visṛjya saśaraṁ cāpaṁ śokasaṁvignamānasaḥ (47)

sañjaya uvāca – Sañjaya said
arjunaḥ – Arjuna; *evam* – in this manner; *uktvā* – having spoken; *saṅkhye* – in the middle of the battlefield; *saśaram* – along with arrows; *cāpam* – the bow; *visṛjya* – casting aside; *śoka-saṁvigna-mānasaḥ* – with his mind completely overcome by sorrow; *ratha-upasthe* – on the seat of the chariot; *upāviśat* – sat down

Sañjaya said:

> Having spoken in this manner in the middle of the battlefield, Arjuna, whose mind was completely overcome by sorrow, sat down on the seat of the chariot casting aside his bow and arrows.

Because Sañjaya was narrating the whole dialogue between Kṛṣṇa and Arjuna to Dhṛtarāṣṭra, the entire *Gītā* is actually in the form of narration by Sañjaya although it was really Vyāsa who was speaking. There is a particular style involved here, which we need to be aware of. There are quotations within quotations. Throughout the *Gītā*, we have to remember that Sañjaya was describing what happened on the battlefield to Dhṛtarāṣṭra. Here, Sañjaya first quoted Arjuna and then, in this verse, Vyāsa reminds his reader that Sañjaya was talking to Dhṛtarāṣṭra.

Arjuna had been standing in his chariot in order to see all the people with whom he was to fight. Finding his own people on all sides, he concluded that it would be better for him to be killed. Having thus spoken to Kṛṣṇa, Arjuna sat down in the chariot, which was in the middle of the battlefield right between the two armies.

This verse also provides a few more details concerning Arjuna's condition. Putting his bow and arrows aside, Arjuna sat back, his mind completely overwhelmed by sorrow. He felt sadness because the situation was so sad. That he had come to fight with his own people was not a happy thought.

Although he was sad, Arjuna did not run away from the battlefield because something inside told him that perhaps there was some defect, some fallacy, in his thinking. He was a man of *dharma*. He had been well brought up and his present thoughts were all coloured by his vision. There was some truth in his argument; but, at the same time, *dharma* was involved in it. Hence, it was not easy to resolve the issues involved.

Arjuna was a person who was supposed to take care of law and order. He had a job to do. One that was mandated by the *śāstra*, by the society, by the crown, and for that reason he did not run away from the battlefield. He could have set out for the Himalayas, the distance from Kurukṣetra not being much. It would, therefore, have been very easy for him to go. However, he did not run away because he knew that there was some problem with his thinking. Instead, he sat there, in the chariot, in the middle of the battlefield, so that Kṛṣṇa could talk to him.

We sometimes tell someone that we do not want to do something, but still we listen to the other person's point of view. Why? Because we have a doubt about what we want or do not want. Otherwise, we would not be availabe for discussion. That Arjuna sat there indicates that something was telling him that there was a fallacy in his thinking and that he stood to be corrected. And he was ready for it.

The first chapter of the *Gītā* ends with these words:

ॐतत्सत् ।
इति श्रीमद्भगवद्गीतासूपनिषत्सु ब्रह्मविद्यायां योगशास्त्रे
श्रीकृष्णार्जुनसंवादेऽर्जुन-विषाद-योगा नाम
प्रथमोऽध्यायः ॥१ ॥

oṁ tat sat.

iti śrīmadbhagavadgītāsūpaniṣatsu brahmavidyāyāṁ yogaśāstre śrīkṛṣṇārjuna-saṁvāde'rjuna-viṣāda-yogonāma prathamo'dhyāyaḥ (1)

oṁ-tat-sat – Om, Brahman is the only reality; *iti* – thus; *śrīmad-bhagavadgītāsu* – in the *Bhagavadgītā*; *upaniṣatsu* – in the *Upaniṣads*; *brahmavidyāyām* – in the knowledge of Brahman; *yoga-śāstre* – in the *yoga-śāstra*; *śrīkṛṣṇa-arjuna-saṁvāde* – in the dialogue between Śrī Kṛṣṇa and Arjuna; *arjuna-viṣāda-yogaḥ nāma* – called the '*yoga*, topic of Arjuna's sorrow'; *prathamaḥ adhyāyaḥ* – first chapter

Om, Brahman, is the only reality. Thus ends the first chapter called *arjuna-viṣāda-yoga*[48] – having the topic of Arjuna's sorrow – in the Bhagavadgītā which is in the form of a dialogue between Śrī Kṛṣṇa and Arjuna,

---

[48] *yoga* here in the compound '*viṣāda-yoga*' means topic; one of the many meanings of the word. The same meaning is in all the following titles of chapters.

which is the essence of the *Upaniṣads*, whose subject matter is both the knowledge of Brahman and *yoga*.[49]

Traditionally, the words, '*oṁ tat sat*' go before this line. '*Oṁ*' is the name for Brahman and Brahman alone is the reality; *tat sat*. This expression indicates a conclusion. After all that is said and done, the reality is only Brahman – *Oṁ tat sat*.

Śrīmat means that which is endowed with all kinds of wealth including *vidyā*, that which gives you everything. The word *śrīmat* here is prefixed to Bhagavadgītā and is used for emphasis. *Śrī* means all wealth and *śrīmān*[50] can be the title for the *guru*. Here, Bhagavān plays the role of *guru*. *Bhaga* is the six-fold absolute virtues, as we have seen, and Bhagavān is, therefore, the one who has absolute *śrī*. All wealth belongs to Bhagavān as does all-knowledge, fullness, dispassion, overlordship, power, fame – the six-fold *bhaga*. The one who has these virtues is called Īśvara, the Lord, otherwise called Bhagavān. Thus, Bhagavān is a definition of Īśvara. And the one who can really be called as '*Śrīmān*' is Bhagavān alone. The title *śrīmat* is used here because Bhagavān has assumed the role of a teacher in the *Gītā*.

---

[49] Here the word '*yoga*' refers to anything a person needs in terms of preparation of the mind that is needed for the assimilation of this knowledge. Since the *Gītā* discusses all these along with the *brahma-vidyā*, it is also referred to as a *yoga-śāstra*.

[50] *śrīmān* is the nominative singular form in the masculine of the noun base, *śrīmat*.

The chapters and verses of the Bhagavadgītā have the same vision as that of the *Upaniṣads*. Therefore, the Bhagavadgītā is referred to as the *Upaniṣad,* the reference here being to the *Gītā* that is yet to come, since the actual *Gītā* has not yet begun. The *Upaniṣads* are the self-knowledge that destroys *saṁsāra,* a life of becoming, sorrow. The *Gītā* also destroys sorrow. By giving Arjuna self-knowledge, the *Gītā* removed his sorrow that is highlighted in the first chapter. Therefore, the *Gītā* is equated to the *Upaniṣads* whose subject matter is *brahma-vidyā,* knowledge of Brahman.

The *Gītā* is not simple psychotherapy; it is much more than that. It deals with what Brahman is, revealing the reality of the self, the self as Brahman. Being identical to the *Upaniṣads*, in terms of its subject matter, the *Gītā* cannot but be *brahma-vidyā,* knowledge of Brahman. It is also *yoga-śāstra* because it talks about *yoga* for maturity, preparing the mind for the knowledge.

Yoga-śāstra means *karma-yoga-śāstra* which includes disciplines, values, religious rituals, prayers, and so on. Performing duties is *yoga.* Also when the *Gītā* talks about *bhakti,* it is *yoga.* When it talks about *karma* to be done with *bhakti,* it is all *karma-yoga.* Even when it talks about *sannyāsa* it is *jñāna-yoga.* Since *sannyāsa* can also be a means for an end to be achieved, it is *yoga. Sannyāsa* as an end is the knowledge that 'I am Brahman and not a *kartā* or *bhoktā.*' All of this will be analysed later.

The *Gītā*, then, is both *brahma-vidyā* and *yoga-śāstra*, which is purely *karma-yoga,* implying devotion as well as all other disciplines that are used as means for preparing the mind for the self-knowledge. Also, included in this closing line are the words, 'in the dialogue between Kṛṣṇa and Arjuna –*śrīkṛṣṇārjuna-saṁvāde*.' It is because the dialogue had already started in the first chapter. The subject matter of this chapter was Arjuna's lamentation, his sorrow, his grief, his despair; thus the title, 'The *yoga* of Arjuna's Sorrow – *arjuna-viṣāda-yogaḥ*.'

Of course, the title of the chapter does not imply that the first *yoga* we are to practice is sorrow! The word '*yoga*' has various meanings, as can be seen from the synonyms given in dictionaries. *Yoga* is *nirodha*, control, or mastery. It also means *upāya*, a means of achieving something. Any form of meditation, *dhyāna*, is called *yoga*. And a connection, *saṅgati*, meaning a subject matter, *viṣaya*, is also called *yoga*.

Each of the eighteen chapters of the *Gītā* has the word '*yoga*' in its title, beginning with Arjuna's sorrow. Therefore, the correct meaning of the word '*yoga*' here is *saṅgati*, connection or subject matter. For instance, in the fifth chapter, *jñāna-karma-sannyāsa* is the *viṣaya*, the subject matter, which is not to suggest that it talks about a *yoga* called *jñāna-karma-sannyāsa* is to be practised. The *Gītā* talks about *karma*, about knowledge, *sannyāsa*, meditation, devotion, the vision of the cosmic person, the division between the knower and the known and so on. What is this division? Is there a division? – this is the topic of the thirteenth chapter called *kṣetra-kṣetrajña-yoga*.

So, the word '*yoga*' in the chapter titles, does not refer to the practice of *yoga*, but to the subject matter. It must be clearly understood because there is a lot of confusion about its meaning. Some people maintain that despair is necessary, and without it, we cannot come to spiritual life. Thus, we must work ourselves into despair! Despair is not something we need to work for; everyone has it. When we have to go to the tenth floor of a building and find out that the elevator is not working, despair begins! Despair need not be practised. We are despair; we are born of despair alone. We are brought up in despair, continue to be in despair, and are despair to everyone else.

The purpose of this first chapter of the *Gītā* was to describe the particular type of thinking, which will lead to self-knowledge. How you think, what leads you to a particular type of thinking, what kind of heart you must have in order to do this enquiry, *vicāra* – all these are necessary to know. Therefore, the chapter reveals Arjuna's nobility, his commitment to *dharma*, and his confusion.

A mature person can be confused and, therefore, Arjuna's confusion represents anyone's confusion. This confusion can lead to a certain type of thinking and to questions about what I really am. A person has to be led to this type of thinking, which is why a chapter about Arjuna's despair was included in the *Gītā*.

When Śaṅkara wrote his *Gītā-bhāṣya*, his commentary on the *Gītā*, he ignored this chapter and the first few verses of the second chapter. A *bhāṣya* comments only on that which requires explanation. Because the beginning of the *Gītā* can easily be understood by anyone who can understand by just reading, Śaṅkara's *bhāṣya*, commentary, is restricted to that which had to be discussed – the *Gītā* itself starting with '*śrībhagavān uvāca*' in the eleventh verse of the second chapter.

The subject matter of the first chapter, then, leads to the second chapter. Arjuna's *viṣāda*, despair, led to his *vicāra*, enquiry. *Viṣāda* can lead one either to enquiry or to escape, including suicide, death being another means of escape. In Arjuna's case, it led him to *vicāra*; Kṛṣṇa made sure that it did and, therefore, we have the *Gītā*.

Alphabetical index of verses

Text	Chapter	Verse	Vol	Page
daṇḍo damayatām asmi	*10*	*38*	*6*	*426*
dambho darpo'bhimānaśca	*16*	*04*	*8*	*176*
daṁṣṭrākarālāni ca te mukhāni	*11*	*25*	*7*	*53*
dātavyam iti yaddānam	*17*	*20*	*8*	*271*
divi sūryasahasrasya	*11*	*12*	*7*	*25*
divyamālyāmbaradharam	*11*	*11*	*7*	*24*
duḥkham ityeva yatkarma	*18*	*08*	*9*	*35*
duḥkheṣvanudvignamanāḥ	*02*	*56*	*2*	*324*
dūreṇa hyavaraṁ karma	*02*	*49*	*2*	*287*
dṛṣṭvā tu pāṇḍavānīkam	*01*	*02*	*1*	*176*
dṛṣṭvedaṁ mānuṣaṁ rūpam	*11*	*51*	*7*	*101*
devadvijagurupрājñapūjanaṁ	*17*	*14*	*8*	*252*
devān bhāvayatānena	*03*	*11*	*3*	*76*
dehī nityam avadhyo'yam	*02*	*30*	*2*	*178*
dehino'smin yathā dehe	*02*	*13*	*2*	*62*
daivam evāpare yajñam	*04*	*25*	*4*	*208*
daivī hyeṣā guṇamayī	*07*	*14*	*5*	*351*
daivī sampadvimokṣāya	*16*	*05*	*8*	*180*
doṣairetaiḥ kulaghnānām	*01*	*43*	*1*	*238*
dyāvāpṛthivyoridam antaraṁ hi	*11*	*20*	*7*	*40*
dyūtaṁ chalayatām asmi	*10*	*36*	*6*	*422*

For a list of our other publications,
please visit the website at:
www.avrpt.com

...or contact :

ARSHA VIDYA RESEARCH
AND PUBLICATION TRUST
32 / 4 Sir Desika Road,
Mylapore Chennai 600 004
Ph : 044 - 2499 7131
Email : avrandpt@gmail.com
Website : www.avrpt.com

ARSHA VIDYA GURUKULAM
Anaikatti P.O.
Coimbatore 641 108
Ph : 0422 - 2657001
Fax : 0422 - 2657002
Email : office@arshavidya.in
Website : www.arshavidya.in

SWAMI DAYANANDA ASHRAM
Purani Jhadi, P.B.No. 30
Rishikesh, Uttaranchal 249 201
Telefax : 0135 - 2430769
Email : ashrambookstore@yahoo.com
Website : www.dayananda.org

ARSHA VIDYA GURUKULAM
P.O. Box 1059. Pennsylvania
PA 18353, USA
Ph : 001 - 570 - 992 - 2339
Email : avp@epix.net
Website : www.arshavidya.org

ARSHA VIDYA TIRTHA
R-17 Yudhishthir Marg, Behind Secretariat
C scheme Jaipur. 302005
Ph : 0141 2228766

Our publications are also available at all leading bookstores and downloadable through the 'Teachings of Swami Dayananda' APP for Android and Apple devices.

Printed in Great Britain
by Amazon

37509215R00170